The Week the World Stood Still

Inside the Secret Cuban Missile Crisis

Sheldon M. Stern

Stanford University Press, Stanford, California

Stanford University Press
Stanford, California
© 2005 by the Board of Trustees of the
Leland Stanford Junior University. All rights reserved.

Printed in the United States of America

Library of Congress Cataloging-in-Publication Data

Stern, Sheldon M.
   The week the world stood still : Inside the secret Cuban Missile Crisis /
Sheldon M. Stern.
      p.   cm. — (Stanford nuclear age series)
   Rev. and condensed version of: Averting 'the final failure' :
   John F. Kennedy and the secret Cuban Missile Crisis meetings. 2003.
   Includes bibliographical references and index.
   ISBN 0-8047-5076-9 (cloth : alk. paper) —
   ISBN 0-8047-5077-7 (pbk : alk. paper)
      1. Cuban Missile Crisis, 1962.   2. Kennedy, John F. (John Fitzgerald),
   1917–1963.   3. National Security Council (U.S.)—History—20th century.
   4. United States—Foreign relations—1961–1963—Decision making.
   5. National security—United States—Decision making.   I. Stern, Sheldon M.
   Averting 'the final failure'.   II. Title.   III. Series.

E841.S758   2005
972.9106'4—dc22   2004020532

This book is printed on acid-free, archival-quality paper.

Original printing 2005

Last figure below indicates year of this printing:
14   13   12   11   10   09   08   07

Designed and typeset at Stanford University Press in 10/12.5 Sabon

Contents

(Six pages of photographs follow page 36)

The Week the World Stood Still

CHAPTER ONE

The JFK Cuban Missile Crisis Tapes

In the summer of 1973, the nation was captivated by the televised "Watergate" hearings into charges of illegal activities in Richard Nixon's White House. On July 16, presidential aide Alexander Butterfield revealed that President Nixon had installed a voice-activated taping system to secretly record his meetings and discussions. Congress subpoenaed the tapes but the president refused to comply. The Supreme Court unanimously ordered their release—and the rest is history.

A day after Butterfield's revelation, the John F. Kennedy Library disclosed that audio recordings of presidential meetings and telephone conversations had also been made during the Kennedy administration. These tapes included most of the secret meetings of the Executive Committee of the National Security Council (ExComm) during the 1962 Cuban missile crisis.

The "heroic" version of the Cuban missile crisis had already become well established by the 1970s. This view, encouraged by JFK himself, popularized by the writings of journalists and Kennedy administration insiders, and dramatized in the 1974 film *The Missiles of October*, depicted the courageous young American president successfully resisting nuclear blackmail by the Soviet Union and its puppet regime in Cuba and winning a decisive victory over communism. And, according to this viewpoint, after his sobering experience on the nuclear brink, Kennedy reached out to his adversaries and began the process of détente—reflected in 1963 in his American University speech urging a rethinking of Cold War beliefs, the establishment of the Moscow-

Washington Hot Line, and the ratification of the Limited Nuclear Test Ban Treaty.

This heroic viewpoint, however, did not last. In the wake of opposition to the Vietnam war and the declassification of key foreign policy documents from the 1960s, critical historians (often called "revisionists") uncovered new details about JFK's "secret war" against Cuba, particularly Operation Mongoose, that included sabotage and subversion against the Cuban economy, plots to overthrow and/or assassinate Castro, and "contingency plans" to blockade, bomb, or reinvade Cuba.

In addition, after the fall of the Soviet Union in the early 1990s, new evidence available from Soviet archives suggested that Nikita Khrushchev's original explanation for shipping missiles to Cuba had been fundamentally true: the Soviet leader had never intended these weapons as a threat to the security of the United States, but rather considered their deployment a defensive move to protect his Cuban allies from American attacks and as a desperate effort to give the U.S.S.R. the appearance of equality in the nuclear balance of power.

JFK's covert war against Cuba had clearly contributed to instigating the missile crisis. Nonetheless, as the ExComm tapes reveal, when faced with the real likelihood of nuclear war, Kennedy used all his intellectual and political skill to prevent the outbreak of hostilities. The president helped steer American policy makers and the two superpowers away from a nuclear conflict. A hawk in public, he actually distrusted the military, was skeptical about military solutions to political problems, and was horrified by the thought of nuclear war. The confrontational JFK depicted by the revisionists is all but imperceptible during the secret ExComm meetings. The president measured each move and countermove with an eye toward averting a nuclear exchange—which he somberly declared would be "the final failure."

The published transcripts of these secret tapes provide essential insights into the ExComm decision-making process, but they also reflect the flaws in the tapes themselves: frequent interruptions, garbled and rambling exchanges, baffling noises, overlapping comments, conversational dead ends, and a great deal of repetition. By their very nature, transcripts must endeavor to present *all* the words and can be dense and impenetrable to the non-specialist. However, the condensed interpretive narrative in this book, about half the length of the original full-length version, seeks to bring these discussions to life as a clear, coherent story, making the essence of the discussions completely understandable to general readers and especially to young people.

The narrative format aims to transform a complex and often redundant primary source, the ExComm tapes, into a more usable secondary source by concentrating on essentials and citing only the indispensable material. Readers can follow themes, ideas, issues, and the role of specific individuals as never before possible. The key moments of stress, doubt, decision, resolution—and even humor—are, in effect, emphasized by separating them from the background chatter and repetition of the unedited tapes, helping the reader to grasp as completely and accurately as possible the meaning, intent, and human dimension of these spontaneous discussions. The participants, obviously, did not know how this potential nuclear showdown would turn out, and their uncertainty, strikingly captured in narrative form, often gives the discussions the nerve-wracking quality of a work of fiction. But, of course, this unique story—permanently documented on audiotape—is not fiction.

My experience with presidential tapes began soon after I became historian at the John F. Kennedy Library in 1977. I initially edited some of the president's recorded telephone conversations—my first in-depth experience listening to White House recordings. Then, in the early 1980s, as part of my preparation for conducting a series of oral history interviews on foreign policy in the Kennedy administration, I began listening to the Cuban missile crisis meeting tapes. The Kennedy Library was preparing for their eventual declassification, and I was almost certainly the first non-member of the ExComm to hear precisely what happened at *all* these meetings; I was definitely the first professional historian to hear all these tapes.

It is difficult to describe the intellectual and physical demands of working on these recordings. I sat for hours at a time, wearing headphones, in front of a Tandberg reel-to-reel tape deck, the state-of-the-art equipment of the period, my foot on a pedal that allowed me to fast-forward, reverse, play, or stop the tape. The clunky and heavy Tandberg unit was difficult to move and operate; and, since it did not have a real-time timer, finding a specific moment on a tape could be incredibly frustrating. The first tape I played actually sounded like an FM radio station without frequency lock, the voices almost drowned out by intense background hiss. Dolby noise reduction appeared later in the 1980s, but the Kennedy Library never used this type of technology in order to avoid altering the originals. I listened to copies made directly from the White House originals.

To complicate the task even further, the recordings were also marred by distracting sounds: a smoker emptying his pipe into an ashtray on the table, water being poured from a pitcher into a glass, coughing, sneezing, nose-blowing and throat-clearing, the ringing of a telephone, the siren of an emergency vehicle passing on the street, the shouts of children at play on the White House grounds, and, most frequently, secondary conversations and people talking at the same time. In addition, there were persistent clanking noises on many tapes that sounded remarkably like a venting steam radiator. I checked the weather charts for that week and confirmed that it was too mild in Washington for White House radiators to have been overheating. To this day, I don't have a clue about the source of that exasperating noise.

These complications frequently required listening to the same words scores of times (in some cases, unfortunately, without success). Some voices were much harder to pick up because the speakers were seated at the opposite end of the table from the microphones concealed in wall fixtures behind the president's chair in the Cabinet Room. But, after a few very frustrating days, I began to develop an ear for the task and patience for the work. To my great relief, I also discovered that the first tape I played had not been typical. (Some tapes had likely deteriorated due to poor storage and preservation.) The project became more and more fascinating but always required absolute concentration (for example, I routinely disconnected my telephone). I quickly learned that missing even a second or two could alter both the speaker's intent and the historical record. There is a world of difference between someone saying "ever" as opposed to "never," or "I think" as opposed to "I don't think."

Reviewing these tapes required detailed knowledge of the Cold War era, familiarity with the views of the participants, the attentiveness to pick up even fragmentary remarks, and the ability to recognize voices. (I had interviewed many of the participants for Kennedy Library programs and was very familiar with most voices.) Some of the voices were distinctive, such as the Boston twang of the Kennedy brothers or the soft southern drawl of secretary of state Dean Rusk. However, the sound quality of each voice could vary from meeting to meeting depending on where each individual sat in relation to the microphone or even from slight imperfections in the speed at which the tape was recorded. The White House taping device was technically primitive by today's standards. McGeorge Bundy, for example, a member of Ex-Comm, listened to some tapes in the early 1980s and could not identify the voices of several of his former colleagues.

The ExComm discussions did not move forward with the momentum of a board meeting with a written agenda; rather, they plodded back and forth, with a great deal of repetition and many dead ends. Many participants often spoke in ungrammatical sentence fragments— no one more than JFK himself. They could be blindly self-righteous and cynical when discussing, for example, American covert actions against Cuba, but also remarkably idealistic in expressing moral doubts about a sneak attack on Cuba. Often, the most important decisions, such as choosing the blockade as the first step in the American response, happened without an explicit statement at any recorded meeting. Everyone simply recognized that the president had decided and acted accordingly.

Listening to these tapes, in any case, was the historian's ultimate fantasy—the chance to be the fly on the wall in one of the most dangerous moments in human history, and to know, within the technical limits of the recordings, *exactly what happened*. Even at the most frustrating moments, when I had to accept that I could not make out a key remark or exchange, I realized how fortunate I was to have the opportunity to study these one-of-a-kind historical records.

JFK's share of the responsibility for the onset of the crisis does not diminish his cautious and thoughtful leadership once the situation had reached a potentially fatal flashpoint. The ExComm tapes prove conclusively that John Kennedy played a decisive role in preventing the world from slipping into the nuclear abyss. If the ExComm decisions had been made by majority vote then war, very likely nuclear war, would almost certainly have been the result. The tapes reveal that a peaceful resolution was far from inevitable; the crisis could easily have ended in catastrophe despite the best intentions of leaders in Washington and Moscow. Of course, as we now know, JFK did have some essential help from his counterpart in the U.S.S.R. Khrushchev too, resisted pressure, especially from his ally Fidel Castro, to escalate the crisis.

There are, apparently, no Khrushchev tapes. The Kennedy tapes, however, present a unique opportunity to observe presidential leadership in the most perilous moment of the Cold War. Many presidents have faced extremely grave crises, but never before or since has the survival of human civilization been at stake in a few short weeks of dangerous deliberations, and never before or since have secret discussions such as these been recorded and preserved. And, given the collapse of the Soviet Union and the end of the Cold War, the Cuban missile crisis will hopefully remain the only "case study" of a full-scale nuclear showdown between military superpowers.

There is, unfortunately, no definitive explanation for why President Kennedy installed the first effective White House taping system. Evelyn Lincoln, JFK's personal secretary, recalled that the president was enraged after the 1961 Bay of Pigs operation in Cuba when several advisers who had supported the plan in closed meetings claimed later to have opposed it; she also maintained that the president simply wanted accurate records for writing his memoirs. Robert Bouck, the Secret Service agent who installed the recording devices, claimed that the president asked him to set up the taping system but never gave a reason. It seems reasonable that Kennedy's decision did reflect a desire to create an accurate source for preparing his memoirs after he left the White House. These explanations, however, fail to explain why JFK did not begin taping for more than a year after the Bay of Pigs.

In the early summer of 1962, Bouck installed taping systems in the Oval Office and the Cabinet Room. The actual recording device was in the White House basement. The president did not have access to the tape recorder itself; that is, he could not personally press the play, record, stop, or rewind buttons. JFK could only turn the system on or off in the Oval Office by hitting a switch concealed in a pen socket on his desk, in a bookend near his favorite chair, or in a table in front of his desk. The Cabinet Room switch was installed on the underside of the conference table in front of JFK's chair. The Oval Office microphones were hidden in the knee well of his desk and in a table across the room; the Cabinet Room microphones were mounted on the outside wall directly behind JFK's chair in spaces that once held light fixtures. A separate Dictaphone taping system was later installed in the Oval Office, and possibly in the president's bedroom, to record telephone conversations.

Bouck and another agent maintained the recording system and changed the tapes. Since the reel-to-reel tapes could record for a maximum of about two hours, Bouck later installed a back-up tape machine which was automatically activated if the first machine ran out of tape. The agents put the tapes in a plain sealed envelope and turned them over to Mrs. Lincoln for storage.

On November 22, 1963, after receiving confirmation of the president's death in Texas, JFK's younger brother, Attorney General Robert Kennedy, instructed Bouck to disconnect the taping system. Two hundred forty-eight hours of meeting tapes and twelve hours of telephone conversations were eventually turned over to the John F. Kennedy Library. Between 1983 and 2001, all forty-three hours of tape from October 16, the day of the first ExComm meeting, through November 20, the day JFK lifted the blockade around Cuba, were gradually declassified.

RFK appears to have asked Evelyn Lincoln to transcribe some tapes soon after JFK's death, but Bouck does not believe that Lincoln did any transcribing. Eventually George Dalton, a junior naval officer detailed to the White House, using equipment supplied by Bouck, took over this task. However, a document found recently at the Kennedy Library proves that some transcripts, probably by Dalton, existed as early as August 9, 1963. On that date, Lincoln apparently turned over eighteen missile crisis transcripts to Robert Kennedy's secretary in the Justice Department—raising the possibility that RFK, and even JFK himself, might have seen these very rough transcripts or even listened to some of the tapes in 1963. (The "Dalton transcripts" remain classified.)

Since the Kennedy taping system was manually activated (not voice activated like Nixon's), it was easily derailed by human carelessness or error. JFK sometimes recorded trivial discussions, but he failed to record the critical Oval Office confrontation with Soviet foreign minister Andrei Gromyko during the first week of the crisis. He often neglected to turn the machine on until after a meeting had begun and sometimes forgot to turn it off so that the tape ran out. In one case, the tape was left running and recorded the White House cleaning crew.

Inevitably, critics have questioned or even dismissed the historical value of these tapes because the two Kennedys knew they were being recorded and presumably could have manipulated the outcome to enhance their historical reputation. "The [JFK] tapes inherently lie," one commentator charged. "There pose the Kennedy brothers knowing they are being recorded, taking care to speak for history—while their unsuspecting colleagues think aloud and contradict themselves the way honest people do in a crisis." These tapes "do not present pure, raw history" since JFK could "turn the meetings into a charade of entrapment—half history-in-the-making, half-image-in-the-manipulating. And you can be sure of some outright deception . . . [by] the turning-off of the machine at key moments."

This argument is plainly groundless. Perhaps in a recorded phone conversation between two people it might be possible to manipulate the discussion. But, in a meeting of some fifteen people, operating under enormous stress and tension, it would be physically impossible. JFK could turn the tape machine on and off in the Cabinet Room, but he did not have access to the controls he would need for selective recording. And, even if he did, how would he have kept the participants from seeing what he was doing? There was no visible counter, and he could not have seen one unless he stuck his head under the table.

In any case, JFK would never have imagined that the public would ever hear these tapes. He thought of them as private property, *which they were legally at the time*, and could not foresee the Freedom of Information Act, "Watergate," and the Presidential Records Act, which eventually led to opening these confidential materials. He could have picked and chosen from the tapes when he wrote his memoirs— ignoring frequent references to classified national security material and potentially embarrassing personal and political remarks (especially in the telephone conversations). Why would he need to control the content of the tapes when he was certain that historians and the public would never hear them unless he or his estate granted special access?

The "Watergate" tapes also confirm this point: President Nixon knew he was being recorded and nevertheless did *not* try to tailor his remarks for the tapes. Instead, he repeatedly incriminated himself. Why? Because even well into the "Watergate" investigation he never thought that he would or could be compelled by the courts to release these personal and confidential recordings.

Finally, JFK and the other missile crisis participants, we should never forget, *did not know the outcome of the crisis when they were in the middle of dealing with it*. Even if President Kennedy had tried to "pose" for history, how could he have known which point of view would later be judged favorably by historians? What if, for example, the Russians had responded to the blockade, just as the Joint Chiefs had warned, by carrying out low-level bombing raids in Florida or by launching the nuclear missiles in Cuba at the U.S.? Historians today would still be listening to the same tapes (assuming any tapes or historians had survived), but with a very different outlook. It would then be the Chiefs who had turned out to be right; the blockade, just as they had predicted, would have proven to be a feeble and inadequate response, and air strikes to neutralize the missile sites and airfields— which we credit Kennedy for resisting—would appear to have been the best course after all. The same tapes could then be interpreted to make Kennedy look terribly negligent rather than diplomatically reasonable, *if the outcome had been different*.

Robert Kennedy's words on the tapes further highlight the fact that the participants could not know what position would seem right in the 20/20 vision of hindsight. RFK too knew about the taping system, but he took a generally hawkish stance during the meetings, pushing for a tough strategy that would remove Castro and demonstrate American power to the Soviets. Yet, when he decided to write a book on the crisis and run for president in 1968, he downplayed his aggressive posture, painting himself as a persistent dove and conciliator. RFK knew only *after* the crisis had been resolved that a dovish position would be "better" politically and would appeal to a nation deeply divided by the Vietnam War. He could not manipulate his image on the tapes any more than his brother since neither of them knew what was going to happen the next day or even the next hour.

JFK understood that history is not a play. There is no script. As he told the ExComm when the hazardous naval blockade around Cuba was about to go into effect, "What *we* are doing is throwing down a card on the table in a game which we don't know the ending of."

CHAPTER TWO

The Making of the Cuban Missile Crisis

The Cold War: JFK's Crucible

The Cold War is over. The Soviet Union no longer exists. Nuclear war between the two superpowers never happened. Anyone who had dared to predict these developments during the recurrent crises of the Kennedy administration would have seemed hopelessly naïve or just plain foolish.

For young Americans today the Cold War is no longer a fact of everyday life but instead a remote historical curiosity—like World War I or the Great Depression. Students find it difficult to believe that many Americans in the 1960s were convinced that nuclear war with the Soviet Union was inevitable. Indeed, black-and-white film of schoolchildren training to protect themselves from nuclear attack by crouching under their desks and covering their heads with their arms often evokes not merely disbelief, but even laughter.

The United States and the Soviet Union, ironically, had been allies only a generation before during the struggle against Nazi Germany in World War II. It had been an alliance of necessity, the ultimate proof that politics makes strange bedfellows. Both sides, despite mutual suspicion and distrust, recognized that the defeat of the common enemy came first. The alliance had begun to crumble well before the death of President Franklin Roosevelt in April 1945 and the surrender of Hitler's Germany just weeks later.

Historians remain divided, nonetheless, about whether the U.S. or the U.S.S.R. was more responsible for the onset of the Cold War. A debate has raged for decades about whether Roosevelt's successor, Harry

Truman, authorized the use of the atomic bomb against Japan to save lives by ending the war quickly or was instead using "atomic diplomacy" to convince the communist world that America would not be afraid to use nuclear weapons in the postwar world. The idealistic language of the new American internationalism clearly masked a drive for political and economic domination at the dawn of the new nuclear era.

Evidence released from archives in the former Soviet Union, however, has highlighted the role of Joseph Stalin in launching the Cold War. The Soviet dictator, whose reign of terror consumed the lives of many millions of his own people, embodied *both* traditional Russian imperialism and Marxist ideological expansionism:

For Stalin there were always two worlds, not one: his empire, born in the Russian Revolution and representing the Kingdom of Light and the force of the future; and the dying—therefore desperate and aggressive—world outside, against which he wanted to protect it. Any opposition to him from within was perceived as a black threat; any opposition from beyond Soviet borders represented the decadent taint of a passing order.

Stalin insisted on the need for a physical buffer between the borders of the Soviet Union and Western Europe (especially Germany) and took advantage of postwar chaos to prop up satellite governments in Albania, Bulgaria, Czechoslovakia, Hungary, Poland, Romania, and the Eastern zone of divided and occupied Germany. By 1946 Stalin declared publicly that it would be impossible to achieve peaceful coexistence in a world dominated by capitalism.

The U.S. and its European allies recognized that they could not force the Soviets out of Eastern Europe. The Truman administration instead initiated a policy of "containment" to halt the spread of communism. The ensuing struggle between the communist nations, led by the U.S.S.R., and the capitalist democracies of the West, led by the U.S., was fought with large military budgets, propaganda, covert operations, and the use of economic aid to win over neutral nations. The terms "Cold War" and "Iron Curtain" soon entered the American vocabulary.

A series of groundbreaking initiatives shaped American policy in the new Cold War era. The Truman Doctrine, based on the premise that U.S. security interests were international, received bipartisan support in Congress in 1947, granting economic and military aid to governments threatened by "armed minorities or by outside pressures." Congress also approved the Marshall Plan, which supplied thirteen billion dollars between 1947 and 1951 to rebuild war-ravaged Europe, promote free-market economies, and undermine support for communism. Young congressman John F. Kennedy vigorously supported these new Cold War initiatives.

Berlin quickly became the focal point of Cold War tensions. The victorious allies had divided Germany into four zones of occupation (American, British, French, and Soviet). In 1948, President Truman reached accords with Britain and France to merge their zones of occupation into a new republic of West Germany; this agreement included West Berlin, the sector of the German capital occupied by the three Western allies despite the fact that it was located deep within the Soviet (Eastern) zone. Understandably fearful of a strong new Germany, Stalin decided to attempt to remove the Western powers from their Berlin outpost in the Soviet zone by imposing an economic blockade against the Western sectors of Berlin.

Truman ordered a massive airlift (Stalin had not closed air access) to bypass the roads, rail lines, and waterways blocked by the Soviets. Two million people were supplied with food, fuel, and other necessities by a quarter of a million flights around the clock. The Soviet leader finally lifted the blockade in May 1949. The previous month a dozen Western European nations, desperate for nuclear protection against the U.S.S.R. and fearful of a resurgent Germany, had established the North Atlantic Treaty Organization (NATO) to provide for collective defense—an attack on any member nation would be regarded as an attack on all member nations. A divided Germany, especially the tenuous Allied access to West Berlin, became the focus of increasingly bitter tensions which might erupt into war at a moment's notice.

Nineteen forty-nine was a decisive year in the evolution of the Cold War. The U.S.S.R. tested its first atomic bomb, shattering the American nuclear monopoly which had existed since the end of World War II. The U.S. joined NATO—the first "peacetime" military/mutual security alliance in American history. Mao Zedong's communist forces seized control of mainland China. Early the next year, President Truman asked the National Security Council to undertake a study of American foreign policy for the new Cold War era. The resulting report, NSC-68, argued that the United States had to assume world leadership in resisting the spread of "communist slavery." This commitment to defeat communism and avoid repeating the 1938 appeasement of Hitler at Munich had a profound influence on the generation that had fought in World War II and would be echoed in John Kennedy's inaugural address in 1961.

In 1957, the Soviet Union stunned the West by successfully launching Sputnik, the first man-made satellite to orbit the Earth. This technical breakthrough suggested that the U.S.S.R. was also capable of developing intercontinental ballistic missiles that could undermine the U.S. guarantee to protect Europe against Soviet aggression. The Eisenhower administration offered its own ICBMs to the NATO allies, and agreements were reached to deploy Thor missiles in England and Jupiter missiles in Italy and Turkey.

The Kremlin worked unsuccessfully to block the deployment. President Dwight Eisenhower conceded privately that the Jupiters could be very unsettling for the U.S.S.R. and declared that if the Soviets made a comparable move in Mexico or Cuba, the U.S. might have to take direct military action. Eisenhower was indeed prescient. The "most acute and dangerous confrontation" of the Cold War, "the closest we ever came to a nuclear exchange," began thousands of miles from Europe or Berlin and just ninety miles off the coast of Florida.

The Cold War and Cuba

In the first hours of 1959, Cuban guerrillas led by Fidel Castro ousted Fulgencio Batista, a brutal military dictator with close ties to U.S. business and the Mafia. Initially, Castro seemed a heroic figure to many Americans. At the 1959 New Year's Eve celebration in Times Square, when word flashed that Castro had entered Havana, a loud cheer erupted from the crowd. In April, Castro visited the U.S. as a guest of the American Society of Newspaper Editors and aroused genuine interest in Washington, in New York, and at Harvard University, where nearly nine thousand people turned out to hear him speak and a dinner in his honor was hosted by the dean of arts and sciences, McGeorge Bundy. Castro was also interviewed on American television.

However, suspicions about Castro intensified quickly when he summarily executed hundreds of Batista supporters, waffled on setting a date for free elections, seized American property without compensation, and suppressed freedom of expression and political opposition. Cuba also became increasingly dependent on Soviet military and economic assistance.

Cold War issues inevitably dominated the 1960 presidential campaign. President Eisenhower had been humiliated in May when a U-2 spy plane was shot down over the Soviet Union. The pilot, Francis Gary Powers, was captured, tried, and convicted of spying. The president, after denials, finally admitted the truth, but he refused to apologize. Soviet premier Nikita Khrushchev denounced Eisenhower, cancelled an upcoming summit in Paris, and withdrew an invitation to the president to visit the U.S.S.R.

Senator John F. Kennedy, the Democratic nominee, was harshly critical of the administration for failing to prevent the creation of a communist outpost in Cuba. The administration, in fact, was already supporting CIA efforts to sabotage and destabilize the new Cuban regime and to assist Cuban dissidents in creating a government in exile. The CIA had also initiated contacts with the Mafia about killing Castro. Vice President Richard Nixon, the Republican candidate, also promised to upgrade U.S. military forces and resist Soviet expansionism around the world, particularly in the Americas. Kennedy narrowly won.

In a January 1961 speech Khrushchev praised the Cuban revolution and declared that armed efforts to achieve national liberation from colonialism and imperialism were "sacred wars" which deserved the support of the Soviet Union and the world socialist movement. The speech was read by Kennedy's inner circle and may have contributed to the strident tone of his inaugural address—which drew a razor-sharp line between the "free world" and the communist world.

President Eisenhower broke diplomatic relations with Cuba shortly before leaving office. Khrushchev, however, eagerly embraced Castro as a symbol of the forward-looking and inevitable advance of world communism. A potentially explosive situation was rapidly developing in American-Soviet-Cuban relations which would make the next three years among the most crisis-filled periods of the Cold War.

In the months between the election and the inauguration, Kennedy was briefed about an Eisenhower administration plan to have the CIA secretly train anti-Castro exiles to attack Cuba. American intelligence specialists predicted that many Cubans would join an attempt to oust Castro and install a non-communist government friendly to the United States. JFK, despite doubts about concealing American participation, approved the plan, believing the invasion could be explained as an independent action by guerrillas backing internal Cuban opposition to Castro. Secretary of State Dean Rusk even told a colleague, "Don't worry about this. It isn't going to amount to anything." Asked if it would make the front page of the *New York Times*, Rusk replied, "I wouldn't think so."

About 1,500 exiles of Brigade 2506 landed at Cuba's Bay of Pigs on

April 17, 1961. Two days of U.S.-backed air strikes had destroyed barely 15 percent of Castro's combat aircraft, leaving the invaders exposed to air attacks. As the plan quickly unraveled, Kennedy cancelled further air strikes. The invasion was crushed by Castro's military, and all the invaders were either captured or killed.

Kennedy was denounced in the communist world, the Third World, and Europe. The influential Cuban exile community in Miami and New Orleans festered with anger over the president's refusal to commit American air power to save the doomed invaders. Kennedy assumed personal responsibility for the fiasco (and later joked that his public approval ratings went up). Castro, in the wake of his stunning triumph, proclaimed Cuba's commitment to communism.

This humiliating setback would have profound consequences for the Kennedy administration, sharpening JFK's lifelong skepticism about the military and doubts about "experts" in the intelligence community. "How could I have been so far off base?" he asked White House special counsel Theodore Sorensen. "All my life I've known better than to depend on the experts. How could I have been so stupid, to let them go ahead?" However, the president, passionately encouraged by his brother Robert Kennedy, also developed a preoccupation, if not an obsession, with getting rid of Castro and erasing this blot on the Kennedy record.

Evidence released over the last decade has substantiated the administration's growing hostility to Castro. Later in 1961, for example, Richard Goodwin, a member of JFK's Latin American Task Force, was approached by Castro's number-two man, Ernesto "Che" Guevara, at a meeting in Uruguay. Guevara suggested that Castro might be willing to discuss reducing tensions. JFK interpreted this apparent peace feeler as a sign of weakness and accepted Goodwin's advice to have the CIA turn up the pressure on Castro. Cold War ideology, combined with personal anger over the Bay of Pigs, had created a powerful incentive for the Kennedys to launch a "secret war" to get even in Cuba.

In November, JFK authorized the creation of Operation Mongoose to undermine the Cuban regime and economy with covert operations and sabotage—including blowing up port and oil storage facilities, burning crops (especially sugarcane), and even assassinating Castro. Mongoose was no fly-by-night scheme run by ultra-right extremists, as depicted in Oliver Stone's film fantasy *JFK*. It became one of the largest operations in CIA history. Robert Kennedy insisted that the Bay of Pigs had to be expunged and kept close tabs on Mongoose activities directed by the Special Group (Augmented). He also established close ties to U.S-backed anti-Castro groups and invited their leaders to his home. Richard Bissell, CIA director of operations who had been working on Cuba since 1959, considered RFK a fanatic on the subject of Castro.

Historians have argued for decades about whether President Kennedy personally authorized plots to assassinate Castro. JFK definitely discussed eliminating Castro with associates and journalists, but also worried that killing the Cuban leader would increase tensions with the Soviet Union. CIA plots continued, but efforts to find a "smoking gun" directly linking JFK to these schemes miss the point. "All one can say is that the obsession with Castro, and Robert's constant goading of the CIA, created a climate in which CIA officials might have been forgiven for believing that the higher authorities would not be unhappy with the Cuban leader's demise." RFK's pressure on the CIA to deal with Castro sent an unmistakable signal to intelligence operatives—notwithstanding JFK's doubts. The need to provide the president with plausible deniability also made a written order unwise and unnecessary.

In 1962, the Kennedy administration implemented a full economic embargo against Cuba and pressured Latin American nations to break relations with Castro and expel his government from the Organization of American States. In addition, an Operation Mongoose timetable was in place to provoke a "popular revolt" in Cuba as a justification for American military intervention. Cuban and Soviet agents, however, had infiltrated anti-Castro exile groups and were aware of these covert efforts. "Contingency" plans for a blockade, air strikes, and/or an invasion were in place well before the discovery of Soviet nuclear missiles in Cuba—although it is uncertain whether JFK would have implemented these plans without Khrushchev's October gamble.

Thirty years later, former defense secretary Robert McNamara could understand why Soviet and Cuban leaders expected an imminent American invasion. But, in 1962, the three antagonists were unable to comprehend their adversaries' viewpoint. Americans called this episode the "Cuban missile crisis"; the Soviets dubbed it the "Caribbean crisis"; but the Cubans labeled it the "October crisis" because it represented only one incident in more than a year of unremitting U.S. threats to Cuba. "From the Cuban perspective, the October crisis was just one of many."

Nuclear Confrontation in Cuba

Nikita Khrushchev, before meeting with Kennedy in Vienna in June 1961, told the Politburo that he was planning to push hard for concessions in Berlin and elsewhere. He believed that JFK was immature, untested, and especially vulnerable after the Bay of Pigs. Khrushchev's belligerent behavior in Vienna convinced JFK that the Soviets would only respect American toughness in Cuba and Berlin, and he endorsed a recommendation to proceed with the deployment of Jupiter missiles in Turkey and Italy.

The construction of the Berlin Wall later that summer, to prevent East Germans from fleeing to the West, took some of the heat off the Berlin issue. JFK and his advisers, nonetheless, never forgot that West Berlin, some two hundred miles inside East Germany, was the Achilles' heel of the Western alliance. The Cuban missile crisis, for the Kennedy administration, was as much about Berlin as Cuba. "It is hard to imagine," in the post–Cold War world, "the fear and passion that once surrounded the very word, 'Berlin.'" President Kennedy was convinced that Khrushchev's October 1962 move in Cuba was the first step in a Soviet plan to threaten nuclear blackmail over the Berlin issue; some advisers worried that he was "imprisoned by Berlin, that's all he thinks about."

Khrushchev, however, was not a passive observer in these escalating tensions between the nuclear superpowers. The Soviet leader was deeply concerned about U.S. covert operations in Cuba and feared that Castro's overthrow would threaten his own hold on power. Several years later, he wrote, "one thought kept hammering at my brain: what will happen if we lose Cuba?" Khrushchev also feared that failure to protect the Cuban revolution would push Castro into closer ties with the U.S.S.R.'s belligerent rival for leadership in the communist world— Mao's China. The Kremlin leader was willing to gamble because he believed that Kennedy did not have the stomach for the ultimate conflict with the Soviet Union.

In the early spring of 1962, during a vacation in the Crimea, Khrushchev brooded over the fact that the newly operational U.S. Jupiter missiles just across the Black Sea in Turkey could reach the U.S.S.R. in a few minutes. Soviet missiles, however, required nearly half an hour to reach the U.S. Soon after returning to Moscow, in discussions with his closest advisers, Khrushchev suggested deploying nuclear missiles in Cuba. The U.S.S.R. had learned to live with U.S. nuclear weapons in

Turkey, Italy, and Britain, and Khrushchev felt that it was time for the Americans to have "a little of their own medicine." In addition, Khrushchev knew that the U.S. had a decisive advantage in ICBMs and warheads capable of reaching the U.S.S.R. and that it would take at least a decade to close the gap. Soviet intermediate-range missiles in Cuba would kill the proverbial two birds with one stone at very modest cost by protecting Castro's communist revolution and appearing to equalize the world balance of power. It was a calculated gamble: "With forty missiles staring at Florida, day and night, no general in the Pentagon would again dare consider a nuclear first strike against the Soviet Union or an attack on Cuba."

Anti-communism had clearly fueled Kennedy administration policy in Cuba, but Marxist ideology had also motivated leaders in the Kremlin. At the Vienna summit, Khrushchev had lectured JFK about the inevitable triumph of world communism: this was not hyperbole or propaganda, the Soviet leader argued, but a scientific analysis of historical development. In presenting his plan to the Presidium, Khrushchev made clear that he was acting to save Cuba and implement the Marxist view of history. He believed that the historical moment for the triumph of Marxist-Leninism was at hand—even his later memoirs are peppered with reflex ideology about "the class blindness of the United States," "the dying capitalist system," and JFK's "goal of strengthening capitalism, while I sought to destroy capitalism and create a new world social system based on the teachings of Marx, Engels, and Lenin." There was little opposition to Khrushchev's plan in the Kremlin.

A delegation of senior Soviet officials traveled to Cuba to propose the plan. To preserve secrecy, they wore civilian clothes, carried false passports, brought no documents, and were forbidden to contact Moscow, even in code. Castro's response was enthusiastic. A five-year agreement for the defense of Cuba, including the deployment of nuclear missiles under Soviet control, was negotiated by both governments later that summer. The entire world was heading for a potentially deadly confrontation between the nuclear superpowers.

Khrushchev had badly underestimated the symbolic importance of historic American power in the Western Hemisphere, going back to the Monroe Doctrine, and was totally unprepared for the intensity of the U.S. response. He also failed to take Castro's shrewd advice to deploy the missiles openly as a legitimate act of bilateral diplomacy (as the U.S. had done in Turkey and Italy). Instead, Soviet duplicity and secrecy virtually guaranteed that the U.S. would conclude that Khrushchev's motives were aggressive. Khrushchev believed that Kennedy would accept the Cuban missiles as a reasonable counterweight to American missiles in Turkey and Italy. But, the Soviet leader simply did not understand the intense American fears of a communist military outpost in the Western Hemisphere that could be used for nuclear blackmail over Berlin and political subversion in Latin America.

Kennedy had naïvely accepted predictions by American intelligence in 1961 that the Cuban people would rise in support of an American-sponsored invasion. Khrushchev, likewise, swallowed the assurances of Soviet "experts" that these huge missiles could be "disguised as coconut palms" and the mounted warheads "crowned with a cap of leaves" to prevent detection. Khrushchev intended to announce the presence of the missiles during a November trip to the U.N. But, he had failed to work out a response in the event that the Americans discovered the missile sites under construction and he was forced to improvise in the pressure cooker of the most dangerous crisis of the Cold War.

In the summer of 1962, Cuba continued to loom large in American politics. Covert operations had failed to reduce Castro's grasp on power, and behind him lurked the potential threat from his Soviet backers. Kennedy had criticized the Eisenhower administration for allowing a Communist base only ninety miles from Florida. Now, the proverbial shoe was on the other foot and conservative Republicans accused Kennedy of ignoring or even suppressing evidence of a Soviet buildup in Cuba. In August, Senator Kenneth Keating of New York, a moderate Republican, charged that the Soviets had begun constructing offensive nuclear missile bases in Cuba. Kennedy was appalled by Keating's charges, which could affect the upcoming midterm congressional elections and might even threaten his own reelection in 1964. Kennedy pressed the CIA for answers, but was told that U-2 reconnaissance photographs revealed only defensive surface-to-air missile sites in Cuba. Early in September, Soviet ambassador Anatoly Dobrynin assured Robert Kennedy that offensive nuclear weapons would not be placed in Cuba. The president wanted to believe these assurances, but he also wanted his adversaries, both Soviet and Republican, to know that he would defend American interests in the Caribbean. JFK warned on September 4 that the introduction of offensive ground-to-ground missiles in Cuba would raise "the gravest issues."

On September 11, the official Soviet news agency, TASS, repeated that all weapons for Cuba were defensive and boasted that Soviet nuclear missiles were so powerful that it was unnecessary to look for sites outside the U.S.S.R. JFK, under constant political scrutiny and unsure about the actual situation on the island, declared at a September 13 press conference that the U.S. would not accept an offensive Soviet base in Cuba.

The first Soviet medium-range ballistic missiles were delivered covertly to Cuba days later. On October 4, ninety-nine nuclear warheads also arrived secretly, containing "over twenty times the explosive power that was dropped by Allied bombers on Germany in all of the Second World War" (some were seventy times more powerful than the primitive atomic bomb which obliterated Hiroshima in 1945). Kennedy's advisers continued to insist that the Soviets would never risk putting nuclear weapons in Cuba since they could already destroy the United States several times over with missiles fired from their own territory. Why would they provoke the U.S. by deploying missiles they did not need in Cuba?

The fact that Khrushchev's vast array of ICBMs was largely a fantasy was a carefully guarded Soviet secret. When Kennedy and Khrushchev met in Vienna the president had proposed that the rivals work together on a joint lunar exploration program. The Soviet leader, despite his bluster about producing these weapons like sausages, turned down the offer. Sergei Khrushchev later pressed his father about the reason: "If we cooperate," the senior Khrushchev admitted, "it will mean opening up our rocket program to them. We have only two hundred missiles, but they think we have many more." Khrushchev believed the Americans might launch a first strike if they discovered this Soviet weakness. "So when they say we have something to hide . . .?" Sergei persisted. "It is just the opposite," his father said with a laugh. "We have nothing to hide. We have nothing. And we must hide it."

Khrushchev's anxiety about a U.S. nuclear first strike was justified. In 1961, in response to concerns that NATO could not protect West Berlin against a Soviet attack, secret plans were prepared for a nuclear first strike against the long-range missile capacity of the U.S.S.R. The plan assumed up to a million Soviet casualties in the initial attack. President Kennedy, despite doubts, read and discussed a "plan to wage *rational* nuclear war." In an October speech, Deputy Defense Secretary Roswell Gilpatric signaled the Soviets that the administration knew that the U.S. had a commanding lead in ICBMs—which likely contributed to Khrushchev's decision to ship nuclear weapons to Cuba as a short-term fix for Soviet strategic inferiority.

The United States had developed and used atomic weapons in 1945 and had enjoyed a nuclear monopoly for the next four years. Stalin, whose paranoia rarely required any connection to reality, had dreaded a preemptive American nuclear attack. Khrushchev gambled in Cuba, at least in part, because he worried that U.S. nuclear superiority, confirmed by forty-five operational Jupiter missiles in Turkey and Italy, could make the U.S.S.R. almost as vulnerable to atomic blackmail as it had been before 1949.

Robert Kennedy chaired an Operation Mongoose planning meeting in early October and demanded an expansion of sabotage and subversion to bring down Castro. Within days, however, Senator Keating claimed publicly to have proof that six offensive intermediate-range nuclear missile bases were already under construction in Cuba. On Sunday, October 14, U-2 spy planes brought back indisputable photographic evidence of MRBM sites in Cuba.

Ironically, McGeorge Bundy had appeared that morning on ABC TV's *Issues and Answers* and insisted that there was no evidence that the U.S.S.R. would install offensive weapons in Cuba. Bundy received the stunning news on Monday evening but waited until early Tuesday morning to brief the president, later explaining that JFK needed an undisturbed night of sleep. Kennedy, still in his pajamas, his face and voice taut with anger, declared, "He can't do that to me." JFK told Bundy to organize a meeting of the National Security Council that morning. He then summoned his brother to the White House. "Oh shit!, Shit!, Shit! Those sons a bitches Russians," RFK exclaimed upon seeing the photos. The Kennedys had attempted to deter Khrushchev by making dozens of secret contacts with Georgi Bolshakov, a Soviet embassy official who was also a colonel in military intelligence. Their efforts had come to nothing.

President Kennedy's October 22 speech announcing the discovery of Soviet missiles in Cuba was artfully misleading—he did not, of course, mention the secret war against Castro. "The purpose of these bases," he warned, "can be none other than to provide a nuclear strike capability against the Western Hemisphere." The ExComm tapes prove, however, that JFK believed the missiles were a political rather than a military challenge. Kennedy, notwithstanding, portrayed the crisis with Castro and his Soviet sponsors in simplistic black-and-white Cold War language that made sense to most Americans: "Our policy has been one of patience and restraint, as befits a peaceful and powerful nation. . . . Our goal is not the victory of might, but the vindication of right."

The Kennedy Paradox

President Kennedy, a prominent historian has argued, was a rigid and uncompromising cold warrior, "more enamored with military than with diplomatic means." "In *all* cases [italics added], Kennedy strove to win" and never abandoned his commitment to "a strategy of annihilation." This attitude was clear in the Cuban missile crisis: "President Kennedy helped precipitate the missile crisis by harassing Cuba. . . . Then he reacted to the crisis by suspending diplomacy in favor of public confrontation." In the end, the nuclear superpowers luckily "stumbled toward a settlement."

One part of this statement about the missile crisis is true: President Kennedy bears significant responsibility for provoking this confrontation—because of the Bay of Pigs invasion, covert plots against Castro, and plans to reinvade Cuba. The Kennedy administration had clearly contributed to polarizing the Cuban issue and had been caught in a political trap at least partly of its own making.

However, much of this assessment of the missile crisis is false. President Kennedy did *not* choose confrontation over diplomacy, and he consistently led the ExComm away from military action; and, fortunately for all of us, he never stumbled. JFK rose above his own Cold War rhetoric and policies during these decisive meetings and audaciously steered the ship of state away from nuclear confrontation.

In September 1961, Kennedy had declared in a speech at the U.N. that "it is absurd to suppose that we would unleash a nuclear war. . . . we believe that a peaceful solution is possible." Khrushchev was so impressed that he allowed the Soviet newspaper *Pravda* to publish an article asserting that "Kennedy had no illusions with respect to nuclear war and he was therefore searching for ways to achieve an honorable peace—although, like any human being, he was not immune to mistakes."

Kennedy and Khrushchev also used secret diplomacy to defuse a potentially explosive confrontation in October 1961. American and Soviet tanks challenged each other at the Berlin Wall's Checkpoint Charlie. JFK made a secret overture to Khrushchev through Bolshakov at the Soviet embassy. Khrushchev agreed to pull back Soviet tanks, the Americans quickly followed, and the crisis eased. "In the future," Sergei Khrushchev later observed, "there would be more than one problem that he [Khrushchev] and the U.S. president would have to solve together."

Did President Kennedy, a scholar recently asked, "single-handedly" prevent World War III during the missile crisis? "Yes, it's pretty much true," he concluded. "John Kennedy behaved more heroically than the standard history books have told—certainly far more heroically than the experts and wise men around him." Another writer agreed that Kennedy "never looked taller" because he had "to be more clever and better informed than his generals and the hawks in his Cabinet and to have the nerve to face them down." A Cold War historian also concluded that JFK's handling of the crisis was "a new profile in courage—but it would be courage of a different kind from what many people presumed that term to mean throughout much of the Cold War."

These assessments point to a dimension of JFK's worldview that has been all but ignored by anti-Kennedy revisionists: namely, his lifelong distrust of military leaders and military solutions to political problems, and, most significantly, his horror at the prospect of nuclear war. This paradoxical dimension of Kennedy's leadership was recently captured by a journalist who knew him well—Hugh Sidey:

I am dissatisfied with some of the modern assessments of him and his presidency. This is not a denial of his flaws, personal or political, many of which were obscured or ignored in those simpler times. It is to say that there was at the core of his stewardship a continuing and serious effort to steady a difficult world. . . . Once in the presidency there is virtually no time for re-education or the deep introspection that might show a president where he is right or wrong and bring about a true change of mind. Events move too fast. A president may pick up more knowledge about a subject or find an expert aide on whom he can rely, but in most instances when he is alone and faced with a crucial decision he must rely on his intuition, a mixture of natural intelligence, education, and experience.

He had read the books of great military strategists—Carl von Clausewitz, Alfred Thayer Mahan, and Basil Henry Liddell Hart—and he wondered if their theories of total violence made sense in the nuclear age. . . . War with all of its modern horror would be his biggest concern if he got to the White House, Kennedy said. . . . If I had to single out one element in Kennedy's life that more than anything else influenced his later leadership it would be a horror of war, a total revulsion over the terrible toll that modern war had taken on individuals, nations and societies, and the even worse prospects in the nuclear age. . . . It ran even deeper than his considerable public rhetoric on the issue.

This "deep core of realism about the world," Sidey concluded, came out of Kennedy's personal past—"that was serious much of the time and was focused on understanding the events and people that drove nations, the preparation of a young man for what was still an ill-defined and distant challenge. . . . Policy at the top comes out of the heart and mind of the president, or at the very least is tempered by his personality. And his convictions and passions are almost always linked to early impressions gained from family and school and youthful experience." During the tense summer of 1961, Sidey recalled, JFK had observed gloomily, "'Ever since the longbow,' he said, 'when man had developed new weapons and stockpiled them, somebody has come along and used them. I don't know how we escape it with nuclear weapons.'"

"There are, I have found, many compartments within the souls of men who rise to great power," Sidey concluded, an assessment that can be documented in the formative years of John Kennedy. The twenty-two-year-old undergraduate, writing a month after the outbreak of World War II, warned his Harvard classmates that the war would be "beyond comprehension in its savage intensity, and which could well presage a return to barbarism." Four years later, the letters written by the twenty-six-year-old junior naval officer from the South Pacific confirm that he was an acute observer of events around him and more dubious than ever about the logic of war: "The day I arrived," Kennedy wrote to his school chum Lem Billings, the Japanese launched "a hell of an attack":

During a lull in the battle—a Jap parachuted into the water—we went to pick him up as he floated along—and got within about 20 yds. of him. He suddenly threw aside his life-jacket + pulled out a revolver and fired two shots at our bridge. I had been praising the Lord + passing the ammunition right alongside—but that slowed me a bit—the thought of him sitting in the water—battling an entire ship. . . . Finally an old soldier standing next to me— picked up his rifle—fired once—and blew the top of his head off. . . . That was the start of a very interesting month—and it brought home very strongly how long it is going to take to finish the war.

His doubts only intensified in a letter to his Danish girlfriend, Inga Arvad:

I would like to write you a letter giving in a terse sharp style an outline of the war situation first hand . . . in which I would use the words global war, total effort and a battle of logistics no less than eight times each . . . [but] it is pretty hard to get the total picture of a global war unless you are sitting in New York or Washington, or even Casablanca . . .

I understand we are winning it, which is cheering, albeit somewhat hard to see, but I guess the view improves with distance . . . I know mine would . . . I wouldn't mind being back in the States picking up the daily paper, saying

'Why don't those bastards out there do something?' It's one of those interesting things about the war that everyone in the States . . . want[s] to be out here killing Japs, while everyone out here wants to be back. . . . It seems to me that someone with enterprise could work out some sort of an exchange, but as I hear you saying, I asked for it, honey and I'm getting it.

But, young Kennedy reserved special contempt for the senior brass supposedly in control of the war:

Dearest Inga Binga, In regard to the food, which I know you know I do regard, as lousy. . . . I have finally found out where those steaks are going that— and I quote—'the boys in the service are getting' end of quote. . . . Well, anyway, a general came aboard and my exec. and I managed to look as weak from hunger as we possibly could which required no great effort, so he finally broke down and invited us for a meal. We went, and they kept bringing in the steaks and the potatoes and the peas and the asparagus and the pie and the beer, all of which I disposed of in a style to which you had become accustomed. . . . Well, when we had finally finished he came out with the statement that he understood we got the same food, only he figured his was probably cooked a little better. . . . Having had a bottle of beer and therefore being scarcely in a condition to carry on an intelligible conversation, and remembering article no. 252 in Naval Regulations, that Generals are seldom wrong and Admirals never, and figuring that the problem of food distribution was a problem that was occupying better minds than the generals' or mine, I merely conceded the putt and went on to the next hole.

I'm certainly glad I came—I wouldn't miss it for the world, but I will be extremely glad to get back. . . . Well honey, I must go and get some of that delightful food, superbly prepared and cuisined, and served in pleasant and peaceful surroundings . . .

Just had an inspection by an Admiral. He must have weighed over three hundred, and came bursting through our hut like a bull coming out of chute three. A burst of speed when he got into the clear brought him against the machine shop. He harrumphed a couple of times, and then inquired, 'And what do we have here?'

'Well, General,' was the answer, 'this is our machine shop.'

'Harrumph, and what do you keep in it, harrumph ah . . . MACHINERY?'

After it was gently but firmly explained to him that machinery was kept in the machine shop and he had written that down on the special pad he carried for such special bits of information which can only be found 'if you get right up to the front and see for yourself' he harrumphed again, looked at a map, and wanted to know what we had *there*—there being a small bay some distance away. When we said nothing, he burst out with, 'well, by God, what we need is to build a dock.' Well, someone said it was almost lunch and it couldn't be built before lunch. . . . After a moment of serious consideration and a hurried consultation with a staff of engineers he agreed and toddled off to stoke his furnace at the luncheon table. . . . That, Bingo, is total war at its totalest.

Don't let anyone sell the idea that everyone out here is hustling with the old American energy. They may be ready to give their blood but not their sweat, if they can help it, and usually they fix it so they can help it. They have brought back a lot of old Captains and Commanders from retirement . . . and they give the impression of their brains being in their tails.

JFK's cynicism about the war erupted regularly: "When I read that we will fight the Japs for years if necessary," he cautioned months later, "and will sacrifice hundreds of thousands if we must—I always like to check from where he is talking—it's seldom out here." He poignantly told Arvad that the "boys at the front" rarely discussed the war but instead talked endlessly about "when they are going to get home." These impressions never faded: "That whole story was fucked up," he told journalist Robert Donovan years later about the war in the Solomon Islands. "You know the military always screws up everything."

The insights of this son of wealth and privilege in 1943 point directly to this "deep core of realism about the world" during the missile crisis:

The war goes slowly here, slower than you can ever imagine from reading the papers at home. The only way you can get the proper perspective on its progress is to put away the headlines for a month and watch us move on the map, it's deathly slow. The Japs have dug deep, and with the possible exception of a couple of Marine divisions are the greatest jungle fighters in the world. Their willingness to die for a place like Munda gives them a tremendous advantage over us, we, in aggregate, just don't have the willingness. Of course, at times, an individual will rise up to it, but in total, no. . . . Munda or any of these spots are just God damned hot stinking corners of small islands in a part of the ocean we all hope never to see again.

We are at a great disadvantage—the Russians could see their country invaded, the Chinese the same. The British were bombed, but we are fighting on some islands belonging to the Lever Company, a British concern making soap. . . . I suppose if we were stockholders we would perhaps be doing better, but to see that by dying at Munda you are helping to insure peace in our time takes a larger imagination than most men possess. . . . The Japs have this advantage: because of their feeling about Hirohito, they merely wish to kill. American energies are divided, he wants to kill but he is also trying desperately to prevent himself from being killed. . . .

This war here is a dirty business. It's very easy to talk about the war and beating the Japs if it takes years and a million men, but anyone who talks like that should consider well his words. We get so used to talking about billions of dollars, and millions of soldiers, that thousands of casualties sound like drops in the bucket. But if those thousands want to live as much as the ten that I saw [his PT boat crew], the people deciding the whys and wherefores had better make mighty sure that all this effort is headed for some definite goal, and that when we reach that goal we may say it was worth it, for if it isn't, the whole thing will turn to ashes, and we will face great trouble in the years to come after the war. . . .

There was a boy on my boat, only twenty-four, had three kids, one night two bombs straddles [sic] our boat, and two of the men were hit, one standing right next to him. He never got over it. He hardly ever spoke after that. He told me one night he thought he was going to be killed. I wanted to put him ashore to work, he wouldn't go. I wish I had. . . . He was in the forward gun turret where the destroyer hit us. . . . I don't know what this all adds up to, nothing I guess, but you said that you figured I'd . . . write my experiences—I wouldn't go near a book like that, this thing is so stupid, that while it has a sickening fascination for some of us, myself included, I want to leave it far behind me when I go.

JFK himself was barely two years older than Andrew Kirksey, the twenty-four-year-old "boy on my boat" killed on PT 109.

John Kennedy's aversion to war, particularly global war, became even more pronounced during the first decades of the nuclear era. In 1947, the twenty-nine-year-old freshman congressman warned of the potential for nuclear catastrophe: "The greatest danger is a war which would be waged by the conscious decision of the leaders of Russia some 25 or 35 years from now. She will have the atomic bomb, the planes, the ports, and the ships to wage aggressive war outside her borders. Such a conflict would truly mean the end of the world." "We should bear in mind," he wrote in 1960, the advice from military theorist Basil Hart: "'Keep strong, if possible. In any case, keep cool. Have unlimited patience. Never corner an opponent, and always assist him to save his face. Put yourself in his shoes—so as to see things through his eyes. Avoid self-righteousness like the devil—nothing is so self-blinding.'"

All his life JFK had a high regard for personal courage and toughness, but, at the same time, he loathed the brutality and carnage of war. He also recognized that although human beings had never been capable of building a stable and peaceful world, war with nuclear weapons was no longer a rational option. Kennedy was as passionately anti-communist as any of his advisers, but he understood that once a nuclear conflict was unleashed, all bets were off. One colleague recalled a briefing by Soviet specialists at which JFK had revealed "a mentality extraordinarily free of preconceived prejudices, inherited or otherwise. ... He saw Russia as a great and powerful country, and it seemed to him there must be some basis upon which the two countries could live without blowing each other up." He once remarked at a White House meeting, "It is insane that two men, sitting on opposite sides of the world, should be able to decide to bring an end to civilization." He was convinced "that there was nothing more important to a president than thinking hard about war."

JFK often mentioned a reported exchange between a former German chancellor and his successor after the outbreak of World War I. "How did it all happen?" the ex-chancellor asked. "Ah, if only one knew," was the reply. "If this planet is ever ravaged by nuclear war—" Kennedy declared in 1963, "if the survivors of that devastation can then endure the fire, poison, chaos and catastrophe—I do not want one of those survivors to ask another, 'How did it all happen?' and to receive the incredible reply: 'Ah, if only one knew.'"

Nonetheless, JFK never lost his ironic sense of humor about such potentially fatal realities in human affairs. After physicist Edward Teller testified against the Nuclear Test Ban Treaty at 1963 Senate hearings, Senator J. William Fulbright told the president that Teller's arguments had been persuasive and may have changed some votes. Kennedy replied with a bemused tone of resignation reflecting that deep core of realism, "There's no doubt that any man with complete conviction, particularly who's an expert, is bound to shake anybody who's got an open mind. That's the advantage of having a closed mind." The Cuban missile crisis provided the supreme test of John F. Kennedy's capacity to have an open mind and, at the same time, to hold fast to his core beliefs about war in the face of unyielding pressure from the "experts" around him.

Key Members of the Executive Committee of the National Security Council

George W. Ball (1909–1994)
Under Secretary of State

Ball worked on the Strategic Bombing Survey during World War II. In 1952 and 1956, he was active in the presidential campaigns of his former law partner, Adlai Stevenson. Several foreign policy papers he wrote for Stevenson's try for a third nomination in 1960 impressed JFK and led to Ball's appointment to the State Department. During the Ex-

Comm discussions, Ball supported a blockade and was among the first to condemn surprise air attacks as an American "Pearl Harbor." However, he also advocated a declaration of war in the early meetings, and during the October 27 discussions he first opposed the Cuba-Turkey missile trade, but switched sides after the shooting down of a U-2 spy plane over Cuba.

McGeorge Bundy (1919–1996)
Special Assistant to the President for National Security

Bundy attended the Dexter School in Brookline, Massachusetts, with classmate John F. Kennedy in the 1920s. He did foreign policy research for Republican presidential candidate Thomas Dewey in 1948, and later worked for the Council on Foreign Relations. In 1953, at the age of thirty-four and without a Ph.D., Bundy became dean of the faculty of arts and sciences at Harvard. A Republican, Bundy worked for the Kennedy campaign in 1960 and was appointed to the top White House national security position. His role in the ExComm meetings is difficult to categorize. Bundy initially supported the blockade but later endorsed bombing the missiles sites already under construction in Cuba. However, he was always eager to stand up for his personal policy choices and sometimes irritated the president. In the later meetings, Bundy stubbornly resisted JFK's willingness to "trade" Soviet missiles in Cuba for U.S. missiles in Turkey because he believed this decision would divide the NATO alliance.

C. Douglas Dillon (1909–2003)
Secretary of the Treasury

Dillon, an investment banker and Republican activist, first served in the Eisenhower administration as ambassador to France. Later, as Under Secretary of State for Economic Affairs, he had some heated personal exchanges with Khrushchev. Even though Dillon had supported Richard Nixon in 1960, Kennedy chose him to lead the Treasury Department in an effort to soften GOP opposition to his economic policies. Deeply suspicious of communism and Khrushchev's motives, Dillon initially supported air strikes on the missile sites as the course of action least likely to provoke Soviet retaliation. He eventually went along with the blockade as the first step in isolating and ousting Castro, but again advocated air strikes late in the second week of meetings. Dillon also vigorously resisted the proposal to remove American missiles from Turkey in exchange for the withdrawal of Soviet missiles from Cuba.

Roswell Gilpatric (1906–1996)
Deputy Secretary of Defense

Gilpatric, a successful Wall Street lawyer, served as assistant secretary of the Air Force in the Truman administration and during the 1950s helped draft a report for the Rockefeller Brothers' Fund calling for an extensive buildup of U.S. weapons and research. Unlike his boss, Robert McNamara, Gilpatric generally supported the JCS view that the missiles represented a military rather than a diplomatic threat and was sympathetic to their proposals to eliminate them by bombing and/or invasion.

Lyndon B. Johnson (1908–1973)
Vice President of the United States

As Senate majority leader during the Eisenhower administration, Johnson had regularly been described as the second most powerful man in Washington. He found the inevitable obscurity of the vice presidency hard to accept and always felt that he did not have the respect of the "best and the brightest" around the president. Despite his initial reluctance to speak at the ExComm meetings, especially when JFK was present, and his uncertainty about the use of force, he did eventually make some important contributions to the discussions on October 27.

U. Alexis Johnson (1908–1997)
Deputy Under Secretary of State for Political Affairs

A career foreign service officer, Johnson served as ambassador to Czechoslovakia during the Eisenhower administration before being appointed to the Kennedy State Department. Johnson, like most members of ExComm, first supported air strikes against the missile sites but ultimately endorsed the blockade. He was not a major participant in the discussions but worked behind the scenes drafting policy papers for the meetings.

John Fitzgerald Kennedy (1917–1963)
President of the United States

JFK, a World War II naval hero in the South Pacific, ran successfully for three terms in the House of Representatives (1946, 1948, 1950) and two terms in the Senate (1952, 1958) before he was narrowly elected president in 1960. Kennedy subtly guided and managed the ExComm discussions without ever appearing overbearing or aggressive. He patiently listened to all points of view and was remarkably tolerant of harsh criticism. His determination to seek a political rather than a military solution, in order to avert "the final failure" of nuclear war, stands in sharp contrast to the Cold War rhetoric and the covert actions against Cuba which he had eagerly pursued since early 1961 and continued to support in his final year as President.

Robert F. Kennedy (1925–1968)
Attorney General of the United States

Robert Kennedy managed JFK's presidential campaign in 1960 before becoming attorney general at the age of thirty-five. RFK played a disproportionately significant role in the meetings because he was JFK's brother and was accurately perceived to be the president's most intimate confidant. Indeed, the loyalty and trust between the Kennedy brothers was unique in the history of the American presidency. If JFK temporarily left the room or did not attend an ExComm meeting, the participants instinctively recognized RFK as the president's stand-in. In the final hours before the October 28 breakthrough, President Kennedy trusted only his brother as a personal and secret emissary to Soviet ambassador Anatoly Dobrynin. Nonetheless, RFK's stance during the ExComm meetings turns out to be much more complicated than the idealized and romanticized view popularized in his 1969 book, *Thirteen Days*. Indeed, RFK, in sharp contrast to JFK, was one of the most consistently hawkish and confrontational members of the ExComm.

Edwin Martin (1908–2002)
Assistant Secretary of State for Inter-American Affairs

Martin held State Department posts in Japan, Korea, and Europe before President Eisenhower named him assistant secretary of state for economic affairs. After moving to Latin American affairs in 1962, Martin played a key role in the OAS resolutions condemning the deployment of Soviet missiles in Cuba and endorsing the U.S. blockade. He was also involved in coordinating covert actions against Cuba and strongly supported the blockade and all necessary steps for removing the missiles.

John McCone (1902–1991)
Director, Central Intelligence Agency

A tough anti-communist and conservative Republican, McCone served as chairman of the Atomic Energy Commission in the Eisenhower administration before JFK named him to head the CIA after the

Bay of Pigs fiasco. He was the first senior administration official to warn that the Soviets were planning to install offensive nuclear weapons in Cuba. McCone regularly briefed the ExComm on Soviet moves in Cuba and updated former president Eisenhower on JFK's behalf. He advocated removal of the missiles by whatever means necessary—including the use of military force. He did, however, break with most of his ExComm colleagues in the final meetings on October 27 by supporting the president's determination to consider a Turkish missile trade.

Robert S. McNamara (1916–)
Secretary of Defense

McNamara, a statistician and business school graduate, worked on the strategic bombing of Japan late in World War II. He became president of the Ford Motor Company in 1960, but only weeks later was offered the top Defense Department post by JFK. He quickly earned a reputation for hard-nosed realism and a grasp of technical issues. Although he supported an invasion at several points in the ExComm meetings, McNamara became the president's ally by openly breaking with the Joint Chiefs and arguing that the Soviet missiles in Cuba posed a political rather than a military threat to the United States. He ultimately resisted surprise air strikes, supported the blockade, and proposed a plan to reduce the chance of a Soviet attack on Turkey by defusing U.S. Jupiter missiles and substituting submarine-launched Polaris missiles. Nonetheless, he opposed the president's support for a direct trade of missiles in Cuba and Turkey and was ready to "*really* escalate" by October 27. He was one of the most articulate and outspoken members of the ExComm.

Paul H. Nitze (1907–2004)
Assistant Secretary of Defense for International Security Affairs

The principal author of NSC-68 in 1950, Nitze was committed to victory over the U.S.S.R. and international communism. He was one of the ExComm's most consistent hawks and argued, contrary to his superior, Robert McNamara, that the Soviet missiles in Cuba had altered the world balance of power. His tense exchange with President Kennedy about tightening JCS procedures so that U.S. missiles in Turkey could not be fired at the U.S.S.R. without a presidential order is one of the most dramatic moments of the ExComm meetings. He was a resolute opponent of the Cuba-Turkey missile trade.

Dean Rusk (1909–1994)
Secretary of State

Rusk, a former Rhodes Scholar, served as deputy under secretary of state in the Truman administration before becoming president of the Rockefeller Foundation from 1951 to 1960. Kennedy offered Rusk the top State Department post on the advice of former defense secretary Robert Lovett. In the first wave of writing after the Cuban missile crisis, RFK and several historians criticized Rusk for lack of leadership in the ExComm discussions. The tapes have proved otherwise. Rusk contributed detailed and thoughtful analyses of diplomatic policy choices throughout the meetings, and, like most ExComm members, shifted positions several times; he generally resisted surprise air strikes, endorsed the blockade, and advised against seizing Soviet ships that had turned away from Cuba. However, he opposed a deal involving U.S. missiles in Turkey and, after a U-2 was shot down on October 27, urged JFK to enforce armed surveillance over Cuba despite the chance of killing Russian personnel on the ground. Later that evening, however, Rusk and JFK collaborated on a secret diplomatic effort, through the U.N., to prevent the outbreak of war.

Theodore C. Sorensen (1928–)
Special Counsel to the President

Sorensen served as speechwriter and trusted political adviser to Senator John Kennedy from 1953 to 1960. Despite the fact that Sorensen was not a foreign policy specialist, Kennedy, who trusted Sorensen's judgment, invited him to participate in the ExComm discussions. Sorensen spoke rarely, but generally came down on the side of caution and diplomacy rather than military force. However, he did join the majority in resisting a Turkish missile swap. He also wrote several important policy option memos during the crisis and was the principal author of JFK's October 22 speech to the nation.

Maxwell D. Taylor (1901–1987)
Chairman, Joint Chiefs of Staff

Taylor served as Army chief of staff during the Eisenhower administration and was chosen as JCS chairman by President Kennedy in 1962. Taylor generally represented the hawkish views of the Chiefs during the ExComm discussions. However, even though he favored bombing over invasion in the early meetings, he eventually shifted ground, even suggesting the possible use of nuclear weapons in Cuba to safeguard American military supremacy in the Caribbean. Taylor reluctantly accepted the quarantine, but always displayed respect for the president and avoided the disdainful tone used by several JCS members.

Llewellyn E. Thompson (1904–1972)
United States Ambassador-at-Large

Thompson served as ambassador to the Soviet Union from 1957 to 1962 and was the only regular member of the ExComm who knew Khrushchev personally. As a result, the president listened with special interest to Thompson's assessments of Soviet thinking and Khrushchev's motives. Thompson's advice, however, was generally hawkish. Despite endorsing the blockade, he supported a declaration of war and the ouster of Castro, advised the president that Khrushchev would never back down, and strenuously resisted a trade of the missiles in Turkey and Cuba in order to preserve U.S. credibility in Europe and to avoid dividing the NATO alliance.

A grim but focused President Kennedy just seconds before addressing the nation and revealing the discovery of Soviet nuclear missiles in Cuba.

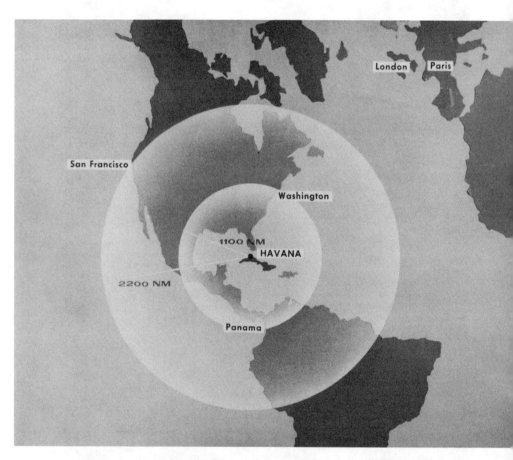

Department of Defense display board showing the range of Soviet MRBMs and IRBMs in Cuba.

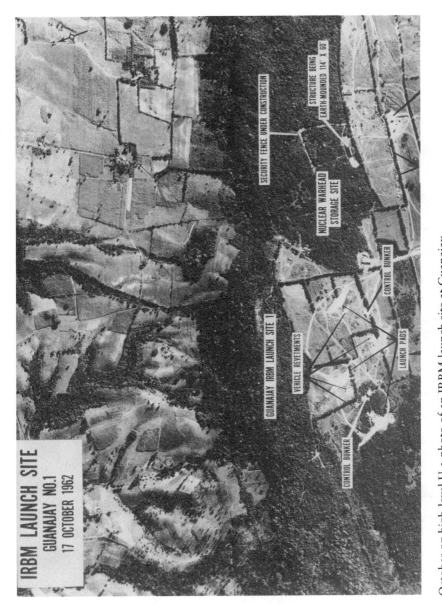

October 17 high-level U-2 photo of an IRBM launch site at Guanajay

October 25 low-level surveillance photo of an MRBM launch site at San Cristobal

The October 29 ExComm meeting (the only meeting photographed), view one. On the President's side of the table (Presidential Seal on the wall behind JFK)— *to JFK's left*: Robert McNamara, Roswell Gilpatric (pen in hand), Maxwell Taylor (not in uniform), Paul Nitze (right end of table); *to JFK's right*: Dean Rusk, George Ball (writing), John McCone's white hair just visible on the left end of the table in front of the fireplace.

The October 29 ExComm meeting, view two. Facing the bookcases on the side opposite the President—*from left to right*: Robert Kennedy (standing), Donald Wilson (partially obscured), Theodore Sorensen, McGeorge Bundy, Douglas Dillon, Lyndon Johnson, Llewellyn Thompson, U. Alexis Johnson.

CHAPTER THREE

The Secret Meetings
of the Executive Committee
of the National Security Council

Tuesday, October 16, 11:50 A.M., Cabinet Room

"How do you know this is a medium-range ballistic missile?"
President John F. Kennedy

In the hours before the first ExComm meeting the president kept to his normal schedule to avoid the public appearance of a crisis. He greeted astronaut Walter Schirra and his family and later met with the White House Panel on Mental Retardation. As the president's advisers entered the Cabinet Room, the human meaning of the situation was made poignantly plain when they found JFK talking with his nearly five-year-old daughter, Caroline. She scurried from the room and the meeting began.

The fifteen men gathering that morning were stunned that the Soviets had taken such a gamble just ninety miles from the Florida coast and infuriated that the administration had been deceived by top Kremlin officials. JFK and his advisers knew, however, that humiliating the Soviets would likely make the situation worse. This was one time when a favorite Kennedy family maxim, "Don't get mad, get even," did not apply.

The tone of the discussions was nearly always calm and business-like—making it difficult for the listener to grasp that the stakes were nothing less than world peace and human survival. The meetings were remarkably egalitarian, and participants spoke freely with no regard for rank. Indeed, there were repeated disagreements with the president—sometimes bordering on rudeness and disrespect. There were also moments of laughter, clearly an emotional necessity in coping with such unrelenting anxiety and uncertainty. The president's "confidence and coolness," one participant recalled, concealed "the deep nervous and emotional energy that you knew was at work within him."

The overriding question was clear at the outset: could the United States eliminate this apparent Soviet provocation without war? JFK assumed that if the U.S. took military action against Cuba, the U.S.S.R. would move against West Berlin. The U.S. would be forced to respond; the Soviets would react in turn—and so on—escalating towards the unthinkable. A reckless or careless move could set in motion an irreversible and catastrophic chain of events.

But before a response could be discussed, one question had to be answered: what exactly were the Soviets doing in Cuba? Nothing in the high-level U-2 photographs displayed at the meeting cried out "missiles!" JFK and most of his advisers had little or no experience in photo analysis, and these objects could easily be mistaken for trucks or farm equipment. Arthur Lundahl, director of the National Photographic Interpretation Center, and missile expert Sydney Graybeal were on hand to explain the evidence. The president pored over the photos using a large magnifying glass, and several participants recalled that the look on his face suggested deep concern and uncertainty. He also hit the hidden switch under the conference table activating the tape recorder.

Deputy CIA director General Marshall Carter began by identifying fourteen canvas-covered missile trailers, sixty-seven feet in length and nine feet in width, photographed on October 14 at an MRBM site in San Cristobal. (CIA director John McCone was attending a family funeral.) Lundahl pointed to small rectangular shapes and whispered to the president, "These are the launchers here."

Carter and Lundahl continued to focus on technical details in the photographs. Finally, President Kennedy, in an almost clinical tone of voice, asked how far advanced the construction had been when the photos were taken. Lundahl admitted that his analysts had never seen this kind of installation before. "Not even in the Soviet Union?" Kennedy pressed. "No sir," Lundahl replied.

The CIA had kept careful tabs on Soviet missile bases, but Lundahl reminded the president that surveillance had been suspended after a U-2 was shot down in 1960. JFK, a junior naval officer in World War II, was not yet familiar with the technical jargon of missile-age weaponry.

"How do you know this is a medium-range ballistic missile?" he asked candidly. "The length, sir," Lundahl responded patiently. "The length of the missile?" Kennedy asked, examining the photo. "Which part?"

Graybeal handed the president photos of missiles from the U.S.S.R.'s annual May Day military parade. JFK asked grimly if the missiles in Cuba were ready to be fired. Graybeal's "no" did not satisfy him and he probed further, "What does it have to be fired from?" Graybeal calmly explained that the missiles could be fired from a hard, stable surface. The sites, however, were being assembled more rapidly than those already observed in the U.S.S.R., and no one could be sure when the missiles would be ready to launch their deadly payloads at military sites or cities in the U.S.

Defense secretary Robert McNamara pressed Graybeal on the key issue implicit in JFK's questions—were Soviet nuclear warheads also in Cuba? "Sir, we've looked very hard," Graybeal replied. "We can find nothing that would spell 'nuclear warhead.'" He added, however, that the warheads could be mounted on the missiles in just a few hours. "It seems almost *impossible, to me*," McNamara insisted forcefully, "that they would be ready to fire *with* nuclear warheads *on the site* without even a fence around it." Graybeal agreed, "We do not believe they are ready to fire." But, even if McNamara's logical conclusion was correct, no one knew how long it would remain correct. General Maxwell Taylor, the new chairman of the Joint Chiefs of Staff, stressed that the sites could become operational rapidly, but Graybeal countered that only one missile had been seen close to launch position near an erector.

McNamara prided himself on examining issues dispassionately and could not believe that the Soviets would risk a military confrontation over missiles that did not have nuclear warheads: "There *must* be *some* storage site there. It should be one of our important objectives to *find* that storage site." Lundahl offered the defense chief guarded assurance that additional U-2 data on the storage sites "may be in our grasp," he added cautiously, "*if* we can find them." General Carter and Secretary of State Dean Rusk contended that the missiles must be equipped with nuclear warheads. "Oh, I think there's no question about that," McNamara affirmed, but "it seems *extremely* unlikely that they are *now* ready to fire, or *may be* ready to fire within a matter of hours, or even a day or two." The bases did not have to be attacked—at least immediately. One decision quickly commanded a consensus: the president should authorize further U-2 flights to locate any other missile bases and the elusive warheads and storage sites.

Rusk soon broke in. His placid, monotone voice and lengthy monologues sometimes tried the patience of his ExComm colleagues, but the soft-spoken diplomat never flinched from the real issue: could the U.S. eliminate these missiles without provoking Soviet retaliation, especially in Berlin, which could spark a conventional or even a nuclear war? "Mr. President," Rusk began gravely, as if delivering a professorial lecture, "this is an overwhelmingly serious problem. It's one that we, I think all of us, had not *really* believed the Soviets could carry this far." Military action in Cuba, he warned, would affect U.S. forces and allies around the world, adding "there's no such thing, I think, as unilateral action by the United States. . . . So I think we have to think *very hard*" about whether to remove the bases with surprise air strikes or "decide that this is the time to eliminate the Cuban problem by actually moving into the island."

Rusk recommended seeking OAS support under the Rio Pact and warning Castro directly that the Soviet Union might betray Cuba for U.S. concessions in Berlin. (The Kennedy administration, in fact, refused to deal directly with Cuba during the crisis.) But, he also urged vigorous support for U.S.-backed guerrilla forces working to "create maximum confusion on the island." In a somber tone of voice, Rusk urged choosing a quick strike or alerting "our allies *and Mr. Khrushchev* that there *is* an utterly serious crisis in the making here because Mr. Khrushchev may not himself really understand that or believe that at this point. I think we'll be facing a situation that could *well* lead to general war."

McNamara echoed Rusk's concerns about the risks in any course of action but insisted forcefully that air strikes in Cuba had to be carried out *before* the missiles became operational: "*if* they become operational *before* the air strike, I do not believe we can state we can knock them out before they can be launched, and *if* they're launched, there is almost certain to be chaos in part of the East Coast or the area in a radius of six hundred to one thousand miles from Cuba." Less than an hour into their first meeting, the president and his advisers were confronting the possibility that millions of Americans might be only hours away from a nuclear attack.

McNamara's advice was technically detailed and well thought-out, and the president respected its value. The defense secretary contended, in a cool and confident tone, that the U.S. must be prepared for air strikes on the missile sites, airfields, aircraft, and nuclear storage sites. The bombing would last several days and result in hundreds or even thousands of Cuban casualties; he did not mention possible Soviet casualties. The air attacks would be followed by a full air and sea invasion within seven days. Finally, he called for military mobilization and a possible declaration of national emergency. The defense chief did not address how Khrushchev might respond if the U.S. bombed the missiles, killed Cubans and Russians, and landed thousands of marines in Cuba.

General Taylor deepened the uncertainties facing the president by rejecting McNamara's assumption that aerial intelligence could provide precise data on the operational status of the missiles *before* an attack. He also acknowledged that the first air strikes would not destroy "a hundred percent" of the missiles. Nonetheless, Taylor urged retaining the element of surprise by striking the missiles "without any warning whatsoever." He also added a step to McNamara's plan: once these weapons are destroyed, "we should indeed prevent any more coming in, which means a naval blockade." The JCS chairman, a veteran of the bloody invasion of Italy in 1943, also cautioned the president against McNamara's view that air attacks must be followed by an invasion: "as to whether we invade or not, I think that's the *hardest* question militarily in the whole business, and one that we should look at very closely before we get our feet in that *deep mud* of Cuba."

Rusk, recognizing Taylor's admission that *all* the sites could not be destroyed immediately—*before* some operational missiles could be fired—cautioned that if the Russians "*shoot those* missiles," before, during, or after air strikes, "we're in a general nuclear war." McNamara added a sobering qualification: "If we saw a warhead on the site and we knew that that launcher was capable of launching that warhead, frankly I would *strongly* urge against the air attack ... because I think the *danger* to this country in relation to the *gain* that would accrue would be *excessive*. ... *If* we're talking about an air attack, I believe we should consider it *only* on the assumption that we can carry it off *before* these become operational."

Several military options had emerged in the initial discussions: air attacks on just the missile bases; air strikes on the missiles, surface-to air sites (SAMs), MiG fighter planes, airfields, and nuclear storage sites; an invasion to remove Castro from power; a naval blockade. At that moment, the consensus was clearly hardening around some military response. But the risks involved in all these options were also becoming unsettlingly plain.

One central question remained unresolved—what was the Soviet motive for a nuclear showdown over Cuba? "There must be some major reason for the Russians to set this up," JFK speculated. "Must be that they're not satisfied with their ICBMs." Taylor agreed that Soviet short-range missiles in Cuba provided a supplement to "their rather defective ICBM system." JFK and his advisers, however, never took seriously Khrushchev's goal of protecting Castro because their Cold War convictions all but dictated an explanation: Berlin and the nuclear balance of power.

JFK also worried that a blockade might be useless because additional missiles could be brought in by submarine. McNamara advised telling the Soviets in that event, "You'll take them out and you'll carry on open surveillance." But, he cautioned, several hundred air sorties would be needed just to wipe out the missiles and the MiGs, and the U.S. might still be vulnerable to conventional or nuclear attack by Castro's air force flying low to avoid radar: "It would be a *very* heavy price to pay in U.S. lives for the damage we did to Cuba."

The discussion returned to Soviet motives. The deployment in Cuba, Rusk suggested, might signal Khrushchev's resentment about American missiles based in NATO countries: "we don't *really* live under fear of his nuclear weapons to the extent that he has to live under fear of ours. Also, we have nuclear weapons nearby, in Turkey and places like that." America's top policy makers generally did not understand how troubling the Turkish missiles were to Khrushchev; nor were they well informed about them. The president asked, "How many weapons do we have in Turkey?" "We have how many?" Bundy repeated, and McNamara, also unsure of the specifics, replied, "About *fifteen*, I believe to be the figure." Bundy responded tentatively, "I think that's right." It required genuine independence of mind for Rusk to cite CIA director McCone's belief "that Khrushchev may feel that it's important for *us* to learn about living under medium-range missiles, and he's doing that to sort of balance that political, psychological flank."

No one was prepared to believe that Khrushchev might also be trying to protect Cuba from another U.S. invasion. Berlin, instead, seemed to provide the key to Khrushchev's motives in Cuba. "For the first time," Rusk asserted, "I'm beginning *really* to wonder whether Mr. Khrushchev is entirely rational about Berlin. U Thant [U.N. acting secretary general] has talked about his obsession with it. And I think we have to keep our eye on that element." Perhaps, Rusk speculated, the Soviets "*grossly* misunderstand the importance of Cuba to this country" and are planning to use American military action against Cuba as a justification for seizing West Berlin.

Bundy scornfully dismissed Khrushchev's argument that the missiles in Cuba were defensive—insisting that failure to locate the warheads "doesn't make them any less offensive to us." But Treasury Secretary C. Douglas Dillon expressed doubts that U.S. allies would back an attack on Cuba to eliminate a threat Europe had been facing for years. "The prospect of that pattern," Bundy noted grimly, "is not an appetizing one." Rusk too expressed sympathy for NATO jitters about facing war "without the slightest consultation, or warning, or preparation."

President Kennedy was dubious that NATO could be warned before air strikes: "warning them, it seems to me, is warning everybody." The Soviets might announce that they will fire the missiles if attacked: "Then whadda we do? Then we don't take 'em out. Of course, we then announce, 'Well, if they do that, then we're gonna attack with nuclear weapons.'" Bundy stressed the political advantage in limiting the strikes, "in surgical terms," to the missiles alone, and Deputy Under Secretary of State U. Alexis Johnson cautioned that attacks on the missiles, MiGs, and airfields would make it "*very* difficult to convince anybody that this was *not* a preinvasion strike." JFK noted again that the Soviets could still bring in missiles by submarine; and, given Taylor's indication that air strikes could not destroy *all* the missiles *before* they were armed, the U.S. might end up under actual rather than potential nuclear attack. President Kennedy and his advisers were gradually realizing that there might not be a quick "surgical" fix in Cuba.

After a brief discussion about preventing leaks from the discussions, JFK asked about the sources of Senator Keating's charges, and Bundy recommended interviewing Keating to "check out his data." JFK invited Vice President Lyndon Johnson to voice his thoughts, and the politically savvy Texan advised the president not to count on the OAS, the NATO allies, or the Congress, saying "We're not gonna get much help out of them."

President Kennedy summed up the options on the table: attacking the missile sites; air strikes against the missiles, the SAMs, the MiGs, and the airfields; the first two choices plus a naval blockade; and consulting with the allies before the strikes. Attorney General Robert Kennedy, dissatisfied with all these options, spoke up for the first time. RFK was an ardent supporter of plans to subvert or eliminate Castro. Now, speaking directly to his brother, he defended the invasion option raised earlier by McNamara. "You're droppin' bombs all over Cuba if you do the second [inclusive air strike]. . . . You're gonna kill an awful lot a people, and we're gonna take an *awful lot* a heat on it." Only an invasion could justify the military and political risks from so much destruction and loss of life.

The president asked how long it would take to mount an invasion. McNamara repeated that it could be done seven days after air strikes. "You could get six divisions or seven divisions into Cuba," the president asked skeptically, "in seven days?" Taylor outlined plans to send in 90,000 men in five to eleven days. "Do you think 90,000 are enough?" the president replied, always concerned about military overconfidence. "At least it's enough to start the thing going," Taylor replied somewhat evasively.

JFK also wondered about how the Cuban people would react to a U.S. invasion, and McNamara speculated that if the air strikes triggered an uprising "of the free [anti-Castro] Cubans" it might be possible to send in troops in less than a week. "Is it *absolutely* essential," RFK insisted, "that you wait seven days after you have an air strike?" Taylor explained that positioning ships and troops for an invasion might sacrifice the element of surprise, but RFK suggested that tension over Berlin could be used to explain these steps, and it would be better, "If you could get it in, get it started, so that there wasn't any turning back." The president also expressed concern about the missiles reaching "ready-to-go" status and Bundy added ominously that more sites would likely be discovered. McNamara sided with Taylor, noting "we haven't been able to figure out a way to shorten that five- to seven-day period while maintaining surprise in the air attack."

As the meeting began to wrap up, despite concerns about Soviet retaliation, a consensus for action against the missiles seemed solid. JFK also appeared willing to attack the MiGs to prevent bombing reprisals in the southeastern U.S.: "I would think you'd have to presume they'd be using iron [conventional] bombs and not nuclear weapons. Because, obviously," he remarked, perhaps engaging in wishful thinking, "why would the Soviets permit nuclear war to begin under that sort of half-assed way?" "I think that's reasonable," McNamara agreed.

After some discussion about informing French president Charles de Gaulle and West German chancellor Konrad Adenauer, JFK declared, "I don't think we've got much *time* on these missiles. ... We're *certainly* gonna do number one [the limited air strike]. We're gonna take out these missiles." He also agreed to move forward with planning for more inclusive air strikes and even for an invasion. The president also instructed that information about the missiles be kept "as tight as possible" in the government, "but what we're gonna do about it really ought to be . . . the tightest of all because otherwise we'll bitch it up."

RFK continued to press for an invasion: "How long would it take to take over the island?" Taylor explained that it was "very hard to estimate, Bobby," suggesting that resistance could be contained in five or six days, but months would be needed to clean up loose ends. The president, despite the lessons he had presumably learned from the Bay of Pigs about predictions by intelligence experts, wondered aloud if the CIA could provide forecasts of how the Cuban people would respond to American military intervention.

Bundy urged his colleagues to leave by the East Gate in order to avoid being observed from the Press Room near the West Gate. After some discussion about when John McCone could return to Washington and brief former president Eisenhower, under whom he had served, the meeting broke up with an agreement to reconvene at 6:30 P.M.

The military planning endorsed by the ExComm continued in the hours after the first meeting. President Kennedy hosted a previously scheduled luncheon for the Crown Prince of Libya, attended by U.N. ambassador Adlai Stevenson; later he showed Stevenson the U-2 photos. During the afternoon, Dean Rusk met with senior State Department officials and Robert McNamara conferred with General Taylor and the Joint Chiefs on the military options discussed that morning.

Robert Kennedy told Richard Helms, CIA deputy director for planning, of the president's dissatisfaction with the progress of covert operations in Cuba. He also discussed possible ground attacks on the missile sites by anti-Castro guerrillas and pledged to give more personal leadership to Operation Mongoose—including daily morning meetings with the Special Group (Augmented), which he chaired, for the duration of the crisis. Military action against the missile sites seemed imminent and all but inevitable.

Tuesday, October 16, 6:30 P.M., Cabinet Room

"I don't know quite what kind of a world we live in after we've struck Cuba and we've started it."
                                    Secretary of Defense Robert McNamara

General Carter revealed that several sites in Cuba would soon be capable of launching up to twenty-four missiles with a range of 1,100 miles.

JFK, perhaps thinking (like RFK) about a guerrilla ground attack, asked if the sites were vulnerable to rifle fire. "Highly vulnerable," McNamara declared. Carter reiterated that warheads and storage facilities had not been located, but JFK returned to the key issue: "General, how long would you say we had before these . . . will be ready to fire?" The bases could be complete in two weeks, Carter explained, but individual missiles "could be operational much sooner." McNamara noted that U-2 flights would soon cover the entire island, and Carter added a bit of good news: "It would *appear* that we have caught this in a very early stage of deployment."

The president, perhaps hoping the photos had been misinterpreted, asked Carter if there was any doubt that these missiles were offensive. "There's no question in our minds, sir," Carter replied. "They are not a camouflage or a covert attempt to fool us." Bundy refused to drop the president's point, insisting that it could be "*really* catastrophic" to make "a bad guess" about the power and range of these missiles. After Carter and McNamara presented more technical data, Bundy reluctantly backed off.

Rusk, however, joined by Edwin Martin, assistant secretary of state for inter-American affairs, again proposed a diplomatic effort to convince Castro that the Soviets were angling to betray Cuba for concessions in Berlin. Martin even suggested hinting that the U.S. might assist Castro in throwing the communists out of Cuba. Rusk warned that military action in Cuba could alienate NATO and lead to the overthrow of several Latin American governments, "And we could find ourselves isolated and the alliance crumbling."

President Kennedy asked for the military's perspective. Taylor reported that the Chiefs favored eliminating the missile sites and the Soviet fighters "with one hard crack." The general cautioned, "We'll never get it all" in a first strike and will need several days to complete the job. The vital question remained unanswered: would the missiles still standing after the first air attack be fired?

McNamara, eager to systematize the discussions, summarized three possible courses of action: negotiations with Khrushchev; unlimited air surveillance of Cuba plus a naval blockade and an announcement that the U.S.S.R. would be attacked if Cuba took offensive action against the U.S.; the JCS plan for air strikes on the missile bases, SAM sites, MiG fighters, and airfields, followed by an invasion. The defense chief cautioned that military action was "*almost* certain" to lead to Soviet reprisals—particularly in Berlin. "It may well be worth the price," he argued. "Perhaps we should pay that." He also suggested rather half-heartedly that Khrushchev might be discouraged from reprisals by U.S. military mobilization and a declaration of national emergency.

The political and military cards were now clearly on the table. JFK acknowledged that announcing the discovery of the MRBMs would deprive the military of a surprise strike, but reasoned that Khrushchev must know "that we're gonna *find out.*" Bundy reminded the commander-in-chief that Khrushchev had been "*very, very* explicit" in the official TASS statement on September 11 about the dangers of such a deployment. "That's right," JFK replied, overlooking U.S. covert operations in Cuba. "He's initiated the danger, really, hasn't he? He's the one playing God, not us."

McNamara warned that the "*minimum* risk" from an advance warning would be the dropping of conventional high-explosive bombs along the East Coast. Taylor agreed that Florida was particularly vulnerable. JFK speculated that one strike would probably not do a great deal of damage, but Dillon countered, "What if they carry a nuclear weapon?" The president was genuinely startled by the suggestion, "Oh, you assume they wouldn't do *that.*" "I just don't see that possibility," Rusk observed, but "we could be just *utterly* wrong." "We certainly have been wrong," JFK conceded, "Not many of us thought that he was gonna put MRBMs on Cuba." "Except John McCone," Bundy and Carter pointed out, and Kennedy muttered, "Yeah." (McCone had predicted that the deployment of defensive surface-to-air missiles in Cuba was a prelude to introducing offensive missiles.)

Bundy questioned whether the missiles were militarily significant: "How gravely *does* this *change,*" he rapped the table for emphasis, "the strategic balance?" McNamara boldly distanced himself from the Chiefs under his authority: "Mac, I asked the Chiefs that this afternoon. In effect, they said 'substantially.' My own personal view is, not at all." General Taylor argued that it made a great deal of difference if these missiles were in Cuba rather than the Soviet Union, and Bundy retorted with a laugh, "Oh, I asked the question with an awareness" of the political realities.

The Soviets could put so much firepower into Cuba, JFK predicted, that an attack might be too risky—allowing Khrushchev to "squeeze us in Berlin." Or, "You may say it doesn't make any difference if you get blown up by an ICBM flying from the Soviet Union or one that was ninety miles away. Geography doesn't mean that much." But, when Bundy observed that attacking Cuba could escalate to all-out war,

Kennedy made a startling admission, "That's why it shows the Bay of Pigs was really right, if we'd *done* it right." JFK, abruptly morose, hesitated for several seconds and muttered, "I would... better and better, worse and worse...," but trailed off inconclusively.

Taylor insisted that the strategic situation had changed dramatically: "a quarter of a million American soldiers, marines, and airmen" are preparing "to take an island we launched 1,800 Cubans against a year and a half ago"—prompting someone to laugh in the background. RFK argued that inaction could lead to nuclear blackmail, and, JFK added, make Cuba appear "coequal with us." Dillon worried about appearing "scared of the Cubans," and Martin agreed that the U.S. could not sit back "and let 'em do it to us—that is more important than the *direct* threat." Martin's view reflected classic Cold War doctrine: even the appearance of weakness would encourage Soviet aggression.

The president, nonetheless, conceded that his rhetoric had contributed to the crisis: "Last month," he began, in a rather jocular tone as several people chuckled in the background, "I said we weren't going to [accept offensive missiles in Cuba], and last month I should have said we don't care. But when we said we're *not* going to, and then they go ahead and do it, and then we do nothing"—he suddenly became very somber—"then I would think that our risks *increase*." "They've got enough to blow us up now anyway," he added gloomily, "After all, this is a political struggle as much as military."

JFK again pondered announcing the discovery of the missiles before taking military action. Martin warned that once the secret is out, "you're going to have a ton of instability in *this* country" unless you act quickly. "Oh, I understand *that*," JFK retorted. Taylor and McNamara pointed out that the missiles might be hidden quickly or fired between an announcement and an attack. Under Secretary of State George Ball urged a warning, "more for the appearance than for the reality," since the Soviets would never accept an ultimatum.

A limited strike on the missiles, JFK contended, was politically more defensible than a general air strike "into the city of Havana. . . . Now I know the Chiefs say, 'Well, that means their bombers can take off against us.'" In that event, Bundy argued firmly, "*they* have made a general war." The political advantages of a small strike, he continued, "are *very* strong. . . . It corresponds to 'the punishment fits the crime,' in political terms. We are doing only what we warned repeatedly and publicly we would *have* to do."

JFK finally concluded that plans should move forward for the general air strike—which did not preclude deciding later to do only the limited strike. RFK asked again, "Does that encompass an invasion?" "No," the president replied firmly. "I'd say that's the third course." JFK did agree to Dillon and Taylor's insistence on including the SAM sites in a general air attack to clear access to the airfields. McNamara, sensing JFK's uneasiness about a general strike, advised waiting for new photography: "The president does not have to make any decision . . . *except* the decision to be prepared." He also recommended preparing "a *specific* strike plan *limited* to the missiles and the nuclear storage sites. . . . We ought to provide you that option." Kennedy agreed.

Doubts, however, had clearly unsettled the defense chief. "I *don't* believe," he asserted, "we have considered the consequences of *any* of these actions satisfactorily, and . . . I'm not sure we're taking all the action we ought to take now to minimize those. I don't know quite what kind of a world we live in after we've struck Cuba and we've started it. . . . How do we *stop* at that point? I don't *know* the answer to this." Ball affirmed that deadly consequences could erupt anywhere in the world, and McNamara quickly agreed.

Taylor, nonetheless, boldly announced that the JCS "feel so strongly" about the dangers in the limited strike "that they would prefer taking *no* military action" rather than lose the advantage of surprise and expose civilians to an attack from Cuba. JFK gently but firmly disagreed: if the airfields are attacked, "I mean you're right in a much more *major* operation, therefore the dangers of the worldwide effects . . . are increased."

The president, maneuvering "to get this thing under some degree of control," boldly appealed to Taylor's earlier doubts about an invasion, "Let's not let the Chiefs knock us out on this one, General"—a striking thing to say to the JCS chairman. JFK then put Taylor on the spot with a leading question: "But you're not for the invasion?" and got the answer he seemed to want: "I would not at this moment, no sir." McNamara reiterated that air strikes could trigger an uprising in Cuba which might force an invasion, but Alexis Johnson countered that in a limited attack on military targets, "People would just stay home and try to keep out of trouble."

The pugnacious Robert Kennedy had no interest in limited air strikes. He predicted that Khrushchev would reintroduce the weapons after the bombing. In that event, McNamara declared, a blockade would have to be established. "Then we're gonna have to sink Russian ships," RFK responded, "Then we're gonna have to sink Russian submarines." It was better to stand up to Khrushchev now and face the consequences—"we should just get into it, and get it over with and take our losses."

McNamara again recommended discussing the consequences of military action. JFK repeated that the missiles did not increase Soviet strategic strength and mused about Soviet motives: "After all, Khrushchev demonstrated a sense of caution over Laos [by accepting a coalition government in 1961]. Berlin, he's been cautious." Ball noted that Khrushchev was coming to the U.N. in November and might be hoping to trade the missiles for concessions in Berlin. "One thing that I would *still* cling to," Bundy affirmed, "is that he's not likely to give *Fidel Castro* nuclear warheads." "But what is the advantage of that?" JFK persisted. "It's just as if we suddenly began to put a *major* number of MRBMs in Turkey. Now that'd be *goddamn dangerous*." "Well, we did it, Mr. President," Bundy retorted, and JFK replied lamely, "Yeah, that was five years ago. But that was during a different period then." (In fact, Kennedy had decided in 1961 to proceed with the deployment in Turkey and Italy.)

Bundy speculated that Khrushchev's generals had been pressing for a chance to increase their strategic capability. Ball conceded that Khrushchev was aware of the deficiency of Soviet ICBMs but concluded hopefully, "I think Khrushchev *himself* would never risk a major war on a fellow as obviously erratic and foolish as Castro." RFK, however, suggested using the U.S. naval base at Guantanamo Bay to stage an incident justifying military intervention: "You know, sink the *Maine* again or something." (Castro had been warned after diplomatic relations were broken in 1961 not to interfere with the base— guaranteed by a 1934 treaty.)

Taylor urged the president to delay deciding on a schedule for military action until *all* the intelligence had been received. "No, I haven't," JFK replied. "I just think we ought to be *ready* to do something, even if we decide not to do it. I'm not saying we *should* do it." The president was obviously hedging his bets and displaying far more caution than his younger brother. Bundy too opted for caution, recalling McNamara's concern: "Our principal problem is to try and imaginatively to think what the world would be like if we do this, and what it will be like if we don't." "That's *exactly* right," the defense chief interjected. "We ought to work on that tonight."

After a brief discussion about securing the release of the Bay of Pigs prisoners in Cuba, Bundy raised a sensitive issue. "We have a list of the sabotage options, Mr. President. ... I think it would need your approval. I take it you *are* in favor of sabotage." Bundy asked about mining international waters, which could impact neutral and friendly vessels, or whether it would be wise to mine only Cuban waters, since "mines are very indiscriminate." JFK, in a vague reference to covert activities coordinated by the Special Group (Augmented), asked, "Is that what they're talking about, mining?" "That's one of the items," Bundy confirmed, "most of them ... will simply be deniable internal Cuban activities." The president urged delaying any steps which could antagonize neutral or friendly nations. "I don't think we want to put *mines* out right now, do we?"

JFK then summed up the issues to be discussed the next day—a warning before bombing; a decision on military choices; and a possible approach to Khrushchev—but also mentioned his upcoming campaign trip to Connecticut. Bundy, worried that the "cover will grow awfully thin" after constant meetings at the White House, suggested gathering at the State Department during JFK's brief trip.

The president turned to his scheduled October 18 meeting with Soviet foreign minister Andrei Gromyko. He wondered about giving the stone-faced diplomat an indirect ultimatum, but assumed he would deny there were missiles in Cuba. "I can't understand their viewpoint," JFK admitted, citing his September 4 and 13 warnings. "I don't think there's any record of the Soviets ever making this *direct* a challenge ... since the Berlin blockade." Bundy countered, correctly as the evidence later proved, that the Soviet decision was likely made before September, adding skeptically, "I wouldn't bet a *cookie* that [Ambassador] Dobrynin doesn't know a *bean* about this." President Kennedy, nervously and audibly slapping his knee, was intrigued: "You think he *does* know." (JFK sometimes slapped his knee or tapped his teeth in stressful situations.) But RFK, who had spoken with Dobrynin, concluded firmly, "He didn't know ... in my judgment."

The president was baffled by Soviet behavior. He was trying, nonetheless, despite his Cold War mindset, to understand what Khrushchev *thought* he was doing. He agreed to press Gromyko on the TASS statement that offensive weapons would not be sent to Cuba, again nervously slapping his knee as he recalled that the Soviets had backed away after China had shelled islands controlled by Taiwan in 1958 and had accepted a ceasefire in Laos. JFK had never pretended to be a Soviet "expert," but his irritation finally burst to the surface: "Well, it's a *goddamn* mystery to me. I don't know enough about the Soviet Union, but if anybody can tell me *any other time* since the Berlin blockade where the Russians have given us so clear a provocation, I don't know what it's been. . . . Now maybe our mistake was in not saying sometime before this summer that if they do this we must act." Kennedy had wondered aloud, only minutes earlier, if his pledge to take action against missiles in Cuba had contributed to inciting the crisis. Now he wondered if he had not been threatening enough!

As the meeting broke up, a course of action was still far from clear, and the president questioned whether even the administration's top Soviet experts could really explain Soviet behavior. Finally, he prompted some laughter with a quip about his political trip: "I wonder what we're gonna say up in Connecticut?" and again asked Carter when his ·boss, John McCone, would be returning to Washington. JFK neglected, perhaps intentionally, to turn off the tape recorder as he left.

Several advisers remained behind, and, no longer concerned about determining what the president was thinking or how he might respond to their advice, began to talk more informally. McNamara suggested preparing a list of targets and the number of air sorties required to destroy them, "not because I think that these are *reasonable* alternatives," but to give the president specific military options. "The most *important* thing," he stressed, is to prepare a written appraisal of the world *after* military action. "I think any military action *does* change the world," Bundy agreed. "I think *not* taking action changes the world [and] . . . these are the two worlds that we need to look at." He also suggested getting the views of former ambassador to Moscow, Llewellyn Thompson.

Earlier in the meeting, the defense secretary had laid out the military choices—despite doubts about whether they were worth the price of Soviet retaliation. Now, he asserted, with uncharacteristic passion, "It's not the chances of success. It's the results. . . . I'll be quite frank, I don't think there *is* a military problem there." "That's my honest [view] too," Bundy interjected. In an authoritative tone it's hard to imagine he would have used if the president were still present, McNamara declared, "This is a domestic *political* problem. . . . We said we'd *act*. Well, how will we *act*? Well, we want to *act* to prevent their use"— with air surveillance, a blockade, and an ultimatum to Khrushchev that any missile fired from Cuba would mean "a full nuclear strike" against the U.S.S.R. "Now this alternative doesn't seem to be a very *acceptable* one," he teased. "But wait until you work on the others!" Some strained laughter broke out.

Ball suggested that enforcing a blockade would also require signifi-cant military action. But Carter, describing a blockade as "a series of single, unrelated acts, *not* by surprise," echoed McNamara's doubts about bombing Cuba. "This comin' in there on Pearl Harbor just frightens the *hell* out of me as to what goes *beyond*." Bundy, clearly puzzled, asked, "What goes beyond what?" Carter replied, "What happens beyond that? You go in there with a surprise attack; you put out all the missiles. This isn't the *end*; this is the *beginning*." It was the first time, but not the last, that surprise air strikes against Cuba would be compared to the 1941 Japanese attack on Pearl Harbor.

McNamara urged his colleagues to consider, "What do we expect *Castro* will be doing after you attack these missiles? Does he survive as a political leader? Is he overthrown? Is he stronger, weaker? How will *he* react? How will the Soviets react? How can Khrushchev *afford* to accept this action without *some* kind of rebuttal? . . . Where? How do we react in relation to it? . . . How does this affect our allies' support of us in relation to Berlin?"

The morning meeting had ended with a consensus for the use of force. During the afternoon, however, reservations, especially by the president and McNamara, had contributed to a growing awareness of the dangers of military action. The question raised by General Carter could not be answered easily: if the U.S. attacked Cuba, especially without warning, where would it end?

That evening the president was the guest of honor at a dinner party for Charles "Chip" Bohlen, who was preparing to leave for France to be-come U.S. ambassador. The president seemed distant and withdrawn and, entirely out of character, hardly mingled with the other guests. Rusk went to the State Department for further discussions which lasted until midnight. McNamara spent the night at the Pentagon.

The next morning, Adlai Stevenson sent a note to the president ar-guing that the Soviet missiles in Cuba would be regarded around the world as a quid pro quo for U.S. missiles in Turkey. He urged the president to remain open to negotiations on all nuclear bases before using force.

President Kennedy kept to his regular schedule to keep the press and the Soviets from realizing that a crisis was imminent. He also author-ized CIA director McCone, who had just returned, to brief General Eisenhower. The president then left for Connecticut to campaign for Democrats in the midterm elections.

The ExComm met at the State Department, joined by Truman administration secretary of state Dean Acheson. (The meeting was not taped.) McNamara, according to the minutes, expressed concern that a warning before air strikes would sacrifice surprise. However, he also argued that air strikes on the missile sites would not be fully effective and invasion was too drastic as a first step. He seemed to be drifting toward the blockade option. Ambassador Thompson, supported by Taylor and McCone, argued that Khrushchev's goal was to gain leverage on Berlin. Ball urged restraint because Khrushchev did not understand American concerns about Cuba. Acheson, however, took a hard line, insisting that air strikes would eliminate the nuclear threat and demonstrate American resolve to Khrushchev. He did not discuss a Soviet response in Berlin or Turkey, or what might happen if the U.S. failed to destroy all the missiles in the first strike. The JCS prepared plans for bombing the missiles, the SAMs, and Soviet aircraft.

And, there was an ominous new development—early on October 18, U-2 photos turned up evidence of intermediate-range ballistic missile sites in Cuba. The IRBMs had a range of more than two thousand miles, about twice that of MRBMs, and carried far deadlier warheads. Soviet IL-28 strategic bombers, with a range of more than seven hundred miles and the capacity to carry nuclear payloads, were also discovered. The ExComm reconvened with a renewed momentum for swift military action.

Thursday, October 18, 11:00 A.M., Cabinet Room

"Now the question *really* is what action we take which *lessens* the chances of a nuclear exchange, which obviously is the final failure."
President John F. Kennedy

McCone, joining ExComm for the first time and perhaps trying to impress the president, boasted that the six reconnaissance missions flown the previous day had produced "a strip of film one hundred miles long, twenty feet wide." Someone can be heard reacting with a whispered "Oh my God!" McCone added rather smugly, "Quite a job!"

Arthur Lundahl then reviewed the new photos, explaining that the configuration of the launch pads and the control bunkers "has been the thing that has suggested to our hearts, if not our minds, the kind of thing that might accompany an IRBM." The president, clearly concerned, asked to see the photos, and Lundahl can be heard handing them over; for some twenty seconds the room remained eerily silent as President Kennedy examined the new evidence. Lundahl also pointed out twenty-two crates containing IL-28 bombers: "We've just caught them, apparently, at the start of the assembly operation."

President Kennedy, likely recalling the furor over doctored pictures shown at the U.N. during the Bay of Pigs debacle, asked about releasing the U-2 photographs: "would it not be possible to demonstrate this to the satisfaction of an untrained observer?" Lundahl downplayed the idea but agreed with Bundy and McNamara that some photos of "missiles lying on trailers . . . could, I think, very clearly impact on people."

Rusk, his voice obscured at first by the clatter of Lundahl clearing away his materials, explained that the new intelligence "changes my thinking on the matter." The Soviet buildup is not "just an *incidental* base" but "a *formidable* military problem," and failure to respond "would undermine our alliances all over the world, very promptly." The secretary of state read from the president's September 4 warning to the Soviets and all but challenged JFK to live up to his words. If we do nothing, he warned, the Soviets would "feel that they've got it made as far as intimidating the United States is concerned," which would undermine "the support that we need for the kind of foreign policy that will eventually secure our survival."

On the other hand, Rusk counseled that military action against Cuba might provoke Soviet reprisals in Berlin, in Korea, or "against the United States itself." If the U.S. challenged the Soviet decision to embark "upon this *fantastically* dangerous course," he declared, "no one can *surely* foresee the outcome." But the normally impassive Rusk also counseled that the public would only support war as a last resort, not as a first option. He recommended "consultation with Khrushchev" even though he did not expect the Soviet leader to back down, "But at least it will take *that* point out of the way for the historical record, and just might have in it the seeds of prevention of a great conflict." Rusk recommended seeking support from the Rio Pact nations and predicted that "there would be no real difficulty in getting a 2/3 vote in favor of necessary action." Finally he raised the possibility of a declaration of national emergency or a declaration of war—bolstering his position by reading from a letter left by Bohlen before his departure for Paris.

McNamara, in sharp contrast, abandoned his cautious October 16 stance and endorsed the JCS plan: "We consider nothing short of a full invasion as practicable military action, and *this* only on the assumption that we're operating against a force that does not possess operational nuclear weapons." President Kennedy, surprised by the defense secretary's about-face, asked "Why do you change? . . . Why has this information changed the recommendation?" McNamara declared that there were too many targets, including some that had not even been located, to be destroyed by air strikes; the Cubans could seize Guantanamo or bomb the east coast of the U.S., and "I think we would find it hard to justify" these casualties in relation to the limited gains from air strikes.

The president questioned this rationale, pointing out that air strikes could be carried out in a day, but an invasion would last many days and increase tensions. Taylor stressed again that 100 percent of the missile sites could not be destroyed from the air, but JFK persisted. "I would think you'd *have* to go on the assumption that they're not gonna permit nuclear weapons to be used against the United States from Cuba unless they're gonna be using them from everyplace." McNamara replied ominously, "I don't believe the Soviets would authorize their use against the U.S., but they might nonetheless be used." He was obviously concerned about an accidental launch, a rogue action by Russian or Cuban personnel, or a deliberate decision by Castro.

The defense secretary reiterated his continuing personal disagreement with the JCS: "it's not a *military* problem that we're facing; it's a *political* problem; it's a problem of holding the alliance together; it's a problem of *properly* conditioning Khrushchev for our future moves." These factors, including "the problem of dealing with our domestic public," now justified the JCS insistence on an invasion.

President Kennedy, coming as close to lecturing as he ever did at these meetings, contended that the allies regarded Cuba "as a fixation of the United States and not a serious military threat. . . . They think that we're slightly demented on this subject. . . . A lot of people would regard this as a *mad* act by the United States which is due to a loss of nerve" since these missiles do not really alter the strategic balance of power.

Taylor, despite JFK's stance, reversed his earlier opposition to an invasion because the missiles would soon become operational: "We can't take *this* threat out by actions from the air." "You mean," Bundy interposed, "you're gonna have to take the island." "Yes," Taylor affirmed, "you can't destroy a hole in the ground." He did concede that warning Khrushchev could be politically useful. JFK, joined by Bundy, cautioned that the Soviets might hide the missiles in nearby woods, but McNamara and Taylor concluded that a twenty-four-hour warning would not make much difference. "Say we sent somebody to see him," Kennedy speculated, "[and] he was *there* at the beginning of the twenty-four-hour period." How long "before Khrushchev's answer could get back to us?" Thompson estimated that a reply in code could take five to six hours, but Rusk felt it would be faster to transmit a message directly through Ambassador Dobrynin.

McCone reported that since Raul Castro and Che Guevara had failed to negotiate a bilateral defense pact with the U.S.S.R. during a visit to Moscow in July, it was difficult to predict the Soviet response to a U.S. attack on the bases. (U.S. intelligence did not know that a five-year re-newable agreement to defend Cuba had been successfully concluded—but not formally signed.) JFK wondered aloud whether the Soviet re-sponse "would be measurably different if they were presented with an accomplished fact [or] . . . given a chance to pull 'em out." The president then floated a trial balloon, echoing Stevenson's suggestion of the previ-ous day: "If we said to Khrushchev . . . 'if you're willing to pull them out, we'll take ours out of Turkey.'" No one responded to JFK's first intima-tion that he might consider trading missiles in Cuba and Turkey.

Thompson, ExComm's Soviet specialist, criticized bombing "because you'd have killed a lot of Russians" and instead endorsed the blockade, predicting that the U.S.S.R. would probably not run a blockade barring only offensive weapons, especially if it was backed up by a declaration of war. He also tried to educate the president on the Soviet worldview: "The Russians have a curious faculty of wanting a legal basis despite all of the outrageous things they've done." The ambassador suggested that Khrushchev would threaten nuclear war, but JFK countered that he would "grab Berlin." Thompson felt Khrushchev was more likely to re-act to air strikes in Cuba by attacking a U.S. base in Turkey before saying, "'Now I want to talk.'" Khrushchev's purpose, he reasoned, was to "try to negotiate out the bases" in Cuba *and* Turkey.

RFK, still pushing an invasion, cautioned that a blockade could be-come "a very slow death" over months and would still require stopping Russian ships and shooting down Russian planes—and, JFK added, at-tacking submarines. Thompson predicted Khrushchev would say, "'What are you getting so excited about? The Cubans asked us for the missiles to deal . . . with the threat to Cuba.'" But, despite scoffing at this defensive argument, Thompson admonished the president: "You want to make it . . . as easy as possible for him to back down." If he re-plies, "'This is *so* serious, I'm prepared to *talk* to you about it.' We could scarcely refuse . . . if you have a world war being threatened."

JFK repeated, however, that a blockade would not stop work on the missiles already in Cuba.

McCone reported on briefing Eisenhower; the former president felt that an offensive Soviet base in Cuba was intolerable but rejected a conventional invasion and endorsed going "*right* to the jugular first" with a "concentrated attack *right* on Havana first" to take out the government "with a *minimum* loss of life and of time." Perhaps emboldened by Eisenhower's tough stance, Thompson judged that "since Castro's gone this far in conniving" in deploying the missiles, "it seems to me that . . . Castro has to go." Despite his earlier suggestion that Khrushchev might seek to negotiate, Thompson concluded gloomily, "I don't think he could ever just back down."

The discussion seemed to be going around in circles when the president probed again: "The only offer we would make . . . giving him *some* out, would be our Turkey missiles." This time JFK picked up limited support: Bundy affirmed that a message should be "in Khrushchev's hands" at the moment the air strikes begin stating "that we understand this base problem and that we *do* expect to dismantle our Turkish base." But, when Rusk objected that a Cuba-Turkey exchange "would be quite serious," Bundy backed off—explaining that a missile swap was only "one way" of minimizing the danger since "this is a political *not* a military problem."

McNamara, always the hard-nosed realist, stressed that several hundred Soviets would be killed in surprise air strikes—at a minimum. "Killed?" Bundy asked. "Killed. Absolutely!" the defense chief replied. "We're using napalm, 750-pound bombs. This is an *extensive* strike we're talking about." "Well, I hope it is!" Bundy avowed—in contrast to his doubts two days earlier about attacking Cuba. McNamara predicted that Khrushchev would demand withdrawal of U.S. missiles from Turkey and Italy—but doubted that would be enough after Russian personnel had been killed in Cuba. "I think they'll take Berlin," Dillon grumbled.

Ball, alarmed by McNamara's casualty estimate, urged the president to consider the "sense of affront" from surprise air strikes, even among America's allies. He urged a twenty-four-hour warning to give "Khrushchev *some* way out. Even though it may be illusory, I think we *still* have to do it." A strike without warning "is like Pearl Harbor," he declared, echoing Carter's doubts on the first day. "It's the kind of conduct . . . one might expect of the Soviet Union. It is *not* conduct that one expects of the United States." The mood of the meeting darkened as the president calculated that Khrushchev would "grab Berlin any-way" and McNamara admonished, "once you start down that course," it's possible that Khrushchev "outmaneuvers you."

JFK repeated that the allies would feel the U.S. had lost Berlin be-cause of missiles in Cuba, "which, as I say, do not bother them." "I think he moves into Berlin," RFK added grimly. "What do we *mean* exactly?" McNamara asked. "Do they take it with Soviet troops?" "That's what I would see, anyway," JFK replied. "I think there's a real possibility of that," McNamara admitted: "We have U.S. troops there. What do they do?" "They fight," Taylor asserted. "And they get over-run," JFK predicted. "Then what do we do?" RFK queried. "Go to general war," Taylor pronounced, "assuming we have time for it." "You mean nuclear exchange?" the president remarked bleakly. "Guess you have to," Taylor declared.

JFK conceded that NATO would be undermined by U.S. action in Cuba, but "if we don't take any action...there will be a more gradual deterioration." Rusk, Dillon, and Bundy dissented in unison, warning that deterioration would be "very rapid" if the U.S. failed to act. Presi-dent Kennedy responded with stark eloquence: "Now the question *really* is what action we take which *lessens* the chances of a nuclear ex-change, which obviously is the final failure." He then added pensively, "And, at the same time maintain some degree of solidarity with our al-lies." The fact that JFK thought of nuclear war as "final" is not sur-prising. But, as the leader who might be faced with the decision to use these weapons, the resulting nuclear holocaust would be *his* failure—a fact that clearly weighed heavily on his mind.

"Now, to get a blockade on Cuba," JFK asked, focusing on practical steps to avert a nuclear exchange, "would we have to declare war on Cuba?" A cacophony of voices declared "yes," for diplomatic, legal, and political reasons. The president seized the initiative, insisting "I think we *shouldn't* assume we have to declare war. . . . Because it seems to me if you're gonna do that . . . it doesn't make any sense not to in-vade. . . . We do the message to Khrushchev [and] . . . launch the block-ade. If work continues, then we go in and take them out. We *don't* de-clare war." Ball contended that a blockade without a declaration of war was illegal, and Bundy called it "an act of aggression against ev-erybody else." "Including our allies," Ball insisted. "I don't think any-body who gets excited because their ships are stopped under these con-ditions," JFK snapped, "they're not very much help to us anyway."

Ball pressed for an ultimatum that "work *must* stop on the missile sites or you *take them out*." The blockade, he declared, in words much like RFK's, could become "rather a slow agony," increasing the "fears and doubts in the minds of people here." Bundy lectured the president: "your whole posture" must reflect that Khrushchev has done "unacceptable things from the point of view of the security of the hemisphere." With or without a declaration of war, he admonished boldly, "You will, in fact, get into the invasion before you're through . . . either way."

McCone reflected that Soviet ships "would go right through" the blockade, and Thompson surmised that Khrushchev might observe the blockade but instead choose to risk "the *big* action in Berlin." Rusk speculated that Khrushchev could be deterred if he knew the U.S. would respond; "Or maybe he's a little crazy and we can't trust him." The president hypothesized aloud about how the crisis might have played out in reverse: if Khrushchev had warned the U.S. against deploying missiles in Turkey and, after they were put in, destroyed them. "To me," JFK mused, "there's some advantages to that if it's all over"—without further escalation.

At this stage the president still assumed that air strikes on the missiles were likely. He suggested announcing the discovery of the sites without revealing the administration's plans: "It isn't Pearl Harbor in that sense. We've told everybody. Then we go ahead . . . and we take 'em out and [we say] that we don't want any war." He stressed that the strikes would take place on Saturday, because "Sunday has historic disadvantages," a sardonic reference to December 7, 1941—the watershed date of their lives.

Robert Kennedy, evidently rattled by the Pearl Harbor analogy, retreated from his belligerent posture for the first time: "I think George Ball has a hell of a good point," that giving the Russians a warning would affirm "what kind of a country we are." Rusk assured the president that a warning would be better than "carrying the mark of Cain on your brow." For fifteen years, RFK avowed, the U.S. had tried to prevent a Russian first strike. "Now . . . we do that to a *small* country. I think it's a hell of a burden to carry." The president acknowledged that a warning would give Khrushchev a chance to "get these Russians outa there"; the point was to "get these missiles," not to kill Russians. Once military action started there was no guarantee that it could be stopped at all, and the Soviets might still "get a couple of them [nuclear warheads] over on us anyway." A measured American response, JFK hoped, would lead to a measured Soviet reaction.

Ambassador Thompson was less hopeful, recalling that Khrushchev had been impetuous when the U-2 was shot down in 1960 and had personally escalated tensions over Berlin. The president pondered what "we'd be trying to get out of him" with a warning before the air attacks. Rusk was emphatic: since Kennedy was taking political risks, Khrushchev, "in order to keep the fig leaf on for the president," must cease work on the bases and withdraw Soviet technicians. Sorensen stressed that any delay in dismantling the sites was unacceptable.

Thompson remained skeptical about dealing with Khrushchev, but seemed to warm to JFK's hints about a Jupiter missile deal, since the U.S. could protect Turkey with submarine-launched Polaris missiles. He even suggested inviting Khrushchev to the U.S. for talks: "This won't wait for your trip [to the U.N.] in November, come on over," he chuckled. Otherwise, he added, "it seems to me you're playing Russian roulette, you're flipping a coin as to whether you end up with world war or not."

President Kennedy contended that it would be less dangerous for Khrushchev to respond to a strike on the missiles by attacking the Jupiters in Turkey; but, it would be quite different if the Red Army responded to an invasion of Cuba by invading Turkey. And, he cautioned, "nobody knows what kind of a success we're gonna have with this invasion. Invasions are tough, hazardous. . . . Thousands of Americans get killed in Cuba and I think you're in *much more* of a *mess*." But, he observed gloomily, "It may be that his response would be the same; nobody can guess that." And there was another wild card—Castro himself. If the Cubans attacked Guantanamo, JFK reasoned, with or without a go-ahead from Moscow, "we're gonna have to invade." Taylor assured the commander-in-chief, "We may have a *big* fight around the place, but . . . we can hold Guantanamo." RFK, still drawn to an invasion, asked, "How many days *after* [bombing] would you be prepared to invade?" "Seven to ten days," McNamara reiterated.

Before these grim possibilities had to be confronted, the practical details of a pre-strike notification to Khrushchev had to be arranged— whether to go through Dobrynin or send an emissary to the Kremlin. Bundy and Thompson predicted that Khrushchev would respond by calling for a summit meeting. Kennedy was not thrilled by the prospect: "then he's gonna be talkin' about Berlin." Ball and Dillon argued that a summit could provide political cover with NATO, world opinion, and history. But Bundy urged the president not to agree to a meeting without a halt to construction of the missile sites.

The president's previously scheduled meeting with Soviet foreign minister Andrei Gromyko later that afternoon had taken on enormous importance. Taylor and Rusk advised trying to get Gromyko to lie about the presence of offensive missiles in Cuba, but RFK worried that he might argue instead that these weapons offset U.S. missiles in Turkey. Rusk rejected the comparison, insisting that the Jupiter deployment was a direct response to Soviet aggression and Stalin's policies. "It makes all the difference in the world." "How many missiles," JFK probed, "do we have in Turkey?" "Fifteen," plus nuclear-equipped aircraft, Bundy answered, probably having checked since the nearly identical exchange two days earlier.

RFK, still fuming about false Soviet promises, questioned whether the president himself, as suggested by Taylor and Rusk, should try to trap Gromyko: "I suppose the other way is to do it rather subtly with me saying, 'What are you doing in Cuba?'" Taylor, backed by Bundy and Sorensen, added, "If he denies it, you have something that you can confront Khrushchev with later." Rusk speculated that "They *must* know now that we know. They're working around the clock down there."

McNamara summed up the alternatives under discussion: a slow move to military action (an announcement and a blockade) *or* a rapid move to military action (a warning followed by air attacks). He also suggested that ExComm sub-groups prepare plans for minimizing the military price to be paid for each option. Early in the meeting, the defense secretary had eagerly endorsed invading Cuba; but, undoubtedly influenced by JFK's reservations, he no longer listed invasion as an option.

President Kennedy, perhaps sensing an opportunity to nail down the historical record, asked point blank: "Is there anyone here who doesn't think that we ought to do something about this?"—followed by about seven seconds of very loud silence. JFK also claimed that there were more choices than the two listed by McNamara: "As I say, you have the blockade without any declaration of war. You've got a blockade with a declaration of war. We've got strikes. . . . We've got invasion. We've got notification to Khrushchev." ExComm members could not have failed to notice that the president had listed the blockade *without* a declaration of war as first among the available alternatives.

The meeting finally appeared to be winding down. A consensus emerged to review the two principal military/diplomatic options more definitively. The real issue, Bundy repeated, was the "level of readiness" of the missiles. JFK replied that it didn't make "a hell of a difference" how many sites were ready if the Soviets really intended "to fire nuclear missiles at us." "If they were rational, Mr. President," Bundy warned.

McNamara concluded that preparations should be made for air strikes "at the *earliest* possible moment," but RFK and Taylor advised waiting a few more days. "The more time we've got," the general asserted, "the better we can do it." McNamara agreed that a final decision could wait, but "we ought to be ready" in case the missiles become operational. JFK agreed.

The ExComm also recommended that President Kennedy should make his second scheduled campaign trip; if he failed to go, the press would realize that something was up. Ball worried about how to handle leaks, and a consensus emerged to be evasive. "The president," Rusk asked somewhat officiously, "hopes to unify or not, by going on this trip this weekend to hear about the country?" JFK, politician to the core, replied dryly, "I don't unify the country, that's *not* the purpose of the trip." Laughter rocked the table. "I don't think there's any problem about *unifying* the country," Dillon concluded. "This action will unify it just like that."

The conversation continued less formally for several minutes as JFK prepared to leave. Bundy joked about press inquiries concerning the meetings: "I still believe that our best cover is 'intensive review of the defense budget.' Now we haven't had to use it yet," he quipped amidst some laughter. McNamara again urged establishing working groups to consider the military options and especially "how the Soviets are going to respond. *This* is what we haven't done."

The tape recorder was left running again after the president's departure, and some fragmentary conversations, again more animated and less structured, continued for several minutes. Edwin Martin speculated about whether the blockade could bring down Castro and RFK replied sarcastically, "Has a blockade ever brought anybody down?" Rusk, backed by Taylor, insisted that a blockade and air strikes "would be a pretty good-sized wallop." Bundy, however, suggested that the advantage of a blockade without air strikes "is you don't kill any Russians." But Alexis Johnson declared that a blockade without OAS backing and a declaration of war "is about the worst [choice] of all." "You must declare," Bundy pronounced, rather surprisingly since RFK was still present, "I think the president did not fully grasp that."

McNamara emphasized again that the missiles would not be withdrawn from Cuba without a price, and "the *minimum* price" would be removing U.S. missiles from Turkey and Italy. Bundy argued that Castro had to go but McNamara cautioned, "This is something to think about." The defense secretary, almost becoming a stand-in for the president, affirmed that if the alliance was not divided and the missiles were removed from Cuba, Turkey, and Italy, "that's the *best* possible solution. There are many *worse* solutions."

Taylor countered that the "collapse of Castro" should be a top priority and Bundy reiterated, "I'm convinced *myself* that Castro has to go. ... I just think his *demon* is self-destruction, and we have to help him to that." In that case, McNamara responded, the price is going to be higher. "I really think that we've *got* to think these problems through *more* than we have. At the moment I lean to the blockade because I think it *reduces the very serious risk* of large-scale military action from which this country *cannot* benefit." The defense secretary's about-face since the start of the meeting must have been troubling to his more hawkish colleagues.

RFK continued to resist the blockade because it did not halt construction on the missile sites. "We tell them," he remarked sarcastically, "they can build as many missiles as they want?" "Oh, no, no," McNamara countered, "What we say is, 'We are going to blockade you. This is a *danger* to us'" that must be removed. Taylor brusquely asked the defense chief to explain his objection to air strikes. "My real objection to it is," McNamara replied bluntly, "that it kills several hundred Russians." The discussion gradually ran down without a genuine meeting of the minds.

After a few laps across the White House swimming pool, JFK met with Dean Acheson. The former secretary of state urged the president to destroy the missiles immediately with "surgical" air strikes. He dismissed the Pearl Harbor analogy as "silly" and urged JFK not to be taken in by such mush. The Russians, he insisted, understood only strength and the will to use it.

At 5:00 p.m. Kennedy met in the Oval Office with the Soviet foreign minister. (The president, likely because of the extreme tension of the moment, forgot to turn on the recorder during this crucial meeting.) Gromyko lectured JFK about the Bay of Pigs, argued that Cuba did not belong to the U.S., and reiterated Khrushchev's commitment to ending the Western military presence in Berlin. Kennedy later admitted that it had been difficult to resist pulling the U-2 photos out of his desk, but the advantage of having more time outweighed the satisfaction of watching Gromyko's jaw drop. Kennedy repeated his September warn-

ing that the U.S. would not tolerate Soviet offensive weapons in Cuba, but was unable to detect any reaction from the poker-faced Gromyko. From that day on, JFK frequently referred to Gromyko as "that lying bastard."

JFK later discussed military and diplomatic options with former defense secretary Robert Lovett and several advisers in the Oval Office. Lovett endorsed the blockade and, after speculation about possible Soviet reprisals, counseled the president that risks could not be avoided. Later in the evening, the president and the ExComm met for further discussions. Some participants used a tunnel from the Treasury Department to the White House because it was feared that activity in the Cabinet Room during the evening might alert reporters. Instead, the meeting was held in the Oval Room of the Mansion—which had no taping system. (Minutes kept by Bromley Smith, executive secretary of the National Security Council, provide the most reliable record of most unrecorded discussions.)

At the outset of the meeting an agreement seemed to be emerging for a blockade rather than air strikes, but doubts from the previous meetings resurfaced and the fragile consensus began to unravel. The president directed the ExComm to work out plans for implementing a blockade and returned to the Oval Office at about midnight. To preserve details from his discussions with Acheson and Lovett, as well as the unrecorded ExComm meeting, he dictated his recollections directly into the microphones hidden in his desk.

Thursday, October 18, near midnight, Oval Office

"The consensus was that we should go ahead with the blockade."

President John F. Kennedy

"During the course of the day," JFK recalled, "opinions had obviously switched from the advantages of a first strike . . . to a blockade." He was intrigued by the disagreement between Truman's secretaries of state and defense: Acheson had "favored the first strike" against the missile sites, but Lovett had argued that the NATO allies would blame the U.S. for losing Berlin "with *inadequate* provocation, they having lived with these intermediate-range ballistic missiles for years." Lovett's words must have struck a chord with the president, given his own view that NATO regarded America as "slightly demented" over Cuba.

Kennedy also noted that Bundy had urged merely taking note "of the existence of these missiles and to wait until the crunch comes in Berlin." Everyone else, Kennedy recalled, agreed that failure to respond would undermine the U.S. commitment to Berlin, "would divide our allies and our country," and would permit Khrushchev to set up a significant missile arsenal in the Western Hemisphere. "The consensus was that we should go ahead with the blockade," to be tightened "as the situation required."

"I was most anxious," Kennedy stressed, to avoid a declaration of war, "because it would obviously be bad to have the word go out that we were having a war rather than . . . a limited blockade for a limited purpose." It was also decided "that I should go ahead with my speeches so that we don't take the cover off this." He then hit the off switch and presumably tried to get a decent night's sleep.

The National Photographic Interpretation Center had reported on October 18 that two MRBM sites were capable of launching missiles and two IRBM sites could be operational in a month. Early the next morning Taylor briefed the JCS on the developing consensus for a blockade. The Chiefs, exasperated by what they regarded as civilian and presidential indecisiveness—if not spinelessness—again demanded air strikes on the missile sites and airfields, followed by an invasion.

The underlying tension between the JCS and the commander-in-chief was symbolized by the Single Integrated Operational Plan (SIOP), the master strategy for nuclear war redrafted annually by the JCS for approval by the president. In 1961, JFK attended a SIOP briefing by General Lyman Lemnitzer and asked why so many sites in the People's Republic of China were targeted since the Chinese had no nuclear weapons. "It's in the plan, Mr. President," the general explained. Kennedy was livid, later telling Dean Rusk, "And we call ourselves the human race."

First Lady Jacqueline Kennedy had once remarked to JFK that Air Force chief of staff, General Curtis LeMay, "was a 'mad bomber' with 'tunnel vision.'" "It's good to have men like Curt LeMay and Arleigh Burke commanding troops once you decide to go in," the president had nonetheless concluded. "But these men aren't the only ones you should listen to when you decide whether to go in or not." LeMay considered SIOP his "bible" and once replied to a query about how to deal with Cuba by retorting, "Fry it." These strains were bubbling close to the surface as the JCS joined JFK and McNamara in the Cabinet Room.

Friday, October 19, 9:45 A.M., Cabinet Room

"This is almost as bad as the appeasement at Munich."
General Curtis LeMay, Air Force Chief of Staff

The tension in the room was palpable as the meeting began. "I think the benefit this morning, Mr. President," Taylor began, "would be for you to hear the other Chiefs' comments." Kennedy ignored Taylor and began to speak immediately in a clear effort to demonstrate that the commander-in-chief was in charge. Nevertheless, he was hesitant and uneasy, repeatedly tripping over his words: "Let me just say a little uh... first about uh... what the problem is uh... from... at least from uh... my point of view," he began. "I... uh... first uh... wh... uh... I think we ought to think of why the Russians did this." He gradually became more confident, telling the Chiefs that a weak American response would appear to upset the strategic balance of power.

But, he warned, if the U.S. attacked Cuba it would give the Soviets "a clear line to take Berlin," and the NATO allies would condemn the U.S. for losing Berlin because "we didn't have the guts to *endure* a situation in Cuba." "After all," he reasoned, "Cuba is five or six thousand miles from them. They don't give a damn about Cuba. But they do care about Berlin and about their own security. . . . I think it's a *very* satisfactory position from their point of view." A quick air strike, he explained, might neutralize the missiles but increase the risk of the Soviets "taking Berlin by force . . . which leaves me only one alternative, which is to fire nuclear weapons—which is a *hell* of an alternative." JFK's use of the personal pronoun sent a clear message to the Chiefs—the decision was his alone. Taylor explained that the Chiefs agreed that American credibility was at stake. "So that's why," JFK affirmed, "we've gotta respond. Now the question is, what kind of response?"

General LeMay, giving no indication that he had understood the dangers raised by the president, turned JFK's Berlin argument on its head: "I don't share your view that if we knock off Cuba they're gonna knock off Berlin." The Soviets "are gonna push on Berlin and push *real hard*" if the U.S. fails to take military action in Cuba, since they would feel "they've got us *on the run*." Kennedy interrupted to ask about Soviet reprisals after a U.S. attack on Cuba. There would be no reprisals, LeMay asserted confidently, as long as you tell Khrushchev again, "If they make a move [in Berlin], we're gonna fight." The self-assured general moved in for the verbal kill: "This blockade and political action I see leading into war. . . . This is almost as bad as the appeasement at Munich. . . . I just don't see any other solution except direct military intervention, *right now*."

The JCS must have held their collective breath waiting for the president's reaction. The general had gone well beyond giving advice or even disagreeing with his commander-in-chief. He had taken their generation's ultimate metaphor for cowardice, the 1938 appeasement of Hitler at Munich, and flung it in the president's face. And everyone at the table knew that JFK's father, Joseph P. Kennedy, had supported appeasement as ambassador to England in the late 1930s, destroying the elder Kennedy's career and casting a long shadow over John Kennedy's political aspirations.

In a remarkable display of sangfroid, JFK refused to take the bait; he said absolutely nothing. But, an ExComm member who "saw the president right afterwards" recalled, "He was just choleric. He was just beside himself."

The discussion resumed after several seconds of awkward silence. Admiral George Anderson, chief of Naval Operations, assured the president that the Navy could enforce a blockade around Cuba but nonetheless argued, "I do not see that . . . there is any solution to the Cuban problem except a military solution." The admiral warned that the communists had left the U.S. without safe choices: "It's the same thing as Korea all over again, only on a grander scale." He acknowledged the danger to Berlin, but insisted that only a strong U.S. response in Cuba would deter the Soviets from moving against that divided city. JFK tried again to counter this military logic: "They can't let us just take out . . . their missiles, kill a lot of Russians, and not do anything." LeMay repeated disdainfully that the Soviets would back off *only* if the U.S. took a decisive military stand.

General Earle Wheeler, Army chief of staff, increased the pressure by insisting that only bombing, a blockade, *plus* an invasion could protect the United States against a nuclear strike from Cuba. The general warned that Khrushchev might declare Cuba part of the Warsaw Pact during his November trip to the U.N., raising doubts in Latin America about U.S. willingness to respond. In addition, the Soviets had only limited numbers of ICBMs targeted at the U.S., and "this short-range missile force gives them a sort of a quantum jump in their capability to inflict damage on the United States. And so as I say, from the military point of view, I feel that the lowest risk . . . is the full gamut of military action by us. That's it."

Finally, Marine Corps commandant David Shoup told the president that failure to act in Cuba would diminish American power everywhere in the world. Despite dismissing Cuba as "that little *pipsqueak* of a place," Shoup argued that the missiles "*can* damage us *increasingly every day.*" If the U.S. delayed action, more substantial forces would be needed to invade Cuba, making America even more vulnerable to Soviet aggression in Berlin, South Vietnam, and Korea. "You'll have to invade the place," Shoup declared, banging the table for emphasis, "and if that decision is made, we must go in with *plenty* of insurance of a *decisive success* and as quick as possible."

General LeMay, buttressed by the unity of his colleagues, warned the president that the missiles in Cuba could expose the U.S. and Latin America to the threat of nuclear blackmail: "I think that a blockade and political talk would be considered by a lot of our friends and neutrals as bein' a pretty weak response to this. And I'm sure a lot of our own citizens would feel that way too." "In other words," LeMay almost taunted the president, "you're in a pretty bad fix at the present time." "What'd you say?" Kennedy replied coldly. "I say, you're in a pretty bad fix," LeMay repeated smugly. "You're in with me," Kennedy retorted with an acerbic chuckle, "personally."

The president continued to hold his ground, stressing that a limited air strike against the missiles would be seen as far less of an escalation than comprehensive bombing followed by a blockade and an invasion; "We have to assume," he reasoned, that "the Soviet response to each of these would have to be different." He also reiterated that Cuba was not the real issue: "the problem is part of this worldwide struggle where we face the Communists, particularly, as I say, over Berlin." LeMay tried again to personalize his differences with the president: "If you lose in Cuba, you're gonna get *more and more* pressure right on Berlin. I'm sure of that." JFK again refused to be goaded, insisting that the missiles in Cuba did not alter the nuclear threat. Soviet ICBMs might not be fully reliable, he admitted, but even without Cuba they could target U.S. cities and inflict 80 to 100 million casualties: "you're talkin' about the destruction of a country!"

Taylor interjected that the U.S. could never invade Cuba with these missiles "pointed at our head." "Well, the logical argument," the president persisted, "is that we don't really have to invade Cuba. That's just one of the difficulties that we live with in life, like you live with the Soviet Union and China." He reiterated that "the existence of these missiles . . . *adds* to the danger, but doesn't create it." The Soviets already had enough missiles, planes, and submarines, he repeated. "I mean, hell, they can kill, especially if they concentrate on the cities, and they've pretty well got us there anyway." After several JCS officers questioned the security of Guantanamo, the president asked, "How effective is an air strike of this kind, General, against a missile base?" LeMay replied evasively, "Well, I think we can guarantee hitting them."

As the president prepared to leave, General Wheeler observed, "There is no *acceptable* military solution to the Berlin problem, whereas there is in Cuba." A resolution in Berlin, he conceded, lies instead "in the diplomatic-economic-political field, if we put enough pressure on the Soviet bloc." He predicted that the people of Berlin "can survive for a long time" if the Soviets responded to military action in Cuba by cutting off allied access to Berlin—as long as Russian troops don't overrun the city.

"I appreciate your views," the president finally told the JCS. "I'm sure we all understand how rather unsatisfactory our alternatives are." But, he contended again, the advantage of the blockade "is to avoid, if we can, nuclear war by escalation. . . . We've got to have some degree of control." Shoup reminded the commander-in-chief that the Cuban bases were very close to the U.S., but JFK countered, "I don't think that it adds particularly to our danger. I think our danger is the use of nuclear weapons . . . particularly on urban sites." He reiterated yet again that the Soviets already had enough nuclear missiles, planes, and submarines to attack American cities—or would within a year. "The major argument is the political effect on the United States."

McNamara, who had been uncharacteristically silent during this war of words, repeated that just two courses of action were under active consideration, air strikes and a blockade, and urged the Chiefs to recommend procedures for each option. After JFK, McNamara, and Taylor had departed, several officers remained behind. Away, they believed, from prying ears, they expressed disdain for civilian control of military decisions. Shoup lauded LeMay for challenging the president: "You pulled the rug right out from under him." "Jesus Christ!" LeMay responded disingenuously, asking "What the hell do you mean?"

Shoup mocked JFK: "When *he* says 'escalation,' that's it. If somebody could keep 'em from doing the *goddamn thing* piecemeal, *that's* our problem. You go in there and friggin' around with the missiles. You're screwed. You go in and friggin' around with little else. You're screwed." "That's right," LeMay exclaimed. "You're screwed, screwed,

screwed," Shoup fulminated. "He could say, 'either do the son of a bitch and do it right, and quit friggin' around.' . . . You can't fiddle around with hittin' a missile site and then hittin' the SAM sites. You got to go in and take out the goddamn thing that's gonna *stop you* from doin' your job."

"It's very apparent to me though," Wheeler contended, "he gave his speech about Berlin and he equates the two." "That's right," Shoup and LeMay affirmed. "If we sneer at Castro," Wheeler asserted sarcastically, "Khrushchev sneers at [West Berlin mayor] Willy Brandt." The discussion soon trailed off, and the tape ran out as the officers left the Cabinet Room.

Friday, October 19, afternoon and evening

After the meeting, the president derided LeMay's certainty that Khrushchev would do nothing if the U.S. bombed the missiles and killed many Russians. "These brass hats have one great advantage in their favor," JFK fumed. "If we listen to them and do what they want us to do, none of us will be alive later to tell them that they were wrong."

Earlier that morning Bundy had told JFK that after a sleepless night he had concluded that the blockade was inadequate because it would not eliminate the sites already under construction. Kennedy admitted that he was having similar doubts and asked Bundy to keep the air strike option alive. But, Bundy later recalled, "advocates of the air strike wanted to strike everything that could fly in Cuba, and that wasn't exactly what the president had in mind."

JFK left later that morning for a campaign trip to Ohio and Illinois. Before departing, he told RFK and Sorensen "this thing is falling apart" and urged them to try to forge a consensus for the blockade during his absence. At an unrecorded meeting later that day, Bundy revealed that he had spoken to JFK and now supported surprise air strikes. Acheson and Taylor again called for immediate military action to destroy the missiles. McCone and Dillon agreed, and even the cautious Ball seemed uncertain.

McNamara endorsed planning for air strikes but continued to support the blockade as a measured first step. He also admitted candidly, "we would at least have to give up our missile bases in Italy and Turkey and would probably have to pay more besides." RFK, standing in for his brother despite his own combative posture, argued for the blockade because a sneak attack on a small country was not in the American tra-

dition. *A blockade would demonstrate American strength and restraint and give the Soviets a chance to reconsider their rash miscalculation. He nonetheless revealed that his own tough perspective lurked just beneath the surface: "it would be better for our children and grandchildren if we decided to face the Soviet threat, stand up to it, and eliminate it, now." The ExComm seemed to be slipping into deadlock.*

Early the next morning, RFK phoned the president in Chicago and urged him to return to the White House. Press secretary Pierre Salinger announced that Kennedy had a cold and would cancel his remaining political appearances. On the return flight, Salinger, still in the dark about Cuba, asked the president what was going on. "The minute you get back in Washington," JFK promised, "you're going to find out what it is. And when you do, grab your balls."

Saturday, October 20, 2:30 P.M.

Within an hour of his arrival the president met with the ExComm. (The meeting was again held in the Mansion and not taped.) "You should all hope," JFK joked grimly, "that your plan isn't the one that will be accepted." It was clear at the outset that the ExComm remained divided and key participants were wavering between military and diplomatic options. The president pointed out, "there is something to destroy in Cuba now, and, if it is destroyed, a strategic missile capability would be difficult to restore." These words must have encouraged air strike proponents. Perhaps, after Bundy's about-face, JFK was backing away from a blockade.

McNamara, notwithstanding, endorsed the blockade and negotiations for "the withdrawal of United States strategic missiles from Turkey and Italy" and even suggested a possible "agreement to limit our use of Guantanamo to a specified limited time." The defense chief acknowledged that the blockade might create "political trouble" at home, but conceded that a surprise strike was "contrary to our tradition" and a blockade was less likely to provoke a Soviet response "leading to general war."

JFK asked Taylor how many missiles could be destroyed by air action. Taylor broke new ground by asserting that he did not share "McNamara's fear that if we used nuclear weapons in Cuba, nuclear weapons would be used against us." He felt that attacking the missiles was less dangerous than allowing them to become operational and could be the last chance to take them out before they were camou-

flaged. Robert Kennedy abruptly returned to his tough stance of October 16, claiming that "now is the last chance we will have to destroy Castro and the Soviet missiles deployed in Cuba." Bundy handed the president a JCS plan for air strikes.

The president reopened the question of giving advance warning before air attacks and added that he was prepared to live with the Soviet bombers in Cuba since they did not affect perceptions of the nuclear balance of power. RFK shifted ground again, arguing that a combination of a blockade and air strikes "was very attractive to him." If the Russians failed to halt construction during the blockade, he added, air attacks could begin without the Pearl Harbor stigma.

Suddenly, most remaining participants took sides: Rusk endorsed the blockade; McCone, Dillon, and Gilpatric essentially agreed. McNamara warned that air strikes would kill thousands of Russians and Cubans and "the U.S. would lose control of the situation." General Taylor still dissented.

JFK repeated that air strikes could lead to an attack on Berlin and "agreed that at an appropriate time we would have to acknowledge that we were willing to take strategic missiles out of Turkey and Italy if this issue were raised by the Russians." He asserted again that there were no safe choices but the blockade would buy time to monitor Soviet activity in Cuba. If air strikes should become necessary, he endorsed attacking only the missiles and repeated that "we would have to live with the threat arising out of the stationing in Cuba of Soviet bombers."

Rusk affirmed that a surprise air strike "had no support in the law or morality and, therefore, must be ruled out." Ambassador Stevenson agreed but also urged the evacuation of the Guantanamo naval base. Kennedy rebuffed Stevenson's proposal because it "would convey to the world that we had been frightened into abandoning our position." JFK's rejection of Stevenson's "soft" response eventually made the president's willingness to consider trading the Jupiter missiles more palatable to the ExComm hawks—and ironically overshadowed McNamara's earlier hint about accepting a time limit on the use of Guantanamo.

Kennedy authorized the blockade and suggested that "we inform the Turks and the Italians that they should not fire the strategic missiles they have even if attacked." He also urged alerting the JCS that military personnel in Turkey should not launch the Jupiter missiles against the U.S.S.R. without a direct presidential order and that the warheads in Turkey and Italy be dismantled to make an unauthorized launch impos-

sible. He agreed that preparations for invading Cuba should continue.

The president "acknowledged that the domestic political heat following his television speech [to inform the public of the crisis] would be terrific." He also urged reassurances to the Turks and Italians that Polaris-equipped submarines would guarantee their safety after the missiles were withdrawn and asked Paul Nitze "to study the problems arising out of the withdrawal of missiles from Italy and Turkey, with particular reference to complications which would arise in NATO."

Soon after the meeting, JFK chatted on the second-floor balcony with RFK and Sorensen. "We are very, very close to war," he conceded bleakly. White House staff like Pierre Salinger and Evelyn Lincoln were receiving instructions on how to evacuate their families, and the president had asked Mrs. Kennedy to leave Washington with their children (she refused). Summoning up his sardonic wit, JFK grinned and added, "I hope you realize there's not enough room for everybody in the White House bomb shelter." He then instructed Sorensen to prepare a quarantine speech. Taylor returned to the Pentagon and told the JCS that this had not been one of their better days.

New intelligence on the buildup in Cuba revealed that sixteen MRBM launchers were capable of firing missiles in less than eight hours. The president also received an update on civil defense preparations and learned that emergency supplies of food, water, and medicine had not been shipped to shelters across the country; he ordered the distribution to begin immediately. In addition, for the first time, a nuclear warhead storage bunker was photographed in Cuba.

Sunday, October 21, early A.M. through noon

On Sunday, after attending morning Mass, the president was briefed by General Walter Sweeney, head of the Tactical Air Command, on preparations for air attacks. Sweeney admitted that air strikes, at best, would destroy 90 percent of the MRBMs; he conceded that more missiles would be discovered and some could be launched even after the air strikes. JFK's conviction was now firm that this risk to the U.S. was unacceptable.

The Cubans and the Russians had already learned of U-2 flights over San Cristobal and likely suspected before the president's speech that the missiles had been discovered.

Sunday, October 21, 2:30 P.M.

*The ExComm met again in the Oval Room of the Mansion in a final ef-
fort to keep a lid on the crisis. (After the president's speech all meetings
were held in the Cabinet Room or the Oval Office and taped.) The deliberations had entered a new phase. The quarantine had been chosen,
and the meeting began with discussion of the president's speech. JFK
expressed concern about publicly justifying the U.S. missiles in Turkey
and Italy. Rusk explained that the Jupiters had been deployed after Soviet threats against NATO and, since the U.S. had never targeted Cuba
with nuclear weapons, the cases were not comparable. The president
also underscored "the clandestine manner in which the U.S.S.R. had
acted in Cuba." Rusk suggested that it would be useful to call the
blockade a "quarantine," because "it avoids comparison with the Berlin
blockade."*

*General Taylor urged the president to keep all military options open,
and JFK acknowledged that bombing and/or invasion might still be necessary. Kennedy also hinted that it was better "to frighten the United
Nations representatives with the prospect of all kinds of actions and
then, when a resolution calling for the withdrawal of missiles from
Cuba, Turkey, and Italy was proposed, we could consider supporting
such a resolution." He predicted, however, that once the crisis was
public, Khrushchev would speed up work on the sites, announce that
"Soviet rockets will fly" if the U.S. attacks Cuba, and move to push the
allies out of Berlin.*

*Admiral Anderson heightened the president's doubts about military
overconfidence by explaining that the Navy would fire a shot across the
bow or disable the rudder of any ship refusing to stop for inspection.
JFK expressed concern that a ship might be unintentionally sunk, but
the admiral assured him that it was not difficult to disable a ship without sinking it. But Kennedy, a veteran of naval combat, knew all too
well the uncertainties of war at sea. Anderson also asked for authorization to shoot down hostile Soviet MiGs and to attack Soviet submarines
en route to Cuba.*

*President Kennedy theorized that Khrushchev "knows that we know
of his missile deployment" and would be ready with a planned response
(which turned out to be wrong). He again asked Nitze to study pulling
U.S. missiles out of Turkey and Italy. To prevent a failure of communication, the president also recommended that the word "miscalculate"
be removed from his letter to Khrushchev because in Vienna the Soviet*

leader "had revealed a misunderstanding of this word when translated into Russian" and did not seem to grasp that miscalculation by either side could unleash nuclear war. As the meeting ended, the president approached the chief of Naval Operations: "Well, Admiral, it looks as though this is up to the Navy." "Mr. President," Anderson replied confidently, "the Navy will not let you down."

An effort was launched to inform foreign leaders, embassies, and consulates about the imminent blockade. The president also sent personal representatives to brief the leaders of Britain, France, and West Germany.

On the morning of October 22, with the president's speech only hours away, the Cubans and the Soviets realized that something was up when the evacuation of U.S. dependents began at Guantanamo. Two thousand five hundred family members, given fifteen minutes to pack one bag each, were soon on their way to Virginia aboard Navy transport ships. The Soviet Union also learned that American forces were carrying out mock amphibious landings on the island of Vieques, near Puerto Rico. Their goal was to practice liberating the island from an imaginary dictator named "Ortsac" (Castro spelled backwards).

Monday, October 22, 11:00 A.M., Oval Office

"But I think we oughta be looking to the day when they're removed from Cuba, Italy, and Turkey."

President John F. Kennedy

The meeting concentrated initially on drafting the president's speech and preparing for a debate at the U.N. (The quality of this tape is very poor, and the conversation can be heard only in fragments. This narrative attempts to capture the audible high points and the essential flavor of the discussion.)

As the tape began, the president and Rusk were discussing a possible U.N. role in neutralizing nuclear missiles in any country that was not a nuclear power—in effect, Cuba, Turkey, and Italy. "Why don't we go all the way?" the president suggested. "That gives us an excuse to get 'em out of Turkey and Italy?" However, he rejected any proposal to lift the quarantine until the missiles were removed from Cuba. He speculated that the Soviets were not going to fire the missiles anyway, noting, "But I think we oughta be looking to the day when they're removed from Cuba, Italy, and Turkey."

JFK, RFK, Rusk, Bundy, Arthur Schlesinger, Jr., and several others then talked softly among themselves for more than fifteen minutes about points to be considered for the United Nations debate, such as U.N. inspection of ships entering Cuban ports and the removal of "all missiles and offensive weapons" from Cuba. Schlesinger expressed concern that the term "offensive" could be interpreted to include American weapons at Guantanamo—a possibility dismissed by JFK, Rusk, and Alexis Johnson. The president can be heard making handwritten revisions and erasing on his own copy. Finally, satisfied with the draft, he affirmed, "That's it. First class."

The president also asked about including warships from OAS nations in the quarantine, but Rusk pointed out caustically, "Our armed forces think only *Americans* can fight!" The discussion moved on to managing press and public relations after the president's speech. Roger Hilsman, assistant secretary of state for intelligence and research, outlined plans to brief OAS and NATO ambassadors and proposed showing slides of the missile bases without revealing their locations. JFK seemed uneasy about releasing the pictures and suggested background briefings—not directly attributable to anyone in the administration. He also discussed informing key journalists like Walter Lippmann and "Scotty" Reston: "You show these pictures," he instructed, "but we don't release them because of security." Ball prompted some laughter by remarking, "I'd rather not have anything handed out, cause somebody will swipe one, just as sure as hell."

RFK raised the embarrassing prospect that the press might ask about why the missiles had not been detected earlier and needled Hilsman, "Why didn't we detect them a month ago? What is your answer?" Hilsman exclaimed that Senator Keating's informants had misidentified SAM sites as offensive missiles, but he remained enthusiastic about the public relations potential of the photos: "Mr. President, there are some *lovely* photographs, one taken on Sunday, one on Monday [October 14–15], and the *enormous* change between Sunday and Monday, in twenty-four hours!" JFK agreed but cautioned, "we ought to be thinking of all the unpleasant questions" that might come up at the briefings.

The president, preparing to meet shortly with the Berlin Planning Group, asked for details on the Soviet buildup in Cuba—he was told there were one hundred MiG 15 and 21 fighters and about eight thousand to ten thousand Soviet military personnel. He wondered about using a less provocative word in his speech, such as "technicians," but agreed to Rusk and Hilsman's suggestion to stick with "personnel."

Monday, October 22, around noon, Cabinet Room

"I don't think we ought to accept the Chiefs' word on that one, Paul."

President John F. Kennedy

Paul Nitze began the meeting with a briefing on Berlin. Two days earlier JFK had instructed Nitze to have the JCS issue new orders to American personnel on the Jupiter bases in Turkey not to fire their missiles at the U.S.S.R. without a direct presidential order, even if attacked. "The Chiefs," Nitze reported, "came back with a paper saying that those instructions are *already* out." JFK was not satisfied: "Well, why don't we reinforce 'em because, as I say, we may be attacking the Cubans and . . . a reprisal may come on these. We don't want them firing without our knowing about it." Kennedy softly pressed Nitze to be sure that his orders were fully understood. "Can we take care of that then, Paul? We need a new instruction out."

Nitze informed the president that the JCS had made another point in their response: "NATO strategic contact [a nuclear attack by the U.S.S.R.] requires the immediate execution of EDP in such events." "What's EDP?" Kennedy asked. "The European Defense Plan," Nitze answered chillingly, "which is nuclear war." "Now that's why," the president barked, "we want to get on that, you see." Nitze tried to explain, "No, they said the orders are that *nothing* can go without the presidential order."

The commander-in-chief's reservations were obvious: "They don't realize there *is* a chance there will be a *spot reprisal*, and what we gotta do is make sure these fellows [in Turkey] *do* know, so that they don't fire 'em off and think the United States is under attack. I don't think," he pronounced candidly, "we ought to accept the Chiefs' word on that one, Paul." "All right," Nitze mumbled grudgingly. JFK, alert to the barely concealed contempt for his authority and judgment by the JCS during their October 19 meeting, wanted to be sure that the military did not "misunderstand" his orders.

"But *surely* these fellows are *thoroughly* indoctrinated *not* to fire," Nitze bristled, banging the table. Kennedy cut him off with a temperate but firm order: "Well, let's do it again, Paul." The president's intent was clear: *his* orders would be carried out regardless of JCS procedures. "I've *got* your point," Nitze finally retreated. "We'll do it again." Some strained laughter broke out and Bundy wryly told Nitze, "Send me the documents, and I will show them to a doubting master." The laughter briefly grew even louder.

Bundy revisited the need to reassure NATO that the American response in Cuba was aimed primarily at protecting Berlin and European security. "Those are good points," JFK affirmed; the allies must feel that they have been fully informed and consulted so that they don't interpret the blockade as a sign of America's Cuba obsession.

Suddenly, press secretary Pierre Salinger entered the room and handed the president a note. They whispered together before Kennedy revealed in an edgy voice that Gromyko was going to make a statement in a few hours before returning to Moscow. A wave of concern swept across the room. JFK recommended promptly announcing his 7:00 P.M. speech so that the Soviets could not scoop him by declaring that they had shipped only defensive missiles to Cuba. Nitze stressed, "I think it's *awfully* important to get ahead of the Russians," and JFK sparked some laughter by joking, "What else do we have to worry about in Berlin?"

Kennedy was especially concerned that the Soviets would say, "if we do anything about it [the missiles], that they're going to do such-and-such." Perhaps, "They think maybe we're gonna invade Cuba," he speculated. "I think we ought to get to work on this," JFK stressed nervously. "We don't have much time."

Salinger's report was a false alarm. Gromyko made a routine statement at the airport and never mentioned the missiles. The ExComm adjourned until 3:00 P.M.

Military preparations moved forward rapidly. The Strategic Air Command (SAC) put its B-52 nuclear bombers on alert and ordered B-47 bombers dispersed around the country. The JCS raised U.S. military forces to Defense Condition (DEFCON) 3. (DEFCON 5 was routine readiness; DEFCON 1 was war.) The Navy deployed 150 ships, 250 aircraft, and 30,000 men to enforce the quarantine. When Khrushchev learned about the president's speech, he and many in the Presidium assumed that an invasion was imminent: "a feeling of impending doom hung in the air."

Meanwhile, the Presidium authorized General Issa Pliyev, commander of Soviet forces in Cuba, to use Luna tactical nuclear weapons without a direct order from Moscow if required to blunt an American invasion. These missiles had a range of only thirty miles and could not threaten the U.S. mainland. They were designed instead for battlefield use, to destroy an invasion fleet or wipe out forces landing on Cuba's beaches. Each warhead, nonetheless, had about one-seventh the explosive power of the bomb dropped on Hiroshima.

Monday, October 22, 3:00 P.M., Cabinet Room

"Khrushchev will *not* take this without a response, maybe in Berlin or maybe here. But . . . the choices being one among second best—I think we've done the *best* thing at least as far as you can tell *in advance.*"

President John F. Kennedy

The full National Security Council, including the Joint Chiefs, convened in mid-afternoon, joined ominously by Edward McDermott, director of the Office of Emergency Preparedness.

After brief discussion of a message from British prime minister Harold Macmillan and news from McCone that Soviet submarines would soon be in Cuban waters, JFK instructed everyone, in order to promote domestic political unity, to "sing one song in order to make clear that there was now no difference among his advisers as to the proper course to follow." He described the quarantine as "a reasonable consensus" and grimly reminded the NSC that if the wrong choice had been made, they may not have "the satisfaction of knowing what would have happened if we had acted differently."

An invasion might still be necessary, he admitted, after turning on the recorder. "Khrushchev will *not* take this without a response, maybe in Berlin or maybe here. But . . . the choices being one among second best—I think we've done the *best* thing at least as far as you can tell *in advance.*" He stressed, however, that two dangerous matters remained to be settled: "what will we do if the work *continues* on these sites, which we assume it *will* [and] . . . If they shoot down one of our U-2s, do we attack *that* SAM site or all the SAM sites?" But, he added, in case anyone should develop cold feet, "I don't think there was anybody *ever* who didn't think we shouldn't respond." His meaning was plain in spite of his grammar.

"The idea of a quick strike was *very* tempting," he acknowledged, "and I really didn't give up on that until yesterday morning" because of the Pearl Harbor parallel and because all the missiles could not be eliminated. "The job can *only* be finished by an invasion. . . . [and] we are moving those forces which will be necessary in case . . . it looks like that would be the only course left to us." The president also tried to placate the Joint Chiefs: "we would have been able to take out more planes and missiles without warning [but] . . . I think the shock to the alliance might have been nearly fatal, particularly as it would have excused very drastic action by Khrushchev." Rusk agreed, aiming his remarks at the JCS: "if any of our colleagues think that this is, in any sense, a *weak* action, I think we can be quite sure that in a number of hours we'll have a *flaming* crisis on our hands. This is gonna go *very* far, and possibly *very* fast."

Robert Kennedy, as he had done that morning, asked about how to respond to politically damaging charges that action should have been taken earlier. JFK replied that without the hard evidence first available on October 16, NATO would have regarded risking Berlin as proof of "almost a fixation on the subject of Cuba . . . [since] the whole foreign policy of the United States since 1947 has been to develop and maintain alliances *in this hemisphere* as well as around the world. . . . And, of course, no one at that time was certain that Khrushchev would make such a *far-reaching* step, which is *wholly* a departure from Soviet foreign policy, *really*, since I would say the Berlin blockade."

President Kennedy acknowledged that there had been rumors from Cuban refugees, and "Mr. Hilsman, who's in charge of that, says that most of them . . . were talking about these SAM sites, the ground-air missiles. Is that correct?" Hilsman, unsure whether to be flattered or embarrassed, and irritated that RFK had again questioned pre–October 14 intelligence, responded hesitantly, "Yes, sir," and muttered, "I wouldn't say I was in charge." "What?" JFK pressed, and Hilsman repeated, "I wouldn't say that I was in *charge* of the whole thing." Amused by Hilsman's discomfort, Kennedy responded dryly, "Well, whoever," sparking a soft ripple of laughter.

Hilsman reiterated that there had been no confirmation until October 14. But McCone cautioned, "I wouldn't be *too* categoric that we had no information" because "there were some fifteen refugee reports" indicating "that *something* was going on." JFK reminded his colleagues that none of the Eastern European satellites had nuclear weapons on their territory, and "this would be the *first* time the Soviet Union had moved these weapons outside their own" borders. (U.S. intelligence did not know that the U.S.S.R. had briefly deployed nuclear weapons in East Germany in 1959.)

The president was still troubled that critics might ask why he had decided not to attack the missiles. Bundy recommended avoiding references to "the difficulty of hitting these targets" since air strikes might still be necessary. RFK advised sticking to "the Pearl Harbor thing." "It is a fact that even with the air strike," JFK emphasized, "we couldn't perhaps get all the missiles that are in sight." Bundy replied impatiently, "*Entirely true*, Mr. President. But I *don't* think the next few days is the time to talk about it." Kennedy retorted irritably, "Well, I know, but I want everybody to understand it, Mac, if you don't mind. The fact of the matter is there *are* missiles on the island which are not in sight!"

JFK remained worried that critics at home and abroad might try to equate Soviet missiles in Cuba and U.S. missiles in Turkey and Italy, "which the Soviets put up with." Rusk again argued forcefully that the cases were *not* comparable because the U.S.S.R. had first deployed "hundreds of these weapons aimed at Europe." JFK agreed and read aloud from a prepared statement: the secret Soviet move was undertaken to spread Castroism in Latin America and as a "probing action" to test whether Khrushchev could get away with grabbing Berlin. "All this represents a provocative change in the delicate status quo both countries have maintained." Ambassador Thompson confirmed that Khrushchev had "made it quite clear in my last talk with him that he was squirming" not to back down in Berlin. Rusk urged the president to state publicly that the missiles in Cuba represented "a special threat" to the U.S. and the forty-one allies all over the world dependent on American nuclear support.

The president recalled that Gromyko had repeated last week that the Soviets were "getting ready to move on Berlin anyway." The quarantine was not a threat, he began reading again, because it affected only offensive weapons and did not stop food or medicine or threaten war. He cited, as an example of U.S. restraint, "Even today the Soviets inspect our, at least stop our, [truck] convoys going into Berlin." He stopped reading and asked, "People get out, don't they?" Bundy responded, rather condescendingly, "No, sir, the people do *not* get out . . . but *inspection* is *not* the word we want to use." Another participant confirmed that U.S. forces sometimes did get out of the trucks to let the Soviets "look in through the tailgates." JFK seized on this vindication in his wrangle with Bundy: "They *do* let them. Yeah."

"But the central point here is," Rusk demanded yet again, "that we're in Berlin by *right* . . . and agreement of the Soviet Union. They're bringing these things into Cuba contrary to the Rio Pact. There's just all the difference in the world between these two situations." The president seemed confident that he could make a convincing case in the court of world public opinion that the blockade of Cuba was not comparable to the 1948 Soviet blockade of Berlin: "This is not a blockade in that sense. It's merely an attempt to prevent the shipment of weapons there."

President Kennedy was prepared to defend the blockade as a reasonable and restrained response to a Soviet provocation. But, he did not want to hand Khrushchev a propaganda plum by revealing that surprise air attacks had even been considered; he was willing to manage the news to preserve this cover story. "So I think," he ordered brusquely, "we oughta just scratch that from all our statements and conversations, and not ever indicate that that *was* a course of action open to us. *I can't say that strongly enough,*" he demanded, "Now it's gonna be very difficult to keep it quiet, but I think we ought to." RFK suggested saying bombing was rejected as a "Pearl Harbor kind of operation," but Rusk recommended stating simply that air attacks were not done rather than not considered. "Well, I think that's fair enough," JFK agreed.

Taylor, however, raised another public relations issue: "Mr. President, I should call attention to the fact we're starting moves [of troops] now which are very overt, and will be seen and reported on and commented on. And you'll be faced with the question, 'Are you preparing to invade?'" JFK pointed out that it was neither strategically nor politically helpful to "have it hanging over us that we're preparing invasion," but Taylor objected that it's the business of the military to plan for any contingency. The president sought to cool the general's rhetoric: "By plans, I think we mean it in the more . . . not in the military sense but in the...," but trailed off without finishing. He asked instead for a report on how troop movements had been publicized during the Korean War.

As the meeting moved toward a conclusion, Rusk asked whether the president had considered extending "our stop and search program to aircraft, should nuclear weapons be sent to Cuba by air." JFK again moved to reign in the potential for escalation: "I don't think we ought to do it on the aircraft just yet" because if a crisis erupts in Berlin, "we may have to rely on aircraft, and I don't think *we* ought to initiate that." RFK inquired about how to respond to questions about the possible delivery of missiles by air and McNamara advised "saying that we're prepared to quarantine movement of weapons by whatever means, *period.* . . . We'll have to watch this carefully and decide what to do at that time."

Rusk speculated whether the press might ask about a call-up of National Guard and Reserve units or a declaration of national emergency and urged saying, "Not at this time, but that could change in an hour's time." JFK questioned Treasury under secretary Henry Fowler about the impact of the crisis on "the balance of payments, gold, and all the rest." Fowler dramatically underscored the urgency of the situation by asking who would decide "on such a question as the closing of the exchanges should any situation bordering on panic develop in the next day or two."

The administration had to clearly explain, Rusk also contended, that the blockade "is not, from our point of view, an act of war," and the president asked if ships from friendly nations would be stopped "so that we get the precedent established in case we want to extend this to oil and petroleum and so on." Admiral Anderson replied by the book: "I think that we *should* stop and visit and search and play this thing straight," and Rusk concurred, "it has to be *effective*, and to make it *effective*, you stop all ships."

JFK ended the meeting by again demanding complete public silence about all tactical, strategic, or military options. Bundy proposed a standard reply, "No orders have been given." "Thank you very much," JFK added, and turned off the tape recorder.

Just after the meeting, JFK and Rusk met with Ugandan prime minister Milton Obote and several members of his cabinet. The president participated in a discussion of African economic development and resisted attempts by Rusk to shorten the meeting. Later that evening, when Obote watched JFK's speech, he was astounded that the president had appeared entirely normal and composed during their meeting.

The president met at 4:00 p.m. with his full cabinet, most of whom were not members of ExComm, and revealed that offensive missiles had been discovered in Cuba and that he would speak to the nation at 7:00 p.m. Secretary of Agriculture Orville Freeman, after the shocked and silent cabinet members had left, asked if any planning had been done for possible food shortages if the crisis lasted for weeks. Kennedy admitted that the issue had been largely ignored, and Freeman promised to prepare plans to deal with any emergency. In fact, "The government had stocked virtually no public shelters with food and survival supplies. If war came, most Americans would be on their own."

At 5:00 p.m., the president, Rusk, McNamara, Thompson, McCone, Lundahl, and Ray Cline of the CIA met with the bipartisan leaders of Congress—summoned from across the country, since Congress was not in session, and flown to the capital in military aircraft. These experi-

enced Washington hands realized that something major was about to happen, but some resented that they were being informed of the president's decision barely two hours before his speech. JFK had never been an insider in the House, and many of his Senate colleagues had dismissed him as an indifferent senator at best, a playboy at worst. Now, whether they liked it or not, he was the president of the United States. But that did not mean they would passively accept his decisions.

Monday, October 22, 5:00 P.M., Cabinet Room

"The people who are the best off are the people whose advice is not taken because *whatever* we do is *filled* with hazards."
President John F. Kennedy

The meeting began with intelligence briefings. The president undoubtedly watched the faces of his congressional allies and opponents, wondering whether they would support his decision. McCone, reading from a prepared document, did not dodge a troubling admission: "Late in September, persistent reports came to us from refugee sources" about the possible deployment of offensive missiles. Photographic proof, however, was not obtained until October 14. He piled on details: forty-three Soviet bloc ships were in Cuban ports or on their way; twenty-four MRBM launchers (with a range of 1,020 nautical miles) and twelve IRBM launch pads (with a range of 2,200 nautical miles) were under construction; four MRBM sites, with sixteen launchers, were "in full operational readiness." The Soviets had also installed twenty-four SAM bases and had delivered forty MiG fighters and twenty IL-28 nuclear bombers. He asserted that although only one warhead storage site had been identified, "We think it prudent to *assume* that nuclear weapons are now or shortly will be available in Cuba."

The congressional leaders sat in stunned silence as McCone turned the photography briefing over to Lundahl. "Mr. President, gentlemen," he began, "I would seek to very briefly summarize in graphic form the statistics which Mr. McCone has shown to you." Lundahl identified missile installations, IL-28 bombers (most still in crates), MiG fighters on airfields, and the nuclear warhead storage site—"right next to an IRBM launching site." Several muted conversations broke out around the table. Lundahl, clearly proud of his work, concluded: "There's no doubt in our mind of our identification." McCone added, "from a variety of intelligence sources we have concluded that these bases, both the ground-to-air SAM sites as well as the missile sites, are manned by Soviets." "Are there any questions?" JFK asked.

Senator Richard Russell, Democrat of Georgia, the powerful chairman of the Senate Armed Services Committee, questioned whether electronic monitoring had been installed on the missiles. McCone confirmed that radar on the SAMs "has been latching on to our U-2s the last couple of days, and while they have not fired a missile at us, we think that they will within a short time." "*My God!*" Russell gasped. Republican senator Thomas Kuchel of California suggested that a nuclear launch from Cuba would be suicide. "*Yes*, it would be suicide," McCone observed matter-of-factly. Rusk added that such a response would inevitably trigger a "general nuclear exchange."

President Kennedy turned to Ambassador Thompson—who declared that the timing and purpose of the Cuban buildup was to provoke "a showdown on Berlin." Rusk speculated that the "hard-line boys" in the Kremlin had decided to drop "the peaceful coexistence theme." Senator Russell's agitation was becoming apparent: "Mr. Secretary, do you see any other chance that it'll get any better if they keep on establishin' new bases and dividin' our space more and more?" Rusk conceded, "I'm not suggesting that things are getting any better."

JFK tried to appeal to the Republicans in the room by revealing that McCone had briefed Eisenhower. "If we invade Cuba," he explained, "we have a chance that these missiles will be fired—*on us*." Alternatively, Khrushchev might seize Berlin and shatter the unity of NATO because "Europe will regard Berlin's loss . . . as having been the fault of the United States by acting in a precipitous way." But, the president reasoned, "to not do anything . . . would be a mistake."

Beginning tonight, he finally announced, "we're going to blockade Cuba . . . under the Rio Treaty . . . and hope to get a two-thirds vote for them to give the blockade legality." If they refuse, the blockade would be carried out instead with a declaration of war. "In order *not* to give Mr. Khrushchev the justification for imposing a *complete* blockade on Berlin, we're going to start with a blockade on the shipment of offensive weapons into Cuba, but stop all ships." Plans for an invasion were still going forward, but, "if we invade Cuba," he explained, "there's a chance these weapons will be fired at the United States . . . [and] if we attempt to strike them from the air, then we will not get 'em all." But, he admitted, "I *don't* know what their response will be." "If there's any strong disagreements with what at least we've set out to do," he concluded, "I want to hear it." Rusk added that a limited first step "is *very* important in order to give the Soviets a chance to pull back from the brink."

Senator Russell suddenly lashed out: "Mr. President, I could not stay silent under these circumstances and live with myself. I think that our responsibilities to our people demand some stronger steps than that. . . . It seems to me that we're at the crossroads. We're either a first-class power or we're *not*." The Georgian tried to hoist the president on his own petard: "You have warned these people time and again, in the most eloquent speeches I have read since Woodrow Wilson. . . . And you have told 'em *not* to do this thing. They've *done* it. And I think that you should assemble as speedily as possible an adequate force and clean out that situation. The time's gonna come, Mr. President, when we're gonna have to take this gamble . . . for the nuclear war. . . . But I think that the more that we temporize, the more *surely* he *is* to convince *himself* that we *are* afraid to . . . really fight."

JFK, obviously discomfited, suggested that Russell listen to McNamara's military analysis, but the senator cut in: "Pardon me, you had said if anybody disagrees, and I couldn't sit here feelin' as I do." McNamara tried to scotch the senator's criticism by providing details on the blockade, air surveillance, and the reinforcement of Guantanamo and the southeastern U.S. coast.

Russell, nonetheless, became even more perturbed: "Mr. President, I don't wanna make a nuisance of myself, but I would like to complete my statement." Delaying an invasion would give the MiGs a chance "to attack our shipping or to drop a few bombs around Miami or some other place," and when we do invade, "we'll lose a great many more men than we would *right now.*"

"But Senator," JFK explained, "we can't invade Cuba," because it would take days to assemble the necessary forces. Russell insisted that an invasion would present the Soviets with a *fait accompli* and make war *less* likely—the same argument made three days before by General LeMay. JFK, clearly irritated, countered: "We *don't* have the forces to seize Cuba." "Well, we can assemble 'em," the senator retorted sharply. "So that's what we're doing now," Kennedy replied impatiently. "This blockade is gonna put them on the alert"—and weaken our forces, Russell sputtered, "around the whole periphery of the free world."

McNamara attempted again, at JFK's urging, to defend the invasion plan—which would require 250,000 personnel and over 100 merchant ships, preceded by 2,000 bombing sorties. "Bombing sorties with what kind of bombs?" House minority leader Charles Halleck asked; the defense secretary, strikingly, left *all* options open: "Initially, iron [conventional] bombs." McNamara also disclosed that the president had ordered the Pentagon nearly a year before to prepare plans for invading Cuba: "We've reviewed them with the president . . . on *five* different occasions. We're *well* prepared."

President Kennedy, perhaps hoping to isolate Russell, laid out the stark choices: "If we go into Cuba, we have to all realize that we are taking a chance that these missiles, which are ready to fire, won't be fired. Is that really a gamble we should take? In any case, we're preparing to take it. I think, fact is, that that is *one hell* of a gamble." He also made a rather disingenuous appeal for unity, since he had ignored the Congress up to the last possible moment: "I'm gonna have everybody in this room *be* here with us because we all have to decide this thing together." And, he added, "if the Soviet Union, as a reprisal, should grab Berlin in the morning, which they could do within a couple of hours, our war plan at that point has been to fire our nuclear weapons at *them*. So that these are all the matters which we have to be thinkin' about."

The president's summation made Russell even more combative: "Excuse me again, but do you see a time *ever* in the future when Berlin will *not* be hostage to this?" JFK replied bluntly, "No," and Russell demanded, "We've *got* to take a chance somewhere, sometime, if we're gonna retain our position as a great world power."

The senator cited General LeMay's belief that all the missiles could be wiped out from the air. "Now let me just answer that, Senator," JFK shot back, again ignoring his own embargo on discussing military options: all the sites could not be destroyed in a Pearl Harbor–type attack—which might spark a nuclear war if the Soviets retaliated in Turkey.

As a parting shot, Russell cited the president's pledge to act regardless of OAS support: "Now I understand," he added sarcastically, "that we're still waitin' while the secretary of state tries to get *them* to agree to it." "I'm not waitin'," Kennedy snapped. "I'm through. Excuse me," Russell backed off. "So I hope you forgive me, but you asked for opinions." "Well, I forgive you," Kennedy replied defensively, "but it's a very difficult problem we're . . . facing together." "*Oh, my God!* I know that," Russell cut in. "Our authority and the world's destiny will hinge on this decision. But it's comin' someday, Mr. President. Will it ever be under more auspicious circumstances?" "It's foolish to just kick

the whole Rio Treaty out the window," JFK asserted. "Well, I don't
wanna do that!" Russell protested. "I understand the force of *your* arguments," Kennedy conceded, but "if we invade, we take the risk . . .
that these weapons will be fired."

"Are we *absolutely* positive from these photos," Halleck asked, that
this buildup is offensive? "That's correct," the president replied firmly.
McNamara assured Halleck: "you might question the missiles, but you
can't question the IL-28s." "What are they?" Halleck responded. Long-
range nuclear jet bombers, the defense secretary explained. McCone, irritated that his judgment about offensive missiles had been questioned,
interjected: "I think the evidence that these are offensive weapons is
conclusive, *except* for the fact that we *do not* have, *which I said*, positive knowledge that the warhead is actually there."

At that point, the president was handed a letter from the British
prime minister and astutely chose to read it to the congressional leaders.
Macmillan urged the U.S. to recognize that Europeans had lived so long
"in close proximity to the enemy's nuclear weapons . . . that we have
got accustomed to it. So European opinion will need attention." He also
cautioned that Khrushchev "will of course try to trade his Cuba position against his ambition in Berlin"—which would threaten the unity of
NATO. There were no comments on the letter and the discussion
promptly returned to the blockade and the president's speech. Everett
Dirksen, the GOP Senate minority leader, asked softly, "Mr. President,
what will you cover in the speech?" JFK cited "the double-dealing of
the Russian statements," this "basic change in Soviet strategy," and a
demand for removal of the missiles. But, he stressed, "I think it would
be a *great mistake* to talk about invasion"—even though preparations
were moving forward.

The president tried again to placate his most vocal critic: "But, as I
say," he began, "I appreciate the"—he paused for several seconds to
find the appropriate words—"the vigor and the strength of what Senator Russell feels and says." But the strategy failed. Russell reiterated
that delaying an invasion would call into question the president's commitment to stay the course, and "we'd be much more likely to have to
abandon the venture completely, which I greatly feel we will before
we're through." Kennedy started to reply but Russell cut him off: "You
know, the right of self-defense is pretty elemental, and you relied on
that in that very *telling* statement you made . . . and that's what we'd be
doin'."

Another influential southern Democrat, Senator J. William Fulbright, abruptly weighed in against the blockade. An invasion, he insisted, was *less* risky: "I mean legally. I mean it's just between us and Cuba. I think a blockade is the *worst* of the alternatives because if you're confronted with a Russian ship, you *are* actually confronting Russia." An invasion of Cuba "is not actually an affront to Russia."

The president again raised the seizure of Berlin, but Fulbright maintained that it would be better to go to the U.N. or invade Cuba, "A blockade seems to me the *worst* alternative." McNamara intervened to remind the Arkansas senator that an invasion would first require two thousand air sorties against thousands of Soviet military personnel. "That's *quite* different," Fulbright maintained. "They're in Cuba. And Cuba still is supposed to be a sovereign country. It isn't a member of the Warsaw Pact. It's not even a satellite. . . . It's just a Communist country."

Finally, his patience strained, JFK asked, "What are you in favor of, Bill?"

"I'm in favor," the former Rhodes Scholar asserted, "on the basis of this information, of an invasion, and an all-out one, and as quickly as possible." He challenged the president to live up to his September 13 statement that the U.S. would prevent an offensive buildup in Cuba. "An attack on a Russian ship," he reiterated, "is really an act of war against Russia. It is *not* an act of war against Russia to attack Cuba."

The president, clearly frustrated, reminded the Senate Foreign Relations Committee chairman that many Russians would be killed in an invasion: "We are gonna have to shoot *them* up. And I think that it would be *foolish* to expect that the Russians would not regard that as a *far* more direct thrust. . . . I think that if we're talkin' about nuclear war, then escalation ought to be at least with some degree of control." Fulbright persisted, "They have no right to say that you've had an attack on Russia." "Well...," JFK muttered, "In the meanwhile we ought to be assembling all our forces."

As the tense meeting wound down, Kennedy reemphasized that he was not sure *any* strategy would avert nuclear war: "Some people would say, 'let's go in with an air strike.' You'd have those bombs [missiles] go off and blow up fifteen cities in the United States. And they would have been *wrong*. . . . The people who are the best off," he reflected fatalistically, "are the people whose advice is not taken because *whatever* we do is *filled* with hazards." "I'll say this to Senator Fulbright," JFK continued. "We don't know where we're gonna end up on this matter." He cited Ambassador Thompson's belief that attacking the missile bases and killing thousands of Russians would be far more dangerous than stopping their ships. But, he admitted, "Now, who knows that? . . . We just tried to make good judgments about a matter on which everyone's uncertain. But at least it's the best advice we could get. So we *start* here. We don't know where he's gonna take us or where we're gonna take ourselves." "Now just wait, Mr. President," Senator Russell interjected, "the nettle is gonna sting anyway." "That's correct," JFK conceded.

Finally, as the meeting began to break up, Congressman Halleck, a Republican, offered a surprising statement of support to the commander-in-chief: "Mr. President, . . . *I* don't have the background information to make these decisions. *You* do. And I've been glad to speak a piece or two here, but whatever you decide to do." "Well, I appreciate that," the president replied gratefully. Halleck was clearly impressed by the terrible choices facing the president, and this exchange is one of the most surprising and personal moments on the ExComm tapes.

JFK switched off the recorder and headed for the Oval Office to make his televised speech—mindful that all the congressional flak had come from Democrats. He quickly cooled off, however, concluding philosophically that the tough stance by some congressional leaders was much like the ExComm reactions at their first meeting.

At 6:00 p.m., Dean Rusk met with Ambassador Dobrynin at the State Department and handed him the president's speech and a cover letter to Khrushchev. He later recalled that Dobrynin seemed to age ten years on the spot, confirming suspicions that he had been kept in the dark by his government. Dobrynin reportedly also looked sick as he left the State Department.

The president's speech shocked the Kremlin as well. As he awaited word from the White House, Khrushchev later recalled, "I slept on a couch in my office—and I kept my clothes on. I was ready for alarming news to come any moment, and I wanted to be ready to react immediately."

The American public responded to JFK's speech with some signs of panic. Food and emergency supplies disappeared from supermarkets and hardware stores. Long lines were reported at gasoline stations, and there was a run on tires. People across America stood in silent, worried clumps around newsstands, anxiously reading the latest headlines. At Phillips Academy in Andover, Massachusetts, and at the Mount Hermon School to the west, students received phone calls from their par-

ents urging them to come home to be with their families—just in case. Some 10 million Americans also left the nation's cities hoping to find safety "far away from nuclear targets."

At 1:00 a.m., after another exhausting day, Rusk and Harlan Cleveland, assistant secretary of state for international organization affairs, prepared to go home for a few hours of sleep. Cleveland remarked, "I'll see you in the morning," and Rusk replied, "I hope so." Cleveland later recalled that he had been so busy that "the full enormity" of the situation "hadn't hit me until that moment." These words, coming from the usually imperturbable Rusk, struck Cleveland as the emotional "equivalent of screaming."

American intelligence continued to monitor Soviet military activity but failed to detect imminent moves against Berlin or Turkey. The president's speech had ended the secret phase of the crisis, and risky low-altitude photographic missions, providing new details about the Soviet buildup, soon began over Cuba.

Khrushchev's initial response to JFK's speech was angry and confrontational: he ordered Soviet ships to ignore the blockade, placed Warsaw Pact forces on full alert, and cancelled all discharges from the Strategic Rocket Forces, air defense units, and the submarine fleet. Early the next morning, the OAS began debating the quarantine, and the U.N. Security Council prepared for an emergency session. Since secrecy was no longer necessary, all the remaining ExComm meetings were held in the Cabinet Room and recorded.

Tuesday, October 23, 10:00 A.M., Cabinet Room

"Well, my God! . . . I think it was *very* significant that we were here this morning. We've passed the *one* contingency: an immediate, sudden, irrational [nuclear] strike [by the U.S.S.R.]."

Secretary of State Dean Rusk

McCone first discussed new evidence that Russians were solely in charge of the missile sites and piloting half of the MiG fighters in Cuba. The CIA chief also reviewed new Soviet efforts to camouflage the missiles. RFK, just after JFK turned on the tape recorder, reopened the tricky political issue of dealing with Republican charges of duplicity or incompetence for not having acted sooner. He suggested, in a worried tone of voice, that the president might be accused of "closing the barn door after the horse is gone." "I don't think it's realized [by the public and the press]," JFK responded, "how quickly these mobile bases can be set up and how quickly they can be moved."

McNamara reported that he had briefed 125 journalists the previous night, but recommended additional briefings for congressional leaders and reporters "who will be asking this kind of a question." Vice President Johnson suggested that McCone also brief Russell and Fulbright, and, perhaps trying to ease JFK's exasperation from the previous evening, recounted, "I saw your speech with 'em last night and I think that the attitude was much *better* than was indicated here." The president, clearly orchestrating a public relations offensive, urged McCone to meet again with key members of Congress. But, put off by the hostile exchanges with Russell and Fulbright, he griped, "I don't think we oughta bring in too many [members of Congress]. They just feed on each other." McCone offered to call former president Eisenhower to "get permission from him to use *his* name in talking with these congressional people" and to get "his view of this thing as a soldier."

A consensus emerged that anyone speaking for the administration should stress the mobility of the missiles but avoid answering specific questions about military or diplomatic options. "It is of *great* importance," Bundy contended, "unless we get a *clear-cut* decision around *this* table to change," he rapped the table for emphasis, "*we stay right with the president's speech.*" RFK surmised that the speech would blunt criticism "for about twenty-four hours, but we're gonna have difficulty after that." Bundy disagreed, "In the broader sense, I don't think the country's reaction is that we've done too little."

The president requested a CIA analysis of "what the effects of a blockade of everything but food and medicine would be on Cuba . . . and what the political effects would be in Cuba, as well as outside." "Do we want that," RFK asked, "on Berlin too?" JFK, always preoccupied with Berlin, agreed that it would be valuable to know "what the effect would be of a blockade in Berlin *by them.*"

Arthur Lundahl reviewed the previous day's photos which showed that several MRBM launchers were no longer visible. He speculated that they might be hidden in the trees or could have been moved to another locale. The photos strengthened JFK's conviction that stressing the mobility of the missiles could help defuse charges that they should have been discovered earlier. "Let's get that on the record," he urged. McNamara also boasted that twenty-five sets of new U-2 photos had been processed in one day in order to target the missiles for air strikes. The president, evidently impressed, responded, "Do you mind if I have these?" Lundahl and McCone also confirmed that photo reconnaissance now covered 97 percent of Cuba.

McNamara contended that the quarantine proclamation should be issued as soon as possible after OAS action and should be implemented at dawn in order to intercept the first ship, the *Kimovsk,* which had hatches large enough to carry missiles. JFK seemed skeptical: "Wouldn't you guess that anything that has a missile on it would be turned around last night?" The defense secretary insisted that the most unfortunate outcome would be to disable a ship that refused to stop and find "it didn't have offensive weapons on it. That would be a poor way to start."

Quite abruptly, the president, clearly vexed about the prospect of political attacks from the press, the Congress, and NATO after a confrontation at sea, vigorously declared: "There's no action we *ever* could have taken, unless we'd invaded Cuba a year ago, to prevent them being there. . . . So there's *no answer* to this unless you're gonna invade Cuba, *six* months ago, or *a* year ago, or *two* years ago, or *three* years ago! . . . And the *fact* of the matter is there wasn't *anybody* who suggested an invasion of Cuba *at a time* when they *necessarily* could have *stopped these things coming onto the island*!" "So," he continued forcefully, "what *we* are doing is throwing down a card on the table in a game which we don't know the ending of. . . . Some of that you can't put on the record, but it's a *very* legitimate point. There was no way we could *stop* this *happening*." JFK also remarked, with unmistakable annoyance, that the British press "are not even with us *today*." Bundy laughed and observed sarcastically that the *Manchester Guardian* had declared that the administration was wrong about the presence of offensive missiles. "Okay. Yeah. Okay," JFK replied, clearly amused.

This brief lighthearted moment evaporated quickly. McNamara urged the president to sign an executive order extending the tours of duty of Navy and Marine personnel: "We *should* have it signed today." "Right," JFK murmured softly. McNamara also disclosed that Defense Department lawyers had concluded that a proclamation signed that night would become legally effective the following morning.

The defense chief then brought up a far more dangerous issue, which the president had raised the previous day: deciding how to respond if a U-2 was shot down by a SAM missile. McNamara explained that the Strategic Air Command was monitoring the photo missions and would have confirmation "*literally* fifteen minutes after the incident." He emphasized to the president that plans were in place to destroy the SAM site, "*if* that *is* your decision," within two hours, "so that we could announce *almost* simultaneously the loss of the U-2 and the destruction of the SAM site."

The president asked about sending escort planes to "*assure* the cause of the accident," so that he could be certain it resulted from hostile action rather than mechanical failure. He seemed uneasy about making a decision to retaliate "in advance." But, at least for the moment, he put his doubts aside: "I suppose what we do is, when we take out that SAM site, we announce that if any U-2 is shot down, we'll take out *every* SAM site." Taylor, however, advised that it was "highly unlikely that we can *really* identify the guilty SAM site." "I understand," JFK replied, and Taylor concluded, "That doesn't really matter."

Bundy observed that since the decision to strike the SAMs had to be made fifteen minutes after confirmation that a U-2 had been shot down, it was impossible to be certain that the president would be available: "Do you want to delegate that authority *now*," Bundy asked, "to the secretary of defense or do you want to... well what is your...?" The president replied cautiously, "Well, what we want to do is, I will delegate to the secretary of defense on the *understanding* that the information would be *very clear*" that it resulted from military action. "Only if you're unavailable," McNamara assured the commander-in-chief, "and only if it's clear."

JFK and his advisers recognized that the quarantine was only a risky first step. If it failed, military action might still have to be ratcheted up, and the president asked if the resolution being debated by the OAS would also sanction additional surveillance and an invasion. Alexis Johnson and Ball told the president that the resolution was broad enough to encompass practically anything under consideration.

McNamara also confirmed that plans were moving forward for all military contingencies: the JCS, for example, was considering rules of engagement for intercepting Soviet aircraft flying to Cuba. On air strikes, the defense chief contended, "We *do* believe we should have warning the night before" for a dawn strike. However, "In an emergency, it could be done with less warning." McNamara also reported that it might be necessary to charter or requisition two-thirds of the merchant cargo vessels in East Coast ports to obtain the ships required for an invasion. Some concern was expressed that the shipping industry and the economy would be seriously affected. McCone recommended using ships from friendly foreign nations, but Taylor countered that the risks would be too great in an invasion. The president suggested looking into invoking national emergency powers to get around federal laws requiring exporters to use American ships.

The discussion returned to concerns about the credibility of the photographic evidence. McNamara urged implementing low-level reconnaissance later that day "to obtain the evidence to prove to a layman the existence of missiles in Cuba." JFK seemed doubtful about the immediate need for low-level missions unless it was essential "for tactical reasons. I think we've proved it to the layman." Bundy, however, insisted that the photos themselves are "becoming of *great* importance in the international debate" and mentioned that Stevenson had called to say that pictures could be critical at the U.N. McNamara recommended gathering the necessary evidence immediately with missions at an altitude of two hundred feet. The president seemed surprised: "There *is* a question about whether these things really exist?" Bundy argued that merely showing the pictures, without releasing them for publication, was no longer adequate, and backed Stevenson's request to display them at the Security Council meeting. The ambassador had been humiliated by unknowingly using spurious CIA photos at the time of the Bay of Pigs debate and now insisted on having irrefutable proof.

Bundy reported that there was also support at the U.N. for identifying the location of the missile sites, but JFK objected on the grounds that the missiles could be moved. He preferred waiting for an agreement allowing U.N. inspectors to go to Cuba. McCone backed Bundy, referring to skepticism in the European press and mentioning a statement by the president of Mexico: "'*if* the evidence was conclusive, the attitude of Mexico towards Castro and Cuba would change.' And I think we ought to get the conclusive evidence, and I think this is the way to do it." Kennedy finally agreed.

After additional discussion about the dangers of low-level surveillance missions, such as going in under radar, JFK asked about a call-up of reserves. McNamara advised extending the tours of regular Navy and Marine personnel but urged delaying a call-up of Navy reserves. JFK expressed concern about whether everything was being done to prepare for a possible invasion. "We believe so," the defense chief affirmed.

The president unexpectedly launched into an unusual attempt at military micro-management. Almost certainly recalling the destruction of American planes parked closely together on airfields on December 7, 1941, JFK alerted General Taylor, "Everybody's lived in peace so long" in Florida, but the Soviets or Cubans may "take a reprisal. I should think one of their planes would strafe *us*." Taylor reported that LeMay was sending a top officer to assess the situation and explained that airfield space was limited. The former junior naval officer, now commander-in-chief, asked, "Well, for example, they're using the West Palm Beach airport, I wonder? That's a hell of a military airport. And it hasn't been used much." Taylor admitted, "No sir, I don't know." "You might check on that," JFK continued. "West Palm is a pretty good field and it was a big base in the war and it isn't used much now." (Kennedy's familiarity with Florida can be explained by the fact that his parents had owned an estate in Palm Beach since 1933, and part of his PT boat training had been in Jacksonville. He had also been assigned to a base in Miami after returning from the South Pacific.) "If we *do* execute this plan we just agreed on this morning," the president continued, to strike a SAM site if a U-2 is shot down, MiGs from Cuba could "strafe our fields, and we don't want 'em to shoot up *one hundred planes*." Taylor explained almost contritely, "This is one of these rather humorous examples of our over-sophistication of our weapons. We have everything except to deal with simple aircraft coming in low." Some muted laughter can be heard just as the tape suddenly cut off or ran out.

As the new tape began, the discussion had returned to using photos at the U.N. debate later that day. Ball reported that Stevenson wanted "photographs showing locations and dates, and not merely anonymous photographs." Bundy expressed doubts that the Soviets would dare to challenge the photographic evidence, and the president declared sharply, "I would *invite* them to challenge it." He finally instructed McCone and Ball to decide what photos could be used at the U.N.

Kennedy also observed that if Russian reprisals made an invasion inevitable, U.S. forces must be ready to move quickly and again advised invoking emergency powers relating to the use of foreign ships. Thompson urged a delay in stopping Soviet ships until the OAS had approved the blockade because the Soviets were "*much* less apt to run a legal blockade than they are an illegal one. I think that you might want to keep that in mind." "We just gotta tell the OAS to get to it," JFK replied impatiently.

Thompson also reported that the ambassadorial group would meet that day to consider how to respond to possible Soviet actions in Berlin, such as more rigorous inspection of U.S. truck convoys. "I think we ought to accept that," JFK replied; "That's my quick reaction. . . . I don't think we're in very good shape to have a big fight about whether they inspect our trucks." Thompson proposed suspending the convoys, but the president rejected getting into a "pattern where it's tough to begin 'em again. I would rather have 'em inspecting them."

The meeting ended with an agreement to reconvene at 6:00 P.M., when new reconnaissance information would be available. JFK added a plea to "Try to keep these meetings as brief as possible," and left the room. Only a few participants remained and Ball was placing a call to Stevenson when Rusk suddenly returned from the emergency OAS meeting. The secretary of state, noticeably excited, announced, "you might want to just hear this." Ball hung up and Rusk reported that "we'll have the resolution, with a *large* majority, by shortly after three." Several ExComm members exclaimed, "Oh, gee," "Wonderful," "Oh, God," and "Oh, terrific, terrific." McNamara observed that the quarantine could begin at dawn. "Yeah, but don't tell *them* that," Rusk joked. "No," McNamara replied against a background of laughter. (The quarantine went into effect at 10:00 A.M. the following morning.)

Rusk, becoming more subdued, admonished his colleagues: "Don't smile too soon here, boys," but Alexis Johnson exclaimed that if the OAS voted before the Security Council debate, "Oh, that's gonna be a big help. Mmm. Pshewwwww. Our diplomacy is working." Rusk, nonetheless, reflected soberly: "Well, my God! ... I think it was *very* significant that we were here this morning. We've passed the *one* contingency: an immediate, sudden, irrational [nuclear] strike [by the U.S.S.R.]." "Yeah, yeah, yeah, yeah," Johnson murmured. Everyone understood Rusk's relief that they had all lived to see another day. He later recalled waking up that morning and saying to himself, "'Well, I'm still here. This is very interesting.' That meant that the immediate response of the Soviet Union was not a missile strike."

"Tell the Security Council," McNamara teased, "we would be happy to evacuate them to Seattle"—the only area in the continental United States outside the range of the IRBMs in Cuba. Alexis Johnson exulted, amidst laughter, "Oh gee, that's great. Oh, that's great news. That's terrific. We *really* caught them with their contingencies down."

Rusk soon left and several conversations continued among the few people still in the room. Bundy revealed that the president and Rusk had asked Paul Nitze to head a special working group on Berlin. Ball and McCone talked by telephone with Stevenson and urged the ambassador not to reveal too much about how the photos were obtained. McCone also promised to arrange for Lundahl and Ray Cline, deputy CIA director for intelligence, to go to New York to help with the presentation.

"George," McCone quipped, "the question I have on my mind is, if it's this hard to start a blockade around Cuba, *how the hell* did we ever start World War II?" A burst of laughter followed. McCone talked to Cline by phone, speaking over the shouts of children playing on the White House grounds, explaining that Stevenson had displayed faked pictures at the time of the Bay of Pigs, "So he's kind of in trouble up there."

Finally, McCone questioned Jerome Wiesner, JFK's special assistant for science and technology, who had been waiting to discuss upgrading communications between the U.S. and Latin America, and "black box" technology which might be used to detect nuclear weapons on Soviet ships and verify the withdrawal of missiles from Cuba. McCone asked Wiesner to explore establishing twenty-four-hour-a-day radio communications between Washington and key sites in Latin America.

These fragmentary conversations soon ended and the tape ran out.

Rusk's optimism was confirmed when the OAS unanimously endorsed the quarantine proclamation. By the time the U.N. Security Council convened at 4:00 p.m., the rhetoric had begun to heat up on all sides: Stevenson condemned the missiles in Cuba as proof of Soviet plans for world domination; the Cubans denounced the blockade as an act of war; the Soviet U.N. ambassador, Valerian Zorin, ridiculed the U.S. charges and reiterated that only defensive weapons had been sent to Cuba.

Khrushchev's written response to the president's speech arrived that afternoon. He insisted that the weapons in Cuba were intended to prevent U.S. aggression—a proposition never taken seriously within the Kennedy administration. He also rejected the right of any nation to search ships in international waters and urged the president to "show prudence" and pull back from piratical actions that could have "catastrophic consequences for world peace."

Robert Kennedy's secret Soviet contact, Georgi Bolshakov, however, received somewhat more hopeful signals after meeting with journalists closely connected to the Kennedy administration. The reporters claimed that the president was open to a negotiated settlement which would include trading Soviet missiles in Cuba for U.S. missiles in Turkey and Italy. Bolshakov's superiors in Washington delayed relaying this potentially critical information to Moscow until the next day.

Khrushchev learned early on October 24, to his great relief, that the Soviet ship Aleksandrovsk had delivered its cargo of nuclear warheads without incident just hours before implementation of the blockade.

Tuesday, October 23, 6:00 P.M., Cabinet Room

"They're gonna keep going and we're gonna try to shoot this rudder off, or this boiler. Then we're gonna try to board it and they're gonna fire a gun and machine guns. . . . We may have to *sink* it rather than just *take* it."

President John F. Kennedy

Bundy explained that the draft of the quarantine proclamation had been examined by legal experts, but the president nonetheless questioned some language: "The 'Sino-Soviet'? Is that proper," he asked, "to put the Chinese in? Is that necessary and wise?" Rusk replied that the term "Sino-Soviet powers" had been used in the OAS resolution, but Kennedy persisted: "Some reason to put 'Sino' in there? What are the effects of this gonna be...?" No one at the table brought up the increasing tensions between communist China and the U.S.S.R.

For the moment, the president dropped the issue, and the room remained silent for some thirty seconds as the participants reviewed the draft proclamation. JFK asked whether it was necessary to list specific items being interdicted—e.g., "land-based surface-to-surface missiles." The Defense Department lawyer attending explained that the proclamation was the official, legal notice, saying "this is the contraband or this is the illegal thing." McNamara explained that additional items could be added later.

The defense chief raised another thorny question—whether to pursue and board a Soviet ship that was hailed, refused to stop, and sailed away from Cuba. "I *don't* believe," he recommended, "we should undertake such an operation." "Not right now," the president agreed, and McNamara added, "So my instruction to the Navy was, '*Don't* do it.'" "That's right," the president reaffirmed, "cause they'd be grabbing stuff that might be heading home." RFK countered that it would be "a *hell* of an advantage" to seize such a vessel in order to examine the missiles. "They're not gonna choose *this* to have the test case on," JFK repeated, "they're gonna *turn that thing around.*" McNamara noted that the ship under scrutiny was 1,800 miles away from Cuba, and JFK pointed out skeptically, "Do we want to grab it if they turned it around—at 1,800 miles away?" The defense secretary advised delaying a final decision.

It would be "damn helpful," RFK reiterated, to examine Soviet equipment, but McNamara cautioned that the initial objective should be "to *grab* a vessel *obviously* loaded with offensive weapons." Rusk, uneasy about RFK's stance, advised, "if they *do* seem to be turning around, give 'em a *chance* to turn around and get on their way." McNamara however, abruptly reversed his position, calling RFK's idea "an excellent suggestion" and endorsed stopping a ship "*even* if it turns around . . . because it very probably would have offensive weapons on board."

Rusk, notwithstanding, lectured the attorney general: "from the Soviet point of view they're gonna be as sensitive as a *boil* because . . . they think we're really trying to capture and seize and analyze and examine their missiles and their warheads and things. Now the purpose [of the blockade] is to keep 'em out of Cuba. This adds a *very* important element into it." President Kennedy pointed out that in the next twenty-four hours Soviet ships could "refuse to haul to and we have to shoot at 'em, so that's really our problem tomorrow." The administration could delay deciding "whether we start grabbing 'em as they leave. So I think," he concluded bleakly, "we're gonna have all our troubles tomorrow morning." JFK also observed that the U.S.S.R. was now "faced with the same problem we were faced with in the Berlin blockade," deciding just how far to push the crisis. "We've given them as clear notice as they gave us," he recalled. "We had an atomic monopoly [and] we didn't push it." He then added a chilling assessment: "Looks like they're *going* to."

Ball also seemed worried about "picking up Soviet ships *anywhere*," just on the supposition that they're heading to Cuba. McNamara explained that it was important to operate outside the range of the IL-28s (about 740 miles) and the MiGs (about 450 miles) in Cuba. The freighter *Kimovsk* would be the best choice since it was far enough out to be safe from air attack and likely carrying offensive weapons—"*if* we can find it and *if* we can stop it." JFK, sounding far more resigned than enthusiastic, finally declared, "I'm gettin' all set to sign this thing [the quarantine proclamation]."

Kennedy abruptly returned to the question he had raised earlier in the meeting: using the term "Sino-Soviet powers" in the proclamation. Perhaps it would be less provocative, he suggested, to simply say "stop the introduction of weapons" instead of specifying the national origin of those weapons: "Does it hit them *harder* to name them in a way which may not be desirable? Is this more *challenging* than it needs to be?" Rusk suggested, and Kennedy finally agreed, to stick with the language in the OAS resolution.

The discussion turned to the president's written response to Khrushchev's latest message. Bundy circulated a draft letter and JFK asked, "What does Tommy think?" The former ambassador speculated that another message might persuade Khrushchev not to challenge the quarantine. Rusk read aloud a proposed draft letter urging the Soviet leader to avoid gunfire at sea, but concluded that intelligence was not encouraging: "We've had *no* indications," Rusk told the president, "of any Soviet instructions or reactions in any way to pull away." "None at all," McCone confirmed, and Rusk reiterated, "Just the converse." Nitze suggested that the Soviets might stop their ships in order to delay an attack on Cuba or the tightening of the blockade, and "*freeze* the status quo with the missiles there." "Well," JFK replied, "we can always come back and say that's unacceptable." "O.K.," the president finally concluded, "let's send it then. Hell, I don't see that we're giving away much."

Rusk reported sarcastically that Kennedy's speech had prompted two thousand supporters of Lord Bertrand Russell's peace organization to storm the U.S. embassy in London—but there had been no reports of disorder in Havana. The president, however, seemed more concerned about the blockade: "Okay. *Now* what do we do tomorrow morning" if their ships sail through? "We're all clear about how we handle it?" Some strained laughter broke out before JFK's final words, spoken in a sardonic tone suggesting that no one in the room could predict or control the outcome of this likely confrontation at sea. McCone cracked, "Shoot the rudders off of 'em, don't you?"

McNamara urged waiting until the morning before issuing instructions to the Navy: "We *ought* to try to avoid shooting a Soviet ship carrying wheat to Cuba or medicine . . . [and] *try* to pick a ship which *almost certainly* carried offensive weapons *as the first ship*." "The only problem I see, Bob," the president repeated, "that's the one vessel I would think they would turn around." The defense chief countered that ships approaching the quarantine line had yet to change course, and Rusk prompted some laughter by joking, "Well that could well be the baby food ships." (Castro had requested substantial amounts of baby food in negotiations for the release of the Bay of Pigs prisoners—freed in December 1962.) Khrushchev might instruct all ships, "'*Don't stop* under any circumstances,'" McNamara predicted. "So the baby food ship comes up and we hail it," he suddenly burst into laughter, "and they'll think it odd when we shoot it."

"That's still gonna happen," President Kennedy cautioned grimly. "They're gonna keep going and we're gonna try to shoot this rudder off, or this boiler. Then we're gonna try to board it and they're gonna fire a gun and machine guns. . . . We may have to *sink* it rather than just *take* it." "Or they might give orders to blow it up," RFK added. "I think that's less likely," JFK asserted, "than having a real fight to try to board it, because they may have five, six, or seven hundred people aboard there with guns." McNamara reassured the president that most ships targeted for boarding were likely to have small crews.

"What do we do now about a ship that *has been* disabled," Rusk pondered, "and can't go anywhere?" McNamara explained that a crippled ship would be towed to a U.S. prize port. "Well, then we take it," JFK retorted sarcastically, "and we find out that it's got baby food on it." McNamara insisted that the ship would be inspected before being towed, but the president again questioned whether "they'd let us aboard." "That's right," McNamara joked, "it's this baby food ship that worries me." "I say those who considered the blockade course to be the easy way," JFK teased, "I told them not to do it!" An intense eruption of laughter followed and Bundy joked above the din, "We bad guys brought consensus today, everybody fell for it!"—reigniting the hilarity.

The laughter evaporated swiftly as the president returned to the dangers of the blockade: "Well, that's what we're gonna have to do," he pronounced in an abruptly somber tone of voice. It was crucial, he insisted, to provide instructions on how to proceed if a ship was drifting but resisted boarding and inspection. "I don't think we can probably get aboard," he cautioned again, without "a machine gun operation. . . . You have a real *fight* aboard there." McNamara reiterated that freighters had small crews but Rusk quipped, "It's a good reason to send this letter to Mr. Khrushchev, tell him to turn 'em around—not to challenge it." Some chuckles can be heard in the background.

"First," President Kennedy stipulated, "we want to be sure that nobody on our boats have cameras." McNamara disclosed that an order to that effect had gone out earlier that day. (Kennedy wanted to eliminate the chance that photos of a bloody clash on a Soviet ship might become public.) JFK also demanded a clear decision on how to react if a disabled ship resisted boarding: "Do we let them drift around?" he asked. "I think, at that point, Mr. President," McNamara advised, "we have to leave it to the local commander." "Well we don't want to tell him necessarily, 'go aboard there,'" JFK replied. "I think we just have to say, Mr. President," Taylor interjected, that they should "use the minimum force required—" but JFK cut him off forcefully. "I think it misses the point. . . . I don't think he ought to feel that he has to board that thing in order to carry out our orders." "Well he's to keep ships going to Cuba," Taylor countered. "*I think* at the *beginning* it would be better," the president instructed sharply, "to let the boat lie there, disabled, for a day or so, not to try to board it and have a *real* machine gunning with thirty to forty people killed on each side."

McNamara, however, raised a significant complication—it might be necessary to get out of the area quickly after boarding because of nearby Soviet submarines. He also cited Admiral Anderson's concern that a submarine might sink a U.S. aircraft carrier. "I think," the defense secretary appealed to the president, "we're gonna have to allow the commander on the scene a certain amount of latitude" since two carriers, the *Enterprise* and the *Independence*, were already in the area. JFK, tapping the table nervously, silently pondered the request for some ten seconds before finally agreeing, but, he pointedly directed Mc-Namara to personally review all instructions to the Navy, "having in mind this conversation we've just had." "All right, I have," the defense chief assured the commander-in-chief, "and I'll do so again tonight, Mr. President."

The discussion returned briefly to the impact of military action against Cuba on U.S. coastal trade and shipping. McNamara revealed that merchant vessels near Cuba were being warned about a possible attack and given limited air cover. "But," he admitted, "this is a *real* possibility, we'd lose a merchant ship in and around Cuba, *quickly*." The president remained silent for nearly seven seconds before responding, in a particularly weary and strained tone of voice, saying "Okay."

The reel of tape soon ran out. The recording resumed, unfortunately on a tape with very poor sound quality, as Steuart Pittman, assistant secretary of defense for civil defense, was discussing domestic preparations for surviving a nuclear attack from Cuba.

The president's mood already seemed grim after McNamara's warning about the loss of a merchant vessel, but that possibility seemed trivial compared to the civil defense risks. Pittman reviewed the threat posed by a "relatively light nuclear attack" to 92 million Americans living in 58 cities with populations greater than 100,000, in an arc of about 1,100 nautical miles from Cuba. Efforts were underway to stock shelters with emergency supplies and to identify buildings which could provide protection from nuclear blast and radiation.

"Let me just ask you this," JFK interjected, "if we decide to invade Cuba, they may fire these weapons." The president assumed that "people living out in the country, we can take care of them, to the extent that is possible, against radiation." "Can we," he finally asked, "say before we invade, evacuate these cities?" Pittman replied bluntly, as JFK began to tap his knee nervously, that the president's premise was wrong—rural-area civilians could *not* be protected: "If there will be fallout, the only protection that exists *today* is in the cities, and there's little or no protection in the rural areas."

The president retreated to the hope that "we're *not* gonna have an all-out nuclear exchange," but nonetheless acknowledged that ten or fifteen missiles might be fired at the U.S. He pressed Pittman on whether the risk to civilians could be reduced before attacking Cuba: "What is it we oughta *do* with the population of the affected areas *in case* the bombs go off? I just don't see," Kennedy noted with annoyance, "in your statement how you addressed yourself to that question effectively." The quality of the tape suddenly went from poor to inaudible, making it impossible to hear Pittman's response to the president's tough question. In fact, as Alice George has concluded, civil defense planning "was haphazard and, in some cases, almost comical." The U.S. government "had little means of protecting its citizens from total war."

More than ten minutes of largely inaudible conversation followed, dealing in part with civil defense and Nitze's appointment to chair a subcommittee on Berlin.

Soon after, Kennedy signed the quarantine proclamation in the Oval Office: "On the last page, he wrote firmly and boldly his full signature, John Fitzgerald Kennedy—one of the few documents he signed thus, normally using only his middle initial F." Then, as photographers snapped away, he stuck the pen in his pocket, and, very conscious of the historical moment, declared, "I am going to keep this one."

Tuesday, October 23, shortly after 7:00 P.M., Cabinet Room

"Well, it looks like it's gonna be *real mean*, doesn't it? But on the other hand, there's really *no choice*."

President John F. Kennedy

After the signing, the president returned to the Cabinet Room. Only RFK, Taylor, and Bundy were still present. Kennedy, obviously irritated, badgered the attorney general about reports that British prime minister Harold Macmillan had permitted classified U-2 photos to be shown on British television. "Bobby," JFK growled impatiently, "I don't wanna make it look like we're all fucked up here." (The president evidently felt comfortable using an expletive only when he was virtually alone with his younger brother.) RFK suggested saying that the administration was about to release the pictures and the president, eager to pacify U.S. journalists, agreed.

The discussion quickly refocused on Berlin. RFK, calling his brother "Jack," reported that General Lucius Clay had offered to go to West Berlin as the president's personal representative. Clay had played a key role during the 1948–49 Berlin airlift and had become a symbol of American resolve to West Berliners. JFK instead endorsed Bundy's suggestion to keep the general on standby in case the Soviets "squeezed" Berlin in the next two to three days.

Evelyn Lincoln interrupted to say that Jacqueline Kennedy was on the phone, and the president left to take the call. As Taylor and Bundy prepared to leave, RFK joked, "I have a feelin' I don't like to see you people go. You have all the answers!" After a bit more banter, and the sound of the door slamming shut as JFK returned, the Kennedy brothers were alone in the Cabinet Room.

"*Oh, Christ!*" the agitated president burst out, recalling that he had to attend a formal dinner that evening. But RFK quickly zeroed in on the real source of his brother's irritability: "How's it look?" he asked point blank. "Well, it looks like it's gonna be *real mean*, doesn't it?" JFK exploded. "But on the other hand, there's really *no choice*. If they get this mean on this one—Jesus Christ! What are they gonna fuck up next?" "No, there wasn't any choice," RFK declared, "I mean you woulda been *impeached*." "Well, that's what I think," JFK agreed, "I woulda been impeached."

Robert Kennedy pointed to the unanimous OAS vote, after "they kicked us in the ass for *two* years," and the belief in NATO "that you *had* to do it," but did express regrets about inadequate communications with the Soviets. JFK asked about recent contacts with Bolshakov and RFK reported, with a derisive laugh, that Bolshakov had claimed that Soviet ships would run the blockade and that "this is a defensive base for the Russians. It's got nothing to do with the Cubans." JFK responded angrily: "Why are they lying then?" RFK also mentioned that Ambassador Dobrynin had advised ignoring Bolshakov.

As this no-nonsense discussion gradually came to a close, RFK emphasized that press reaction had thus far been "pretty good." "Till tomorrow morning," JFK retorted pessimistically, and RFK agreed "it's gonna get unpleasant" once the blockade was implemented. But, he argued, it was "the luckiest thing in the world" that there had been time to line up OAS support. JFK agreed that if the U.S. had started with air strikes and "had been over there shootin' up everything, then the Russians *really* would tense." With OAS support, RFK reasoned, "It's not just the United States doing it." The Kennedy brothers, as the tape ended, did not have the slightest idea how things would turn out a few hours after sunrise the next morning.

JFK replied to Khrushchev's cable that evening: "I am concerned that we both show prudence and do nothing to allow events to make the situation more difficult to control than it already is. I hope that you will issue immediately the necessary instructions to your ships to observe the terms of the quarantine . . . which will go into effect at 1400 hours Greenwich time October twenty-four."

Fidel Castro spoke defiantly to the Cuban people. He denied the presence of offensive missiles but reasserted Cuba's right to defend itself against American aggression. He also placed the military on the highest level of alert and ordered total mobilization.

Later that evening, RFK, at JFK's suggestion, met with Ambassador Dobrynin at the Soviet embassy. The attorney general denounced the deployment in Cuba and emphasized the president's fury over Soviet duplicity. Dobrynin cabled the Kremlin that "The president felt himself deceived and deceived deliberately." The ambassador wanted his superiors to understand that JFK's anger was personal as well as official. Dobrynin nonetheless told RFK that he had no knowledge of offensive missiles in Cuba and added ominously that Soviet ships heading for Cuba had not been instructed to change course. Soviet ships, in fact, reacted with considerable caution. All the vessels carrying military equipment had slowed down, stopped, or turned around before the quarantine became effective—exactly as President Kennedy had predicted.

Early on the morning of October 24, William Knox, president of Westinghouse Electric International, visiting the U.S.S.R. on business, was summoned to the Kremlin by Khrushchev. The Soviet leader angrily accused the U.S. of aggression and threatened to sink an American naval vessel if Soviet ships were boarded. Knox, as Khrushchev had expected, relayed an account of the meeting to Washington. Meanwhile, McNamara approved a first-ever JCS request to raise SAC bombers to DEFCON 2, the highest state of readiness short of war.

Wednesday, October 24, 10:00 A.M., Cabinet Room

"It seems to me we want to give that ship a chance to turn around.
You don't wanna have word goin' out from Moscow, 'Turn around,'
and suddenly we sink their ship."

President John F. Kennedy

The president and his advisers gathered in the Cabinet Room at virtually the moment that the quarantine proclamation, signed fifteen hours earlier, became legally effective. McCone reported that the Soviets were *not* moving "on a crash basis" to upgrade the combat readiness of their armed forces. But, aerial surveillance confirmed "rapid progress" on the missile sites and buildings for the storage of nuclear materials; also, three ships heading for Cuba had hatches large enough to carry missiles. He also revealed that all Soviet ships were now receiving orders directly from Moscow. He tempered this intriguing but ambiguous development with news that three or four Russian submarines were already in the Atlantic.

"Mr. President," McCone continued, "Mr. Lundahl has two or three [photo] boards of this low-level flight." "May I come around beside you, sir?" Lundahl asked; he can be heard carrying his materials over to the president's place at the table. Lundahl emphasized details visible for the first time on low-level photos, especially Soviet efforts at camouflage. JFK expressed concern that the sites might become difficult to find, but Lundahl predicted that NPIC photo interpreters could locate any camouflaged sites. McCone suggested sending the "most convincing panels" to Stevenson at the U.N.

The discussion returned to possible military risks if the Cubans resisted surveillance flights or Soviet ships challenged the quarantine. Rusk revealed that an intelligence intercept indicated that Cuban forces had been instructed not to fire at surveillance aircraft and that Khrushchev's "public line seems designed to leave him with some option to back off if he chooses." But, Rusk added, it was too soon to say whether the Kremlin would seek to compromise or "risk escalation and the countermeasures that the U.S. plans to make."

McNamara, however, revisited a danger much closer to home: "Mr. President, first a question you raised yesterday" about U.S. aircraft parked tightly together on airfields in Florida. Taylor explained that the JCS was studying plans to protect the planes, but JFK remarked sarcastically, it would be "terrific if fifty to sixty MiGs could come over and really shoot up a lot of the airstrips." "We're making every preparation against that that we can," Taylor repeated. McNamara recommended keeping "a substantially smaller alert force" ready to strike "a SAM site or a limited target in Cuba" on one to two hours' notice and moving the bulk of the planes back to their home bases. They would still be ready to strike Cuba with twelve hours' notice, "But I think this is an acceptable reduction in lead time." The president seemed satisfied.

Everyone at the table, however, recognized that intercepting, boarding, or disabling a Soviet ship might quickly escalate beyond strafing in Florida to reprisals in Berlin or Turkey. McNamara revealed that two Soviet ships, the *Gagarin* and the *Kimovsk*, were approaching the quarantine barrier. The former claimed to be carrying "technical material," he explained, a typical tactic to conceal "an offensive-weapons-carrying ship. . . . Admiral Anderson plans to try to intercept one or both of them today."

But, the greatest menace, the defense secretary added, might be lurking beneath the waves: "There is a submarine very close, we believe, to each of them." "Two submarines," the president muttered. A submarine, McNamara explained, "should be twenty to thirty miles from these ships at the time of intercept. And hence it's a *very* dangerous situation." "Which one are they going to try to get on?" the president pressed. "They are concentrating on the *Kimovsk*," McNamara replied, "but we'll try to get both." The president also asked, "What kind of a ship is going to try to intercept?" A destroyer, McNamara confirmed, clarifying that antisubmarine-equipped helicopters from the aircraft carrier *Essex* would attempt to divert the submarines from the intercept point.

McCone suddenly interrupted this increasingly bleak discussion: "Mr. President, I have a note just handed me . . . through ONI [Office of Naval Intelligence] that all six Soviet ships *currently* identified in *Cuban waters*—I don't know what that means—have either *stopped* or reversed course."

Someone at the table reacted with an audible "Phew!" but Rusk amplified McCone's doubts, asking "Whadda' you mean, 'Cuban waters'?" JFK asked McCone to find out "whether they're talking about the ships leaving Cuba or the ones coming in?" As the CIA director prepared to leave, Rusk quipped, "Makes *some* difference," and some edgy laughter can be heard at the table as Bundy murmured, "It *sure* does."

The president, obviously uncertain about the meaning of McCone's pronouncement, returned to the imminent military contingencies: "*If* this submarine should sink our destroyer," he continued very hesitantly, "then what is our... proposed... reply?" Alexis Johnson evaded the question, reporting instead that a message had been sent to the Soviets outlining standard international procedures, presumably accepted by Moscow, for identifying submarines at sea.

McNamara, however, made the unexpected announcement that he had just set up a new procedure: "We have depth charges that have such a small charge that they can be dropped and they can actually *hit the submarine* without *damaging* the submarine." "They're practice depth charges," General Taylor explained. "When our forces come upon an unidentified submarine," McNamara added, "we will ask it to come to the surface for inspection by . . . using a depth charge of this type and *also* using certain sonar signals which they *may not* be able to accept and interpret. Therefore, it's the depth charge that is the warning notice and the instruction to surface."

Robert Kennedy, who *may* have read a transcript or listened to this tape in preparing his posthumously published 1969 book, claimed that the president was profoundly unsettled by McNamara's cold certainty that these weapons could be used with such precision that the U.S.S.R. would not be provoked to retaliate. The attorney general recalled that JFK covered his mouth with his hand and clenched and unclenched his fist as "we stared at each other across the table."

Taylor reminded the defense chief that sonar would be tried first, but McNamara repeated, "The sonar signal very probably will not accomplish its purpose." JFK finally asked, "If he [the submarine] doesn't surface or if he takes some action . . . to assist the merchant ship, are we just gonna attack him anyway?" "We're going to attack him—" Taylor began, but the president cut him off: "I think we ought to wait on that today, cause we don't wanna have the first thing we attack is a Soviet submarine. I'd much rather have a merchant ship."

McNamara firmly but respectfully disagreed: "I think it would be *extremely* dangerous, Mr. President, to try to defer attack on this submarine. ... We could *easily* lose an American ship. ... The inaccuracy, as you well know, of antisubmarine warfare is such that I don't have any great confidence that we can *push* him away from our ships and make the intercept securely." The president must have been struck by the obvious contradiction between McNamara's acknowledgment of the imprecision of submarine warfare and his confidence about using practice depth charges to harmlessly force a Soviet submarine to surface.

The defense secretary also warned that it would be especially dangerous to limit the discretion of the naval commander on the scene. "I looked into this in *great* detail last night," he pointedly told the president, "because of your interest in the question." But, he admitted, "this is *only* a plan, and there are *many, many* uncertainties." "Okay," JFK yielded, despite his doubts, "let's proceed." (Despite these risks, a practice depth charge was dropped near a Soviet submarine that week and decades later it was learned that the temperature inside the submarine climbed to over 122 degrees; some crewmen lost consciousness, and the irate and frantic Soviet captain nearly fired a nuclear-tipped torpedo at a US aircraft carrier.)

The quarantine was still *terra incognita*, and Rusk returned to a point he had already disputed with the attorney general. He acknowledged that circumstances might change, but insisted that the administration had "to be *quite* clear" that the blockade was intended "to *stop* these weapons from going to Cuba. It is *not* to capture them for ourselves at this stage. I take it that we all understand the *present* purpose." Bundy pressed Rusk on whether there was "*no* priority concern to capture the weapons," but the president decided to return to this issue if and when a ship were actually seized.

RFK unexpectedly raised a pivotal issue: "I *presume* that somebody on the destroyer speaks Russian." McNamara, Bundy, and Gilpatric admitted that they did not have a definitive answer, and the president instructed, "May we get this, as a matter of procedure . . . that you can get a Russian-speaking person on every one of these ships?" "Yes, Mr. President," McNamara responded. "That is being done," Bundy reaffirmed.

"I would think that if we have this confrontation and we sink this ship," JFK speculated darkly, there would be a blockade of Berlin. "Then we would be faced with ordering in air [support] in there, which is probably gonna be shot down. . . . What do we do then?" Nitze responded with a tough scenario reminiscent of his earlier wrangle with the president over the European Defense Plan: "Of course, what we do then," he declared assertively, is "we try to shoot down *their* planes and keep the air corridor [to Berlin] open" and decide whether to also attack "the bases from which the planes come."

McCone's sudden return aborted this tense exchange. "Whadda ya have, John?" JFK asked. The CIA chief reported that the six ships in question were inbound for Cuba, and naval intelligence believed that Moscow had "either stopped them or reversed direction." McNamara suggested that the ships might be those closest to the quarantine barrier and JFK asserted, "If this report is accurate, then we're not gonna do anything about these ships close in to Cuba." (At this point, Rusk may have whispered his now-famous words, "We are eyeball to eyeball, and I think the other fellow just blinked"—although this remark cannot be heard on the tape.)

Sounding recharged for the first time in days, President Kennedy reasoned that if all the ships within a certain distance from Cuba had turned around, that would mean that the Soviets were not picking out only those carrying offensive weapons. "We're not planning to grab any of those, are we?" he asked again. McNamara confirmed that there were no plans "to grab any ship that is not proceeding toward Cuba." RFK and Rusk insisted that the Navy should be instructed not to pursue these ships.

Several participants later recalled that they felt for the first time that the crisis might have reached a turning point; but it was too early to pin much hope on such meager scraps of evidence. "But everyone looked like a different person," Robert Kennedy later wrote. "For a moment the world had stood still, and now it was going around again."

Jerome Wiesner and several technical experts were invited in to report on communications problems with Latin America. He contended that telephone, telegraph, and teletype connections with Central and South American nations were far less adequate than those with Europe. Wiesner had been speaking for nearly six minutes when he suddenly hesitated and stopped. McNamara had begun whispering to the president about new information on Soviet ships heading for Cuba. JFK asked Taylor, "What does the Navy say about this report?" The JCS chief confirmed that several ships were "*definitely* turning back" and others "*may be* turning back."

After pausing for some six seconds, the president made his position clear—a confrontation at sea was to be averted if at all possible: "It seems to me we want to give that ship a chance to turn around. You don't wanna have word goin' out from Moscow, 'Turn around,' and suddenly we sink their ship." He urged immediate contact with the aircraft carrier *Essex* to "tell them to wait an hour and see whether that ship continues on its course in view of this other intelligence. . . . We have to move *quickly*," he instructed, "because they're gonna intercept between 10:30 and 11."

Wiesner resumed his report on communications with Latin America. McNamara called the plan "a magnificent opportunity to break down a diplomatic block which has existed for years," and Rusk concluded "that the *great* United States of America can't face a series of crises without adequate communications." Despite the possibility that a naval clash with the U.S.S.R. might be occurring at that very moment, the discussion was focused on getting congressional appropriations for a new communications network with Latin America—when JFK switched off the tape recorder. Before the meeting broke up, however, Kennedy directed that the United States Information Agency should be represented at subsequent ExComm meetings. (The USIA was founded in 1953 to promote the Cold War foreign policy of the United States.)

At midday, George Ball sent a cable to Raymond Hare, U.S. ambassador to Turkey, and Thomas Finletter, U.S. ambassador to NATO, alerting them that it might be necessary to consider a deal removing the Jupiter missiles from Turkey.

Military intelligence officers carried aerial photos to New York, briefed the justifiably skeptical and suspicious Ambassador Stevenson, and authorized him to share the evidence with some U.N. diplomats.

Around 5:00 p.m., several ExComm members, including RFK, met without the president to review evidence from the first day of the blockade and concluded that the Soviets had decided to avoid the seizure of a ship carrying missiles. Ball recommended, and the president later approved, new orders for Navy vessels on the blockade line: maintain surveillance and make regular reports, but avoid stopping or boarding any ships. The Defense Department also announced that some of the Soviet bloc vessels heading toward Cuba had apparently altered course.

Wednesday, October 24, about 4:30 P.M., Oval Office

"Well, I think the *irony* will be that the Russians led us into a trap."
President John F. Kennedy.

JFK switched on the recorder in the Oval Office as he chatted with several advisers for a few minutes. Nitze cautioned that the NATO allies were "worried about the *conviction* which they can give as to these things [the missiles] *really* being there." The president pointed out that the picture released without authorization in London "is the *best* one that captures that." Nitze also observed that the allies had been asking, "'Why didn't the Russians camouflage?' Well, this demonstrates that the Russians *did* do their best to camouflage them. Using these pictures,

I think, could be *very* helpful." "Well," JFK declared, "I think the *irony* will be that the Russians led us into a trap."

Bundy interrupted to ask for clearance to release the photos, declaring, "The Russians *did* camouflage these things by their standard practice, *very carefully*. They proceeded by night, our agents' reports now indicate—our refugee reports." He recommended using the photos to "back our claim," and JFK approved making them available to the press. After a few additional remarks (someone asserted, "The Russians are *so* crafty") the brief gathering broke up.

Wednesday, October 24, just after 5:00 P.M., Cabinet Room

"Our best judgment is that they are scratching their brains *very hard* at the present time, deciding just exactly how they want to play this."

Secretary of State Dean Rusk

Forty-eight hours had passed since the president last met with the leaders of Congress. In the interim, the crisis had become public and the quarantine had been implemented. JFK must have wondered if this meeting with his former colleagues would be any less difficult. He switched on the tape recorder as Rusk revealed that the state-controlled press in the Soviet Union, perhaps to avoid "war scares," had not informed their own people about the missiles. "We *do* think," he cautioned, "that although the situation is highly critical and dangerous, that it is not *frozen* in any inevitable way at this point." "Our best judgment," he added rather colorfully, "is that they are scratching their brains *very hard* at the present time, deciding just exactly how they want to play this."

McNamara reported that there had been "*no* intercepts" on the quarantine that day "and none were necessary." He also admitted that it was difficult to locate ships en route to Cuba: "There's a tremendous expanse of ocean that we are endeavoring to watch, roughly from the Azores to Bermuda." The defense chief also conceded that he was not sure if any Soviet ships had actually changed course.

Secretary Rusk suggested that information on ships "of special interest" to the U.S. should be kept secret because the Soviets might find it useful. Senate majority leader Mike Mansfield jumped in: "Mr. President, as long as the secretary's brought up . . . withholding information, I was deeply disturbed to read this morning . . . a story by Rowland Evans, which *I think* ought to be discussed here." The article, he explained, cited a claim by Senator Russell that President Kennedy had decided to invade Cuba. Mansfield put Russell on the hot seat: "Dick, I don't know whether you saw this or not?"

The Georgia senator denied leaking the story but turned on his southern charm, congratulating Rusk on "a *magnificent* triumph in the Organization of American States on yesterday. . . . I never would have believed it could've been done." Rusk, amidst laughter, thanked the senior senator from his home state and praised the resolve of "our Latin American friends." The leak in the article, whether or not Russell was responsible, was never discussed again. The senator's more accommodating manner suggested that the leaders of Congress would, at least for the moment, publicly support the commander-in-chief. If the blockade were to fail, however, the president realized that there would be ample opportunity for political sniping at the administration in the mid-term elections.

Republican senators Everett Dirksen and Leverett Saltonstall questioned Rusk about a possible U.N. peace initiative. Rusk declared that since the proposal did not deal with the missiles already in Cuba, efforts were underway to get U Thant to withhold the plan. Dirksen also asked whether Khrushchev might propose a summit conference. "I think it'd be useless," Kennedy declared. "I would too," Dirksen affirmed, "*Absolutely* useless."

The president mentioned his exchange of letters with Khrushchev, but candidly emphasized that the situation was very fluid: the Soviets might turn back some ships carrying weapons, might choose a ship "for a test case, either to have us sink it, or disable it, and have a fight about it;" or they might allow the inspection of ships not carrying offensive weapons. JFK expressed hope that the situation might be resolved in the next twenty-four hours.

Senators Fulbright and Russell, the president's main antagonists only two days before, asked whether the Soviets might try to deliver missiles to Cuba by plane. JFK defended his decision to stop only ships "because the only way you can stop a plane is to shoot it down," and, "with *our* problem in Berlin," that would be a very dangerous step. McNamara added that the Soviets did not have enough large commercial planes to deliver missiles but might use bombers to deliver warheads.

Saltonstall, however, created an awkward moment by asking about the presence of Soviet submarines in Cuban waters. McNamara replied very hesitantly, "I want to answer that, but I want to say that our knowledge of submarines, Soviet Union submarines, in the Atlantic is the *most highly classified* information we have in the Department." Saltonstall tried to back off: "Well, if you prefer not to answer it, don't do it." The normally articulate defense chief became tongue-tied until he was bailed out, ironically, by Senator Russell. The Armed Services Committee chairman recommended keeping this sensitive information off the table. Some self-conscious throat clearing can be heard in the background as Rusk whispered about "a large number" of Soviet submarines but he, like McNamara, resisted giving any specifics.

Dirksen deftly changed the subject—inquiring if the administration was surprised by the slow Soviet response to the quarantine. Rusk, citing Ambassador Thompson, "my chief adviser on this sort of thing," speculated that Khrushchev had planned to come to the U.N. in November, with these missiles "in his pocket," to pressure the president on Berlin. "Our impression *so far* is that we have not caught them with a lot of contingency plans all laid on and ready to go—that this has upset their timing somewhat."

Carl Vinson of Georgia, chairman of the House Armed Services Committee, asked McCone about the number of MiG-21s in Cuba and about the nationality of the pilots. McCone revealed that the latest "*hard* information" suggested that Russians and Cubans were each piloting about half of the nearly forty MiGs. The CIA chief also confirmed that the missile sites were manned exclusively by Russians. He was able to provide one scrap of potentially good news when Dirksen asked whether the Red Chinese had been brought in: "We have *no* information one way or the other on that, Senator."

McNamara reported that the quarantine would "apply to all ships equally," and Rusk noted that several friendly nations were voluntarily turning their ships back. On the prospect of a summit, however, the president became more cagey; only minutes before he had dismissed such a meeting as "useless." But, when pressed by Senator Bourke Hickenlooper, he seemed ready to leave *all* options open: "Well, why don't we wait if the message comes through . . . until we see . . . what it says." The Iowa Republican also cited reports that Khrushchev had ordered his ships to resist the blockade. "Now if that happens," he asked bluntly, "then we're in it, aren't we?" JFK was evasive: "We'll have to wait and see, Senator. I think in the next twenty-four hours we can tell what our problems are gonna be on the quarantine." JFK then arranged to meet again with the leaders of Congress by Monday [October 29] or sooner.

Senator Hubert Humphrey, a Minnesota Democrat, asked for details on the "military equipment and associated materials" covered by the blockade. Senator Russell, however, reverting to his tougher stance, criticized the exclusion of conventional weapons from the list and cited a report that five thousand rifles had just been sent to Cuba. McNamara explained that the rifles were not associated with the missiles and stressed that the quarantine could always be tightened. Senator Fulbright, perhaps emboldened by Russell, signaled that he continued to favor an invasion: "It's *still* my understanding that in seven to ten days *you will be ready* to take *definite* action *if* conditions warrant it?" "That is correct," McNamara avowed. JFK clarified that the rifles had been excluded because "the first collision with the Soviets" should be on offensive missiles "for political reasons . . . this puts us in a much stronger position around the world." But, he admitted, "if they *accept* the quarantine, we will *not* permit these rifles to go through."

The problem of keeping the deliberations secret, raised earlier by Senator Mansfield, suddenly resurfaced. A participant argued forcefully that there should be no comment "in any shape, form, or fashion . . . because otherwise the finger of suspicion points at *every person* who is here." The president did not seem concerned: "I think the security's been awfully good." Senator Thomas Kuchel of California asked if the administration would "require a personal disavowal" from each person attending and the president replied, "I don't think so. I think we can probably do without it."

After agreeing that the congressional leaders would remain on eight-hour standby for another meeting, the participants left the Cabinet Room.

Wednesday, October 24, 6:00 P.M., Oval Office

"If they put the screws on Berlin in the way that Gromyko said they were going to, then I know that we were bound to invade Cuba under those conditions."

President John F. Kennedy

Shortly thereafter, the president turned on the taping device as he chatted in the Oval Office with a few advisers who had just attended the congressional meeting. Former defense secretary Robert Lovett advised "that the *basic* wisdom here is to regard Cuba *really* as an extension of Berlin. . . . Therefore we have to *avoid* in the case of Cuba a *diversion* of attention, and troops, involvement there, at this stage." The advantage of the quarantine, Lovett emphasized, was that it gave the Soviets "a couple of days while they make up their *own* minds what their intentions are." Lovett, like JFK, was also suspicious of military overconfidence, especially the "congenital habit of *overstating* the *ease* as well as the *results* of an air strike." The views of the sixty-seven-year-old Lovett dovetailed with those already expressed by the forty-five-year-old commander-in-chief: "There's no such thing," Lovett explained, "as a *small* military action, I don't think. Now the moment we start *anything* in this field, we have to be prepared to do *everything*." He urged the president to wait until Soviet intentions had become clear.

"There seems to be some disposition on [Konrad] Adenauer's part," JFK observed, "and I think you might even say Macmillan . . . ," but he trailed off indistinctly. Bundy, however, assuming he understood Kennedy's thinking, revealed that [British ambassador] "David [Ormsby-Gore] said he shares that estimate of Macmillan." "That what?" JFK inquired. "That he'd look with equanimity upon invasion?" "Well," Bundy explained, "that he thinks you mustn't have a half-finished job." "Look," Lovett asserted firmly, "when do you tell whether it's half-finished?" "That's *quite* right," Bundy agreed.

McCone also conceded that there was no such thing as a small military action but remained worried that the Russians might trap the U.S. by observing the blockade *and* completing the missile sites. McNamara, however, interrupted with a more upbeat view: "Mr. President, I thought of Cuba as *our* hostage. I think it's just as much *our* hostage as Berlin is a *Soviet* hostage. I think if we can remain *cool* and *calm* here, we've *really* got the screws on 'em." The president replied, "If they put the screws on Berlin in the way that Gromyko said they were going to, then I know that we were bound to invade Cuba under those conditions." But, Lovett interjected, "we can also put the screws on Cuba," and the president acknowledged, "They've committed their prestige much more heavily now—much more than I have in Berlin." "Exactly," Lovett and McNamara affirmed. "Well," JFK wisecracked, "I think then we've got their neck [in Cuba] just like we've got it [our neck] there [in Berlin]."

Kennedy repeated McCone's concern that work might continue on the missile sites despite a successful blockade and the U.S. could be faced with fifty or sixty missiles by November. "Under what conditions," he speculated, "would the Russians *fire* them? They might be more reluctant to fire them," he noted with a touch of *realpolitik*, "if they've already grabbed Berlin than they would be if we suddenly go in [to Cuba]. . . . But anyway, that's what we gotta make a judgment on."

As the conversation began to wind down, the president read aloud U

Thant's proposal for a joint suspension of arms shipments to Cuba and the quarantine. McCone reiterated that any agreement had to include a halt to work on the missile sites and assurances that no missiles would be placed on launchers, verified, Lovett pointed out, by on-site U.N. observers. JFK agreed, but cautioned, "We ought to welcome his [U Thant's] efforts," and Bundy confirmed, "Oh yes, that's the first sentence."

After a few desultory exchanges about briefing important newspaper editors and journalists, the meeting ended and the tape machine stopped recording.

Later that evening, McNamara visited the Navy's blockade control room for an update on approaching ships. He later recalled asking Admiral Anderson:

"'When the ship reaches the line, how are you going to stop it?'

'We'll hail it,' he said.

'In what language—English or Russian?' I asked.

'How the hell do I know?' he said, clearly a little agitated by my line of questioning.

I followed up by asking, 'What will you do if they don't understand?'

'I suppose we'll use flags,' he replied.

'Well, what if they don't stop?' I asked.

'We'll send a shot across the bow,' he said.

'Then what if that doesn't work?'

'Then we'll fire into the rudder,' he replied, by now clearly very annoyed."

McNamara exploded: "'You're not going to fire a single shot at anything without my express permission, is that clear?'"

Anderson replied contemptuously that the Navy had been running blockades since John Paul Jones.

McNamara retorted angrily that "'this was not a blockade but a means of communication between Kennedy and Khrushchev.'" He ordered Anderson not to use force without his permission—which first required direct authorization from the president.

"'Was that understood?'" McNamara demanded.

Anderson's "tight-lipped response was 'Yes.'"

McNamara also stipulated "that he be fully informed minute by minute during an interception so that he could consult with the president, and then the president and he would issue the Navy pertinent further instruction. He then turned on his heels and departed." "That's the end

of Anderson," McNamara told Roswell Gilpatric on the way back to
the Pentagon, "He won't be reappointed. . . . As far as I'm concerned,
he's lost my confidence." McNamara kept his word when Anderson's
term as chief of Naval Operations expired in 1963.

General Taylor, in contrast to the rest of the Joint Chiefs, shared
McNamara's perspective on the quarantine: "President Kennedy, very
rightly in my judgment, wanted to know where every ship was every
morning and to find out just what instructions went to every ship's captain. This appeared to my naval colleagues as being unpardonable intervention in the execution of purely military movements. The argument I made, and I believe correctly, was that this was not really a military situation, but a political situation; it just happened that the power
being used by the government were military toys. . . . This was political
chess and those ships were involved in that kind of game and very properly directed by the master player, the president of the United States."

At 10:00 p.m., Soviet Army intelligence at the embassy in Washington intercepted a JCS order to place the Strategic Air Command on
DEFCON 2 nuclear alert: "In fifteen years of intercepting U.S. military
messages, the Soviet military intelligence service may never have seen
anything like this." A few hours later, journalists Robert Donovan and
Warren Rogers were speculating at a National Press Club bar about an
imminent U.S. invasion of Cuba. Their discussion was overheard by a
bartender and repeated to another customer—KGB agent Anatoly Gor-
sky. The agent relayed the information to the Soviet embassy, which arranged to have an officer waiting when Rogers left the bar. The official
asked if "Kennedy means what he says?" Rogers replied, "You're damn
right, he does." An embassy officer met with Rogers that day to confirm
reports that Kennedy was ready "to finish with Castro." This information was relayed to Moscow and to Khrushchev himself.

A new, tough, and emotional message from Khrushchev soon arrived
at the State Department and was available for the president within an
hour. Khrushchev denounced the quarantine: "I cannot agree to this,
and I think that in your own heart you recognize that I am correct." He
refused to order ships bound for Cuba to observe the quarantine—"the
folly of degenerate imperialism [and] . . . an act of aggression which
pushes mankind toward the abyss of a world nuclear-missile war."
Khrushchev warned that the U.S.S.R. would not relinquish its freedom
to use international waters: "Mr. President, if you coolly weigh the
situation which has developed, not giving way to passions, you will understand that the Soviet Union cannot fail to reject the arbitrary de-

*mands of the United States. . . . try to put yourself in our place and con-
sider how the United States would react to these conditions."* He concluded with a transparent threat: *"We will then be forced on our part to
take the measures we consider necessary and adequate in order to protect our rights. We have everything necessary to do so."*

Less than three hours later, JFK's response was on its way to Moscow.
"I regret very much," the president began, *"that you still do not appear
to understand what it is that has moved us in this matter."* He reviewed
*"the most explicit assurances from your Government and its representa-
tive, both publicly and privately, that no offensive weapons were being
sent to Cuba"* and expressed shock *"that all these public assurances were
false."* He reminded the Soviet premier that *"it was not I who issued the
first challenge in this case"* and urged Khrushchev *"to take the necessary
action to permit a restoration of the earlier situation."*

The movement of military equipment and combat troops to Florida
continued around the clock. More than six thousand vehicles and thousands of tons of weapons and supplies were loaded onto nearly forty
trains, each hauling up to 150 cars. The Defense Department released
voluntary guidelines for reporting these activities, but the buildup was
reported by local press and television stations, and the administration
did not regret that this news would reach the Soviet Union.

In Moscow, after receiving Kennedy's reply, Khrushchev, unbe-
knownst to anyone in Washington, had begun to prepare for a retreat
from the nuclear abyss. *"Moscow would have to find another way to
protect Fidel Castro"* by offering to remove the missiles in exchange for
an American pledge not to invade Cuba and by allowing U.N. inspection of the missile sites. After the Presidium approved this new initiative, Khrushchev announced, *"Comrades, let's go to the Bolshoi Thea-
ter this evening. Our own people as well as foreign eyes will notice, and
perhaps it will calm them down."* He later acknowledged, *"We were
trying to disguise our own anxiety, which was intense."*

Thursday, October 25, 10:00 A.M., Cabinet Room

"This is *not* the *appropriate* time to *blow up* a ship. . . . So let's
think a little more about it."

President John F. Kennedy

Twenty-four hours after the quarantine had been activated, the overriding question remained: would Khrushchev challenge the blockade as

threatened in his latest letter? President Kennedy switched on the recorder as he spoke with USIA acting director Donald Wilson about Cuban jamming of Voice of America radio broadcasts and Castro's denial that Cuba had acquired offensive missiles. JFK asked about dropping photo leaflets over Cuba pinpointing the missile sites. Wilson favored the idea, but it was shelved for the moment because of risks to U.S. aircraft.

McCone reported that construction on the missile sites was moving forward rapidly; Cuba's armed forces remained on high alert, and dissidents were being rounded up. Soviet forces, however, had not been redeployed. He confirmed the "widely known turnaround" of Soviet ships bound for Cuba and noted that several Latin American nations might offer military assistance for the quarantine. The CIA chief also revealed that Sir Kenneth Strong, chairman of the British Joint Intelligence Committee, had examined the photos and informed his government that the evidence was convincing: "I think this is a very useful thing that by coincidence he happened to be here [in Washington]."

McCone also brought up "another almost forgotten subject," the negotiations to free the Bay of Pigs prisoners in exchange for Castro's list of medicine, baby food, and other supplies. Finally, he revealed that "there's great worry *in* Havana, great anxiety among the people." The president asked about getting an analysis of "the state of morale of the people there," whether they know about the missiles, and "their support of the regime." McCone promised to "go into it carefully. We have quite a number of sources."

Attention shifted to the overnight situation on the quarantine line. McNamara revealed that the Soviet tanker *Bucharest* had been permitted to pass through the blockade after identifying its point of origin (the Black Sea), destination (Havana), and cargo (petroleum products). However, the *Bucharest* remained under surveillance and might be boarded later: "I believe," he stressed, "we should establish a pattern of boarding as a quarantine technique and do it *immediately*." The president asked if any other ships might soon be stopped. McNamara explained that the tanker *Grozny*, carrying missile fuel tanks on deck, is "of *great* interest to us" and should reach the blockade line by Friday evening.

McNamara also cited intriguing intelligence suggesting that the Soviets had instructed the Cubans not to fire on U.S. aircraft and had ordered MiGs not to take off from Cuban airfields. The Soviets were also camouflaging the SAM sites, "thereby reducing their readiness because they have to pull these covers off in order to fire effectively." The defense chief urged the president to exploit this military opportunity by setting up low-level surveillance flights which could later be used to initiate air attacks, "with *very* little risk of an incident that we did not wish to incite ourselves."

JFK seemed puzzled by McNamara's reasoning, and the defense chief explained that low-level missions would provide new intelligence and demonstrate the U.S. commitment to stop offensive weapons heading to Cuba and remove the weapons already there. But, they would also establish a pattern of surveillance flights that could quickly be converted into air attacks. This surveillance was critical, he contended, because "the Soviets are camouflaging . . . not *just* the weapons, but various buildings, trucks, all kinds of things."

"It's all gray to me," JFK quipped sardonically, "this whole Russian thing . . . ahh . . . someday!" Some laughter can be heard as he continued, "Why they didn't camouflage it before? Why they do it now and at what point they thought we were gonna find it out?"

"It's an *amazing* thing," McNamara replied, "but *now* I think we're beginning to read their minds," he laughed softly, "*much more clearly* than was true seventy-two hours ago."

"Maybe their minds are clearer," Bundy suggested.

McNamara repeated his proposal to take advantage of Soviet camouflage by initiating low-level surveillance in a pattern that could later disguise air attacks on the missile sites, the IL-28s, the MiG airfields, the SAM sites, and the nuclear storage areas. Taylor also endorsed the proposal: "This low-level is very desirable, Mr. President." The defense chief asked for permission to order the flights immediately. JFK agreed and Taylor left the meeting to personally deliver to the JCS the order for immediate unannounced low-level surveillance flights.

The defense secretary continued to push his rather Machiavellian scheme: if low-level photos, which could be interpreted in three to four hours, confirmed that every site was at least eight hours from launch, "then we have *very* little risk of going in within that eight-hour period." Also, if the U.S. backed a Security Council plan for neutral inspection in Cuba, almost certain to be vetoed by the U.S.S.R., the administration would then have the rationale for converting these unarmed low-level reconnaissance missions into surprise air attacks with almost no risk of retaliation.

Robert Kennedy promptly punctured McNamara's confidence by raising the possibility that the Russians and Cubans might be maneuvering to get the U.S. to fire the first shot before they launched the missiles. McNamara had to admit, "*Possibly*, Bobby, I don't know." He recommended taking only those steps "that'll give us the *option* to do it if we later *choose* to."

The president pondered whether the political situation "is such that we want to let this *Bucharest* pass today without making the inspection. . . . Are we better off to make this issue come to a head *today*, or is there some advantage in putting it off till tomorrow?" Rusk advised against stopping the *Bucharest* a second time. JFK finally decided on giving "sufficient grace to the Soviet Union to get these instructions clear [and] . . . in view of U Thant's appeal, we let this go. . . . I think the *whole problem* is to make a judgment of Khrushchev's message to me last night combined with . . . what is happening at the U.N."

JFK nonetheless asked yet again, "What impression do they get over there [in the Kremlin] that we let this one [the *Bucharest*] go?" The main advantage, McNamara recapitulated, "is avoiding a *shooting* incident over a ship that appears to the public to be an obvious example of a ship *not* carrying prohibited weapons." "I think this is the course to follow," Ambassador Thompson also affirmed, since the Soviets would surely turn the *Grozny* around if the *Bucharest* were boarded.

McNamara recommended announcing that the *Bucharest* had not been boarded because it did not have a deck load and its hatches were too small for missiles. RFK, however, proposed a more politically subtle explanation: "I suppose you could say that obviously, at the present time, the Russians are observing the quarantine. They've sent all their other ships back." JFK reasoned that this strategy could give the administration more time, and Rusk added that it would avoid an incident at sea during the U.N. discussions. "I think," RFK nonetheless persisted, "we have to face up to the fact that we're gonna have to intercept a ship that doesn't have contraband."

The president recognized the political benefit in his brother's point about Khrushchev observing the quarantine: "as Bobby said, the quarantine *to a degree* is already successful. . . . How many ships have turned back?" McNamara, Bundy, and others responded, "Fourteen." "Fourteen ships," JFK continued, "have *turned back* as a result of the quarantine." But, he cautioned, almost using RFK's exact words, "we've got to face up to the fact that we're gonna have to grab a Russian ship and that he [Khrushchev] says he's not gonna permit it. Now, the question is whether it's better to have that happen today or tomorrow." Bundy expressed hope that U Thant might convince the U.S.S.R.

to avoid challenging the quarantine: "It's not likely, but it's conceivable." "In that case," JFK finally decided, "we might as well wait."

The president, nonetheless, had no illusions about avoiding the seizure of a Soviet ship in the next day or two. RFK remarked that the situation at the quarantine line had yet to come to a head and JFK declared, "I think we oughta have a ship available to grab, depending on what happens tomorrow afternoon." "I think you should instruct them, Mr. President," McNamara counseled, "to be prepared to intercept tomorrow during daylight." "And no matter where it might be," RFK added, backed by McNamara.

McCone, on a more hopeful note, cited a CIA report that many Soviet ships had turned around near the Mediterranean, suggesting that they were not regrouping as a convoy to challenge the quarantine. Ball agreed that the early course change indicated that the Soviets did not expect the blockade to be lifted soon. "The other explanation," Nitze countered bleakly, "might be that they're counting on *taking* forceful action against the first one we intercept." "That's right," JFK muttered almost inaudibly.

RFK asked if the *Bucharest* was carrying missile fuel. Not likely, McNamara replied, because missile fuel would be carried on deck. JFK pointed out that the fact that no ships had been stopped was bound to come out, making it increasingly difficult to sit around waiting for the *Grozny*. McNamara again proposed saying that all ships were being hailed and those not carrying prohibited materials, like the *Bucharest*, were allowed through. "It's *extremely unusual* for tankers to carry deck cargo," he pointed out. "This is why the *Grozny* is *so* extraordinary."

There was no evidence other than Khrushchev's latest letter and the Soviet submarines in the Atlantic to indicate that the Russians might try to run the blockade. Wilson wondered if the government should announce that the ships "*have indeed* turned back." JFK agreed—but not until the evidence was confirmed. Rusk advised being careful about giving the impression that most ships had turned back because if the Navy grabbed one, "it will put the bee on us for being..." "Warmongers," the president interjected, finishing Rusk's sentence. "Well, we're caught with one crowd *or* the other," Bundy quipped.

JFK contended that it was risky to make too much of the ships that had reversed direction: "I don't want a sense of euphoria passing around," he counseled. "That message of Khrushchev is much tougher than that." McCone advised the president to stick with the statement from the previous evening: "They've altered their course and we don't know the significance of it." McNamara recommended avoiding public speculation about Soviet ships by confining statements to the day's quarantine activities.

Once a ship had been stopped and the Soviet response was clear, JFK proposed, POL (petroleum, oil, and lubricants) could be put on the contraband list because work on the missile sites was continuing. McNamara advised adding aviation gas as well since the IL-28s were still being assembled. After that, the president made clear, all tankers would be seized: "We first wanna get the test case to be a better one than a tanker," JFK asked, "is that the argument?" and McNamara confirmed, "I think so, Mr. President." RFK worried that the *Grozny* might also turn back, leading Bundy to quip, "Damned few trains on the Long Island Railroad."

The strained laughter that followed lasted only a few seconds. "My God," RFK asserted testily, it would be better to grab a vessel likely carrying missiles even if it had turned around. If a ship "has radioed Moscow that it has turned around and it's still boarded," Rusk disagreed sharply, "*that's bad*." "But they'd let you wait until Lent," RFK joked, provoking another touch of laughter. "Isn't our *purpose*," Rusk reiterated, "to turn it around without shooting, if we *can*?" "The point is," RFK persisted, "we'd like to intercept a ship that had something rather than a lot of baby food for children." Nitze, surprisingly, sided with Rusk: "I think Dean is right," if the ships turn around, "that's fine," but those that reach the blockade must be inspected. "Otherwise *they're* deciding," Bundy declared, "what meets *our* proclamation."

Ball echoed Rusk's doubts: "I think personally it would be a *great* mistake to intercept a ship if it were in the process of turning around." The president, however, worried "whether this procedure is a little *flat*. . . . Is there a political advantage," he conjectured, "in stretching this thing out? That's *really* the question. Are we gonna get anything out of the U.N. or Khrushchev?"

At that point, Bundy proposed turning to Ambassador Stevenson's draft reply to U Thant's proposal to halt the delivery of missiles and suspend the quarantine. Rusk read Stevenson's proposed message aloud and advised that the quarantine should not be suspended until the shipment of offensive weapons and work on the missile sites had ceased. The president's skepticism surfaced immediately: the quarantine could only be lifted, he remarked, "if the U.N. can give, which they *can't* give, adequate guarantees against the introduction of offensive material during this period. . . . but at least it doesn't make us look

quite as negative." JFK seemed eager to fix the blame for the likely failure of the U.N. peace plan on U Thant: "I'd rather stick the cat on his
back. . . . We *can't* take the quarantine off until he offers a substitute,
and he hasn't offered a substitute."

"Why don't we say that in sentence one?" Bundy suggested. "That's an
absolutely fundamental proposition with us." He then summarized the
emerging consensus: the quarantine could be lifted only after a halt in the
delivery of offensive weapons, cessation of work on the sites, and reliable
inspection and verification. "And," Rusk added, "U.N. observers to ensure that offensive weapons are not operational." McNamara, however,
urged his colleagues to remember that the quarantine is also "a form of
pressure" to assure the withdrawal of the missiles already in Cuba.

Rusk spelled out his understanding of the U.N. moratorium proposal: two to three weeks of preliminary talks with the quarantine in
place, followed by a U.N. quarantine and observers to verify that work
had ceased and the missiles were inoperable, and finally, "getting the
weapons out of there." Bundy worried that the status quo might "come
to have a momentum of it's own," and McNamara advised against removing the quarantine, even with U.N. inspection, "*unless* they agreed
to take the weapons out." The president remained very skeptical:
"We're not gonna get anyplace with this thing because . . . there's no
way they can accept with American ships preventing weapons coming
in. In addition, the Cubans aren't gonna take this too well." The message to U Thant was revised again after consultation with Stevenson
and dispatched to the U.N.

The secretary of state shifted the discussion to a Brazilian proposal to
declare Latin America a nuclear-free zone. The president seemed cool to
the idea, asking whether Rusk meant "nuclear-free" or "missile-free"
since the U.S. had proof of missiles in Cuba but no verification of nuclear warheads. Rusk replied that the plan called for making Latin
America nuclear-free, but President Kennedy quickly changed the subject—"What else we got?" Bundy advised reviewing the October 23 letters between Khrushchev and Kennedy and read aloud from the Soviet
leader's message—after mocking his claims "about our immorality, and
that the quarantine's no good, and the OAS is no good." Ambassador
Thompson contended that Khrushchev's letter "indicated preparation
for resistance by force, that is, forcing us to take forcible action."
Bundy then read portions of JFK's reply and the president muttered almost despondently, "And there we are."

Bundy hypothesized that "we *may* be moving into some kind of a de facto, unclarified quarantine." The prospect of a protracted and inconclusive status quo in Cuba alarmed McNamara: in the next twenty-four hours the U.N. might fail to take effective action, there might be no Soviet ships carrying offensive weapons available for interception, and work might continue on the missile sites. In that case, he asked point blank, "What do we do?" "Well," the president cut in, "we first stop a Soviet ship someplace, and have this out on what they're gonna do."

McNamara reiterated that the Soviets might comply with the prohibition on shipping offensive materials to Cuba while they continued the construction of the missile sites: "Now what do we do under these circumstances?" The defense chief answered his own question, recommending an escalation of the quarantine. JFK asked if adding POL would be "the obvious escalation," but McNamara again urged including aviation gas or jet fuel because of the IL-28 bombers: "We don't want to allow any particular period of time to go by that starts to freeze the situation. We want to continue to move toward this ultimate objective of removing the missiles." Bundy tried to pin down a general consensus, "especially the president's own view. I share that view, *very much*, that a plateau here is the most dangerous thing." Several participants expressed agreement, and McNamara recommended drafting a "program of escalation that we might put into effect in the next twenty-four to forty-eight hours."

JFK, impressed by McNamara's logic, reopened the discussion of intercepting the *Bucharest* before it reached Cuba. Bundy countered that it would be damaging to appear to have waffled over seizing the *Bucharest* and recommended, "take her now or . . . let her go." "I agree with Mac, Mr. President," McNamara reaffirmed. "I *don't* think the *Bucharest* is a very useful case for us." Bundy, nonetheless, unflinchingly admonished the president, "there is a *real* case to be made, which has perhaps not been presented as strongly this morning as it *could* be, for *doing* it and *getting* it done. . . . It is *important* for you to know, Mr. President, that there is a *good*, substantial argument and a lot of people in the argument on the other side, *all* of whom will fall in with whatever decision you make." He cited Nitze as an example and the assistant defense secretary promptly took the cue, pushing the president to fully enforce "the *principle* of a blockade . . . against everybody, not selecting ships or the types of ships." Rusk, however, noted that Soviet ships were turning back and urged restraint: "it's already escalated *very*, *very* fast."

JFK's response, at this potential turning point, was disjointed, agitated, and ungrammatical; he stammered out word fragments in rapid-fire stream of consciousness: "Let's wait until . . . we gotta . . . let's come back this afternoon and take this ship. I don't . . . I think we can always . . . your point about, we didn't act, so, 'eyeball to eyeball' . . . We coulda said, 'no, we're waiting for Khrushchev, we're waiting for U Thant' . . ."

His next few sentences, however, were unmistakably clear: "We don't want to precipitate an incident with major new . . . we still have then another six or seven hours [to stop the *Bucharest*]. I think the only argument's for *not* taking it. I think we could grab us one of these things anytime. I don't think it makes a hell of a lot of difference what ship it is. . . . This is *not* the *appropriate* time to *blow up* a ship. . . . So let's think a little more about it." "Right," Bundy conceded.

Robert Kennedy interjected, "Can you take a tanker without blowing it up, Bob?" and McNamara replied confidently, "Yes." Bundy and RFK suggested meeting without the president to discuss expanding the quarantine—just as the tape ran out or JFK switched off the recorder.

That afternoon, the U.N. Security Council convened in New York. Soviet ambassador Valerian Zorin, unaware of Khrushchev's covert deployment, defiantly denied that the U.S.S.R. had placed offensive nuclear weapons in Cuba. He ridiculed Stevenson's "so-called evidence" and demanded to know why President Kennedy had not shown these "incontrovertible facts" to Gromyko during their recent meeting. President Kennedy, after watching the televised meeting, authorized Stevenson to shaft Zorin by displaying the photos.

Thursday, October 25, after 5:00 P.M., Cabinet Room

"Rather than have the confrontation with the Russians at sea, it might be better to knock out their missile base as the *first step* . . . [demonstrating] that we're not backing off and that we're still being tough with Cuba. That's really the point we have to make."

Attorney General Robert F. Kennedy

The intelligence briefing revealed that the Soviets were working swiftly to complete the missile sites and the assembly of the IL-28s. McNamara proposed options for turning up the blockade in order to keep the status quo from becoming frozen in place. The president turned on the recorder as McNamara reported that a passenger ship, the *Völkerfreundschaft*, carrying 1,500 people, including 550 Czech technicians and 25 East

German students, would soon reach the quarantine. He advised letting it pass rather than risk injuring civilians. JFK seemed uneasy about unilaterally observing U Thant's request to avoid an incident at sea when Khrushchev still refused to keep ships away from the blockade line. Sorensen suggested that stopping this East German ship would prove that the U.S. response was "*not a soft* one at all," without directly challenging "the prestige of the Soviets." He also asked skeptically, "How do you tell a missile technician from an agricultural technician?" Bundy claimed that letting the ship through would damage American credibility. The president argued that the decision should ultimately depend on Khrushchev's response to U Thant—he might keep ships out of the area, reject the offer, or fail to respond. "Then," JFK reasoned, "we have to pick up some ship tomorrow, after the shoe drops."

The president exposed his doubts by asking, "What do you think, Bob?" The defense secretary again rejected risking lives on a passenger ship. JFK recognized the political wisdom in McNamara's position, acknowledging that "the only reason for picking *this* ship up is we gotta prove sooner or later that the blockade works." McNamara offered an alternative discussed that morning: intercepting the *Grozny*, "a Soviet tanker with a deck cargo," which could reach the blockade in twenty-four hours. The president seemed receptive since waiting for the *Grozny* would also give Khrushchev another day to consider U Thant's message.

Robert Kennedy, trying to give "another side of it," warned against being trapped in a stalemate while the Soviets completed the buildup in Cuba. "Rather than have the confrontation with the Russians at sea," he suggested impassively, "it might be better to knock out their missile base as the *first step*." RFK sidestepped the Pearl Harbor issue by proposing to warn Soviet personnel "to get out of that vicinity in ten minutes and then we go through and knock [off] the base." This step, he reasoned, would demonstrate "that we're not backing off and that we're still being tough with Cuba. That's really the point we have to make."

No one openly backed RFK's proposition, although Dillon hinted that it seemed logical to confine military action to Cuba itself. "When you *really* step back and look at it," Rusk maintained, "the quarantine is now *fully* effective." Several voices can be heard affirming, "That's right" or "That's correct." "If you wanted to really wait," RFK admitted, the effectiveness of the blockade provided an excuse, "without losing face." McNamara proposed that "we could appear to be forceful" by increasing aerial surveillance during the day and using flares to check on work being done overnight.

JFK appeared to be leaning towards letting the East German passenger ship through and delaying a decision on the *Grozny* until Khrushchev replied to U Thant. If he "announces all the ships [heading to Cuba] are being suspended," the president declared, "that's *that* point." But, he predicted, "I don't think he will, probably." RFK suggested letting the *Grozny*, like the *Bucharest*, through the blockade and then announcing that since most ships had turned back, the quarantine had been successful. "And then what do we do?" JFK pressed, before answering his own question: "Then we need to decide about this air strike again" or add POL to the contraband list. McNamara assured the president, "We have a lot of harassing actions" ("*Exactly,*" RFK interjected) "we could carry out and incidents we can provoke if we'd wish to."

Four days earlier the president had decided that air strikes were too risky because all the missiles could not be destroyed. Now, in response to his brother's suggestion, he resurrected the air attack option if a stalemate at sea gave the Russians time to finish the missile sites. "The only weakness, in my judgment," RFK persisted, "is the idea to the Russians that [we're] . . . backing off and that we're weak." He nonetheless conceded, "It's a *hell* of a thing, really, when you think of it, that fifteen ships have turned back. And I don't think we really have any apologies to make." Sorensen again suggested stopping the East German ship, but RFK seemed impressed by McNamara's point about avoiding harm to the passengers. "Mr. President," Rusk insisted, "since I recommended a blockade, I haven't been very helpful about applying it in particular instances." But, he cautioned, if the Navy stopped, disabled, or sank a tanker or a passenger ship, "I think we're just in a *hell* of a shape." "I assume" Sorensen persisted, "we don't have to sink it."

Walt Rostow, chairman of the State Department Policy Planning Council, spoke for the first time: "The POL thing is *very* serious for them" because of their "100 percent reliance on it and a *very* short supply," and a cutoff would grind their economy to a halt. McCone and RFK countered that the impact would not be felt for months. Rostow cited the German experience in World War II and claimed to have studies backing his stand, but several participants claimed that a Defense Department study had reached the opposite conclusion.

The president finally cut through the increasingly repetitious discussion and decided not to intercept the *Völkerfreundschaft* since the U Thant initiative held out "a chance of *easing* this." "If you try to disable it," he argued, "you're apt to sink it. There are no guarantees when you try to shoot a rudder off, because you either sink it or have it catch fire."

JFK was willing to give Khrushchev more time to respond to U Thant before stopping the *Grozny*, but he nonetheless edged closer to RFK's tougher stance: "I think if the work continues, we either have to do this air business *or* we have to put POL on because we got to begin to bring counterpressure because otherwise the work's going on and *we're not really doin' anything else.*" RFK, heartened by the president's renewed determination, added, "And we've got to show them that we mean it."

As the meeting began to break up, there was some discussion about preventing the Cubans from confusing night reconnaissance flares with a bombing attack. McNamara suggested a "warning ahead of time," and a few people chuckled when someone advised being "sure these missiles aren't on their launchers" when the night missions start.

"What do you think, Tommy?" the president asked the former ambassador. Thompson endorsed the president's quarantine decisions but echoed RFK's theme: "I'm a little troubled by Khrushchev's *strong* letter of yesterday" and want to be sure that we "show him that we're not backing away because of a threat. On the other hand, he *is* backing away, and that tips the balance." RFK agreed, "he *definitely* has," but added cynically, "We retreat an inch and he says, 'six feet to go.'" Thompson recalled a recent conversation in which the Yugoslav ambassador denied "'that Khrushchev thinks you're afraid to act or are weak.'" JFK replied that Khrushchev's motives could range from "frustration over Berlin" to a test of American resolve. "In other words," he reflected, "you can take your choice on these." Thompson agreed, just as the recording stopped.

Sometime after President Kennedy left the Cabinet Room, the tape machine suddenly started recording again. There may have been a technical problem or a delay in switching to the backup recorder, or the tape may have run out and been replaced. It is also possible that RFK, sitting near the president's chair, turned it on for a few minutes of rump conversation—touching on surveillance missions, air strikes, and using Operation Mongoose Cuban operatives to sabotage the missile sites.

The U.N. Security Council meeting continued into the evening, and millions of Americans viewed the televised debate. When Zorin again denied that there were missiles in Cuba, Stevenson angrily pushed aside his notes: "Do you, Ambassador Zorin, deny that the U.S.S.R. has placed or is placing medium- and intermediate-range missiles and missile sites in Cuba? Yes or no—don't wait for the translation—yes or no." Zorin responded scornfully that he was not in an American court-

room and Stevenson countered, "You are in the courtroom of world opinion right now and you can answer yes or no. You have denied that they exist—and I want to know if I have understood you correctly." Zorin replied that he would respond in due course, and Stevenson shot back, "I am prepared to wait for my answer until hell freezes over, if that is your decision." The delegates burst into laughter.

Stevenson then displayed the photos and Zorin, recalling the doctored pictures from the Bay of Pigs, responded, "One who has lied once will not be believed a second time." Stevenson irately challenged the Soviet Union to "ask their Cuban colleagues to permit a U.N. team to go to these sites. . . . Our job here is not to score debating points. Our job, Mr. Zorin, is to save the peace. And if you are ready to try, we are." The response to Stevenson's presentation, in the White House and the nation, was enthusiastic.

Later that evening JFK informed U Thant that the U.S. would try to prevent a clash at sea if Khrushchev kept Soviet ships away from the blockade zone. Meanwhile, Castro delivered another passionate harangue denouncing U.S. surveillance and pledging never to submit to American aggression.

Early the following morning the destroyers Pierce *and* Kennedy *hailed and boarded the* Marucla, *a Soviet-chartered freighter. (The U.S.S.* Kennedy *was named for JFK's older brother, Joseph P. Kennedy, Jr., killed in World War II.) The crew cooperated with the three-hour inspection, and the* Marucla *was permitted to continue toward Cuba. No one had expected that stopping a Soviet-chartered ship would be so uneventful. A new CIA report confirmed nonetheless that construction was proceeding on the missile sites. The massive movement of troops and supplies to southern Florida continued as well, and the press was reporting that an invasion of Cuba was imminent.*

Friday, October 26, 10:00 A.M., Cabinet Room

"The only thing that I'm saying is that we're not gonna get 'em out with the quarantine. . . . We're either gonna trade 'em out or we're gonna have to go in and get 'em out—ourselves."

President John F. Kennedy

The president switched on the recorder as McCone was discussing pressure, particularly from RFK, to expand Operation Mongoose in Cuba. Bundy advised reconstituting Mongoose "as a subcommittee of this committee." JFK acknowledged having discussed with McCone "a crash program" to create a new civil government for Cuba in the wake of a possible invasion. "These are *very* important matters," Bundy agreed, and should be "part of the discussion at the Mongoose meeting this afternoon . . . the paramilitary, the civil government, [and] correlated activities to the main show that we need to reorganize." JFK pointed out that someone at State, CIA, and Defense should be in charge of this planning. "Post-Castro Cuba," Bundy acknowledged, "is the most complex landscape." JFK also suggested identifying doctors and others in the Cuban community in greater Miami "who would be *useful* if we have an invasion," and McCone called for more effective use of "the Mongoose organization" in Cuba.

At that very moment, McNamara revealed, the Navy was on board the Soviet-chartered Lebanese freighter *Marucla,* chosen because "it was a non–[Soviet] bloc ship" that could be boarded "with the least possible chance of violence." "It won't be held long," he promised, and urged that the story "be put out immediately." The defense chief further reported that no ships were near the blockade except for the *Grozny.* "So there's *very* little quarantine activity with respect to Soviet ships that we can anticipate in the next few days."

McNamara also disclosed that work on assembling the IL-28 bombers "has continued at an accelerated pace." Therefore, he told the president, "acting under *your* authority," bomber fuel is being added to the prohibited list. JFK replied that he would rather add POL because it was directly linked to the missiles rather than the bombers and "the missiles are the more *dramatic* offensive weapons." Bundy pushed the president to decide: "The larger question is whether you want at the end to have the bombers there. If you want to get them out, this is as good a time as any to tie them in." But, JFK persisted, "I would rather tie as much as we could to the missiles." "Can't we do them both?" McNamara countered. The president agreed to announce that the U.S. was restricting the delivery of fuel used for constructing the missile sites as well as aviation fuel for the bombers; but, he reiterated, "I think the *missiles* are the *dramatic* one."

Rusk, however, recommended a twenty-four-hour delay in adding POL to give the U Thant talks a chance. Bundy expressed concern about losing momentum and Taylor exclaimed, "Mr. President," since there is clear evidence that work has continued, shouldn't the U.S. respond "with mounting indignation in our voices?" "Yes," McCone muttered in the background, "this is an awfully important point." Bundy tried to pin down a consensus that blockading POL would be "the next step on the line of pressure."

Robert Kennedy, the previous evening, had reintroduced the idea of bombing the missile sites to avoid the danger that work on the bases might continue during a stalemate in U.N. negotiations. Now, on the eleventh day of meetings, those who doubted that the quarantine could neutralize the threat from the bases already under construction picked up important support. "If we follow this track," the soft-spoken Treasury secretary, Douglas Dillon, cautioned, "we'll be sort of caught up in events not of our own control. We will *have to* stop a Soviet ship ... and we might wind up in some sort of a naval encounter all around the world with the Soviet Union which would have *nothing* to do with the buildup of the missile bases in Cuba." Instead, like RFK, he suggested focusing the confrontation on Cuba "by preparing for air action to hit these bases."

No one, not even RFK, openly backed Dillon's position, and Bundy and McNamara pushed his argument aside. The defense secretary, instead, recommended day and night surveillance (using flares) to prove whether construction was continuing on the missile bases. Rusk again urged delaying night reconnaissance "until we've had a crack at the U Thant discussions" and expressed concern that the flares might be misinterpreted because they had been used in the past to prepare for night bombing raids. McNamara contended that an announcement could be made in advance to warn the Cubans about the flares. But, after further discussion, the president sided with Rusk on delaying the night flights: "Why don't we wait on this surveillance until we get the [results of] political talks [at the U.N.]." On the daytime flights, however, he instructed, "Just get them goin'. We can announce it later."

Rusk reintroduced the idea of dropping photo leaflets over Cuba: "One of the possible *outs* here is to produce such pressures there *in Cuba* as to cause something to crack on the island." JFK agreed to release the leaflets fifteen minutes before an air strike, but cautioned, "We don't want to get 'em so used to leaflets dropping that they don't bother to read them when the key moment comes." As someone chuckled, JFK suggested that leaflets would be useful over "Havana, Santiago, and a few other places," and Bundy responded wryly, "There's no need telling the people on the missile sites that there are missiles in Cuba."

Wilson complained about the technical quality of the photographs available for use on the leaflets, and JFK agreed that the USIA could use any picture that had been released—including those at the U.N. John

McCloy urged Wilson to use the May Day parade picture "of the *big* bomb going through Red Square." (JFK had assigned McCloy, a disarmament specialist and a Republican, to assist Stevenson with the U.N. talks and he had flown to Washington with the ambassador for this meeting.) McCloy acknowledged that it isn't "the same missile that we have down there [in Cuba] . . . [but] it's half a city block long . . . [and] there's nothing defensive about *this*." He also proposed that the leaflets stress that Castro was exposing the Cuban people to potential disaster.

In one of his most forceful monologues, Rusk declared that the U.S. must demand an end to arms shipments and work on the bases, as well as making the missiles and warheads inoperable—backed up by on-site U.N. inspectors from neutral nations. "We have to insist upon that *very hard*." He predicted, however, that the U.S.S.R. would instead try "talking indefinitely," while the sites become operational, "And then we are *nowhere*." Effective inspection, Rusk continued, would require at least three hundred personnel from nations with "a technical capacity, to know what they're looking at." He suggested Sweden, Switzerland, and Austria and perhaps Brazil and Canada. "We can't have *Burmese* or *Cambodians* going in there . . . and being led down the garden path." Rusk had evidently forgotten that U Thant, sponsor of the talks, was Burmese.

Secretary Rusk also insisted that the quarantine must remain in place until the U.N. set up a substitute. Dillon, sensing another opening for his earlier suggestion to bomb the bases, contended that if the Soviets rejected these conditions, "that gives you your excuse to take further action." Nitze argued that since U.N. inspectors would not arrive for weeks, the Soviets could demonstrate good faith by separating the missiles from the erectors and moving them "into an open field, where we could get *a view* of them." McCone agreed that "inoperable" had to be more than "just having a switch turned off."

McCloy demanded reversing Rusk's priorities by making inoperability the *first* U.S. condition. He warned darkly that the buildup in Cuba "was for a sinister purpose" and it would be foolish to suspend the quarantine because it could never be reintroduced with OAS support and because "there's a growing momentum of [public] opinion" behind it. The president stressed that "even if the quarantine's 100 percent effective, it isn't any good because the missile sites go on being constructed. So this is only a *first step*." "And have a pistol at your hip by tomorrow," McCloy interjected theatrically.

Rusk reintroduced the plan he had floated the day before to declare

Latin America an atomic weapon–free zone. "We need to study and consider this possibility," McNamara commented; "The Chiefs are *very* cool toward it for a variety of reasons that General Taylor can outline." But, again breaking ranks with the military under his authority, the defense secretary revealed, "I'm inclined to favor it." Buoyed by McNamara's support, Rusk explained that the Soviets had been "supporting nuclear-free zones for years. And they may find in this a face-saving formula." A rejection, however, would be on the record for all the world to see. Taylor, speaking for the JCS, argued that the plan would divert attention from the removal of the missiles. McNamara agreed that the administration could not permit itself "to be maneuvered into a position in which *this* is *the* approach we take in order to achieve the elimination of the missiles from Cuba."

President Kennedy, however, put his finger on a key issue: "Isn't it part of the Brazilian initiative," he asked, "that they would remove these weapons if we would guarantee the territorial integrity of Cuba?" "Very much so," Bundy confirmed. "Well, obviously we're gonna have to pay a price. We're not gonna get these missiles out of there without either fighting them to get 'em out," the president reasoned, "or if that's one of the prices that has to be paid to get these out of there, then we commit ourselves not to invade Cuba."

Rusk turned to yet another long-shot diplomatic initiative, a State Department cable to be delivered to Castro by the Brazilian ambassador in Havana. The message identified two "nonnegotiable" issues between Castro and the U.S.: Cuba's ties to the Soviet Union and support for political subversion in Latin America. "If Castro tries to rationalize the presence of these missiles as due to Cuban fear of U.S. invasion," Rusk explained, the ambassador will reply that the U.S. and the OAS "would not risk upsetting hemispheric solidarity by invading a Cuba so clearly committed to a peaceful course." Rusk admitted that the final sentence "was the seduction, as far as Castro is concerned."

The president objected to language in the cable suggesting that the Soviets were angling to betray Cuba for concessions from NATO: "I don't think that there's enough evidence to indicate *that*. So I think probably that our stating it would be regarded as rather insulting." Rusk explained that Brazil's ambassador would make the argument; "Well if the Brazilians want to say it," JFK agreed, "it's alright." Rusk also repeated Kennedy's view that if the Cubans "*get rid* of these offensive weapons then, I assume, that it is *not* our purpose to invade Cuba."

Nitze did not trust the Cubans or the Soviets and raised the specter of "long, drawn-out negotiations." Several participants proposed deadlines of twenty-four hours or a few days or removal with "great urgency." "One thing I don't like" about Rusk's proposal, McCone grumbled, is that it "insulates Castro from further actions. . . . This does *not* involve a *break* between Castro and the Soviet Union." Rusk held his ground, insisting that the message "would repeat the president's statement that the military-political connection with Moscow is not negotiable, as well as the actions aimed at other Latin American countries. Now," he wished out loud, "*if Castro* were, through some miracle, to get his militia together and turn on the Soviets on these missiles, then this problem is solved, John." "Yeah," McCone replied warily, "that's a big 'if' though." "It's a *very big* 'if', but it's on that *off* chance," Rusk acknowledged, "and that's the purpose of this operation." RFK asked what would happen if "other weapons are sent in there." Rusk conceded that the message "does not give assurances against any kind of rascality."

Bundy warned JFK not to be distracted by secondary issues: "Mr. President," he declared impatiently, "I believe myself that *all* of these things need to be measured in terms of the very *simple, basic, structural* purpose of this whole enterprise: *to get these missiles out.* . . . If we can bring Castro down in the process, *dandy*. If we can turn him on other people, dandy. But if we can get the missiles out..." JFK agreed that "we ought to concentrate on the missiles right now."

Ambassador Thompson nonetheless cautioned, "In my opinion, the Soviets will find it *far* easier to remove these weapons" than accept inspections and would resist putting Soviet technicians under U.N. authority. The president finally put an end to this increasingly repetitive discussion: "We gotta get moving," he instructed. "Let's send this off. It won't matter," he pronounced indifferently. "It won't get any place. But let's send it . . . because time's running out for us. . . . We can't screw around for two weeks" while the Soviets finish the missile sites.

At that juncture, President Kennedy, likely inadvertently, initiated one of ExComm's most rancorous exchanges by asking for Adlai Stevenson's thoughts. The ambassador surely sensed the personal antagonism in the room: Bundy, Dillon, McCloy, McCone, and McNamara were or had been Republicans; RFK had worked in Stevenson's 1956 presidential campaign, but, convinced that the nominee was weak, voted for Eisenhower. JFK himself never forgave Stevenson's ineffectual effort to pull off a third consecutive nomination in 1960.

The ambassador, notwithstanding, launched into a defense of U

Thant's moratorium plan: "I think it's well for you all to bear in mind that the concept of this proposal is a *standstill*." The inoperability of the missiles, he explained, "is *not* a standstill. It includes a reversal of something that has already taken place." But, he added circuitously, "I think it would be *quite proper* to include in our original demands that the weapons be *kept* inoperable."

"Would the work on the sites be ceased?" the president asked skeptically. "Of course," Stevenson replied. Bundy interrupted, barely concealing his patronizing scorn: "Excuse me. You're gonna have to be clear. Are we talking now about the first two days or about the first two weeks" of negotiations? Stevenson explained diffidently that the final negotiations would proceed only after achieving three objectives in the first two days: "*no ships* go to Cuba carrying arms"; "no further construction on the bases and how that's to be policed"; the U.S. "would then suspend our quarantine."

Rusk jumped on an ambiguity in Stevenson's argument: "The work on the bases *stops*—includes the inoperability of the missiles." "Well, that could *not* help," Stevenson responded softly; "I think it would be quite proper to *attempt* to include that, to *keep* them inoperable rather than to say that they should be *rendered* inoperable." "Well, when did they become inoperable?" McNamara bristled, "They're operable now." "*Ensure* that they *are* inoperable!" Bundy demanded stridently. "I'm trying to make clear to you," Stevenson replied, "that this was a standstill" and does not require undoing the work already done. There would be *no more* construction, *no more* quarantine, *no more* arms shipments. . . . But I don't think that there should be any misunderstanding about what was intended here, which was a *standstill* and *only* a standstill."

"What *they* will want in return," the ambassador continued, "is, I anticipate, a new guarantee of the territorial integrity of Cuba. Indeed," he added audaciously, "that's what they said these weapons were for—to defend the territorial integrity of Cuba"—an argument conspicuously missing from the ExComm discussions. Stevenson then dropped the other shoe: "It is *possible* that the price that might be asked of us in the long-term negotiation, two-week negotiation, might include dismantling *bases of ours*, such as Italy and Turkey, that we have talked about."

McCloy had remained silent during Stevenson's presentation but abruptly burst out: "I don't agree with that, Mr. President. I feel *very* strongly about it. And I think that the real *crux* of this matter is the fact that he's got these pointed, for all you know, *right now* at our hearts." *"The quarantine goes on,"* he demanded, rapping the table, *"until we are satisfied that these are inoperable."* Stevenson must have been embarrassed by this attack from his U.N. "assistant." The administration had publicly explained that McCloy had been assigned to the U.N. to add a bipartisan voice to the negotiations. In fact, McCloy was sent to New York because of concern that Stevenson was not tough enough to deal with the Soviets—a view confirmed for many in the room by this exchange.

The president, however, coming strikingly close to Stevenson's position on the Jupiters, declared, "So you've only got two ways of removing the weapons." One way "is to negotiate them out, or in other words, trade them out. And the other is to go in and take them out." McCloy continued emotionally, *"Look,* this is the security of the United States! I believe the strategic situation has *greatly* changed with the presence of these weapons in Cuba." "That's right," Kennedy acknowledged: "The only thing that I'm saying is that we're not gonna get 'em out with the quarantine. . . . We're either gonna trade 'em out or we're gonna have to go in and get 'em out—ourselves."

Bundy eagerly pointed out that the first two days of negotiations under the U.N. proposal *"does* involve a dropping of the quarantine without what I would call adequate momentum. Very far from it!" Rusk seemed somewhat more confident that U.N. monitoring could provide adequate warning "if they were actually raising one of these things on its launcher," but JFK repeated that the quarantine would not compel the U.S.S.R. to remove the missiles: "Why should the Soviets take these things out?" he added pessimistically. "The Soviets are not gonna take 'em out."

McNamara admitted to being confused about the details of the U.N. plan, and Stevenson explained again that U.N. inspectors would confirm that the shipment of weapons and construction of the sites had ceased before the U.S. lifted the quarantine. "Well on that point," McCloy interposed, "I think we've got to insist upon having our *own* people down there. The Soviets are already there." The president suggested that daily overflights could provide assurances, but Bundy disagreed: "Not really, Mr. President. If we're talking about inoperability, we have to *be* there." McCloy reiterated sharply, "You have to have somebody that *knows what these things mean.*"

"The only thing is," the president repeated, the quarantine is not "gonna get 'em out of there." "No sir," Bundy replied firmly, but "if we adopt a course at the U.N. which presumes that they might *stay there*, we've had it." Rusk predicted that "a major back down" by the Soviets was extremely unlikely, and McCone declared that the Soviets "could put these things on their stands" in just a few hours. Stevenson, echoing JFK, pointed out that "the quarantine isn't going to prevent that," and McCone insisted that the U.S. must be prepared to "take such action as necessary" if any hostile move was detected during negotiations. "If there's any violation of the standstill," Stevenson conceded, "it serves them right, all bets are off. We're back to status quo."

Nitze demanded that separating the missiles from the erectors and removing the IL-28 wings was essential for U.S. security during negotiations. "This isn't a *standstill*," McCloy nearly shouted, "until you've got that." Stevenson countered that these details belonged in the long-term negotiations. "No!" Nitze objected, buttressed by several other sharp "No's." "During the negotiations they disassemble, so we're not negotiating under the threat. In your speech," Nitze reminded the president, "you said we wouldn't negotiate under threat." "Have we seen a missile *on* a launcher?" Rusk asked. A chorus of voices responded, "Right next to it." Bundy, clearly aiming at Stevenson, contended that negotiating for the status quo "is *not* in our interest." McCone urged Stevenson to invite Zorin to fly to Cuba and view the bases, and Dillon demanded, "I just don't see how you can negotiate for *two weeks* with these things sitting right next to the launchers."

Stevenson then asked to be excused to take a call from the U.N. "Okay, sure thing," JFK replied. "Why don't you go in my office." (Stevenson took the call alone in the Oval Office—possibly from the president's desk. There is much evidence of animosity between JFK and his U.N. ambassador; the twice-defeated presidential candidate must have experienced mixed emotions sitting in the office he felt *he* deserved to occupy.)

McCloy again demanded finding "sophisticated people" for on-site inspection and a U.S. role in naming them: "I want somebody that *knows* something about this business." Robert Kennedy objected, "I can't *believe* that they'd allow a lot of foreigners runnin' around their missiles." Dillon and RFK also warned that the missiles could be hidden in the woods and Taylor admitted, "We can make 'em account for the one's we've actually seen, but those we've never seen, we have no control." The president observed with unusual bluntness: "Stevenson has this proposal for dealing with the missiles, which nobody's very much interested in." (Stevenson was still on the phone in the Oval Office.)

"But the point is that the blockade is not going to accomplish the job either. . . . What other devices are we gonna use to get 'em out of there?"

Rusk urged the president to resist pressure to relax the quarantine until arms shipments and work on the bases had stopped and the weapons were inoperable. Bundy again revealed disdain for Stevenson: "But it's the *inoperable* that's obvious—it's very important that the governor must get that clearly in his head." (Stevenson had been governor of Illinois from 1949 to 1953, his only elective office.) "It seems to me," JFK replied, "this should provide some direction for the governor this afternoon [at the U.N.]. Then he'll come back and tell us that they won't agree to this and then we continue with the blockade." Bundy also urged the president to mention bipartisan representation at the U.N.—the cover story for assigning McCloy to "assist" Stevenson.

"Mr. President," Taylor demanded again, "shouldn't we be raising the noise level of our indignation over this?" Kennedy agreed, asking McNamara if the most recent photos corroborated that work was continuing on the sites. "They *do* indeed," McNamara replied. JFK pronounced flatly, "and we can't *accept* that." Tomorrow, the president declared, we either add POL to the blockade or "decide to go the other route, the force route." Taylor proposed increasing the pressure by starting night photography, and Bundy suggested convening a working group in the State Department to consider turning up the quarantine. Rusk cautioned that it was essential "to explore the political thing, to be sure that the Soviets have *turned down* these three conditions before we put on the night photography." "Well, that's fair enough," JFK declared. He also instructed that a White House statement be released confirming that work was going forward on the sites—to scotch the impression that the Defense or State Departments were actually calling the shots. Bundy agreed, noting "that the Soviets are saying the U.S. military have taken over at this point."

As the meeting drew to a close, JFK instructed Wilson to drop the photo leaflets over Cuba. He also proposed, citing Dillon's doubts about emphasizing a confrontation at sea rather than the threat in Cuba, "a presentation tomorrow by the Defense Department on air action again. . . . In some ways that's more advantageous than it was even a week ago. I'd like to have us take a look now at whether that can even *be* an option."

Kennedy was becoming less confident that the U.S.S.R. had really "blinked" and was coming under increasing pressure to view Khrushchev's promise to divert ships as a tactical ploy to allow completion of the missile sites. As a result, JFK seemed to be leaning toward breaking the logjam over U.N. negotiations by tightening the quarantine or by bombing the missile bases after all. The ExComm hard-liners, in the wake of the evolving diplomatic stalemate, appeared poised to gain the upper hand.

The meeting dissolved into random conversations as several participants chatted about the planning session at the State Department. JFK switched off the tape recorder.

In the afternoon, ABC News correspondent John Scali met with Soviet embassy public affairs counselor Aleksandr Fomin [his real name was Feklisov] at a Washington restaurant. Fomin, also the KGB chief in Washington, had met with Scali several times in the past, but urgently asked for this meeting. The U.S.S.R., Fomin proposed, might agree to remove the missiles from Cuba, verified by U.N. inspectors, in return for an American commitment not to invade Cuba. Scali reported the discussion to the State Department. Rusk, like Scali, assumed that Fomin was acting on instructions from the Kremlin and perhaps from Khrushchev himself. After getting White House approval, Rusk expressed interest in the scheme but urged Scali to tell Fomin that time was running out. Documents available since the fall of the Soviet Union indicate that Fomin was not speaking for Khrushchev, but a special KGB operation remains a possibility.

At the State Department, an ExComm subcommittee reviewed options for air strikes against the missile sites and the bombers. The JCS, however, urged the president to order more comprehensive strikes. Kennedy also authorized the State Department to move forward on plans to occupy Cuba and establish a civil government after a U.S. invasion. McNamara revealed that Defense Department studies suggested there would be heavy American casualties in an invasion.

Later that day, the National Photographic Interpretation Center confirmed that Soviet technicians were working at top speed to complete the MRBM and IRBM sites. In addition, support equipment used to prepare the missiles for firing had been moved into position near the launchers. Some work appeared to have been done after dark. There were also indications that the U.S.S.R. might be deploying tactical nuclear missiles in Cuba. The Kennedy administration, in fact, never confirmed the presence of these weapons during the crisis. U.S. officials downplayed the likelihood that tactical nuclear weapons would be deployed in Cuba, just as they had discounted the likelihood of MRBMs and IRBMs before October 14. Lundahl, alarmed by this new intelligence, contacted McCone and a private meeting with the president was hastily arranged.

Friday, October 26, around noon, Oval Office

"I'm getting more concerned *all the time*. . . . They've got a *substantial* number of these so they could start at dark and have missiles pointing at us the following morning."

CIA director John McCone

The president was particularly interested in recent Soviet efforts to camouflage the missile sites. "If we hadn't gotten those early pictures," he speculated, "we might'a missed these." The Soviets, he pronounced acidly, "always think *they're* so smart." "Did you see the *London Times*," he asked derisively, "which said we'd misread the pictures?" JFK also seemed intrigued that "you don't see any people" on the sites and asked McCone "to find out what our pilots see themselves," flying at that speed, "compared to what the pictures show." McCone replied, "They don't see very much."

The CIA director did provide some hopeful news: "*I've* concluded it isn't possible to *really* hide these things as we have sometimes thought. They're mobile, but they're not quite as mobile as a tractor-trailer. Furthermore, they're *big*." "This could be fired now?" JFK asked. "No, this can't be fired," McCone explained, before going to the Oval Office door and shouting to Lundahl, waiting with more photos, "Bring all of 'em in, Art."

"We feel there's a *higher* probability of immobilizing these missiles," McCone explained, "*all of them*, with a strike than our thinking has tended in the last few days." But, he admitted, "It won't be *final* because we don't see *all* the missiles for which there are launchers and SAM sites." JFK, thinking as always about Berlin, asked if the U.S. had a missile with a thousand-mile range "that's transportable by plane." Lundahl explained that McNamara had recently made such a claim. "We could," JFK continued, "if we ever had to, fly, say fifteen, into Berlin?" McCone replied confidently, "I think so, yes."

Lundahl can be heard setting up the photo easels. He was obviously gratified when the president recognized a site from previous U-2 photos. "Well, we've got 'em lined up," Kennedy observed, "haven't we?"

"Can one bullet do much to that?" JFK asked, perhaps again pondering a ground attack on the sites. "Well," McCone replied, "if a fella went across there with bullet punctures, it would. It invariably wreaks hell with it." "Would it blow?" the president inquired, and Lundahl explained that fuming red nitric acid in the trucks would be very difficult to contain "if they're opened up."

JFK wondered if the Soviets "may hide *these* pretty quickly." McCone confirmed, "Well, we have evidence that they are"—pointing out additional camouflage details and likely touching on the still unconfirmed presence of Soviet tactical nuclear missiles. President Kennedy asked about the effectiveness of a ground attack on the tactical equipment, and McCone admitted, "No, you couldn't shoot them up." He also estimated that each base had "as many as five hundred personnel on-site with three hundred additional Soviet guards."

As Lundahl noisily gathered his materials and prepared to leave, JFK asked, "What conclusions does this lead you to, John?" McCone, after thanking Lundahl, responded resolutely, "I'm getting more concerned *all the time*. . . . I think that they've got a *substantial* number of these so they could start at dark and have missiles pointing at us the following morning. For that reason, I'm growing increasingly concerned about following a political route unless the initial and *immediate* step is to ensure that these missiles are immobilized by the *physical separation* of the missile . . . from the launcher." "The alternative course," JFK maintained, "is we could do the air strike or an invasion. We still are gonna face the fact that if we invade, by the time we *get* to these sites after a very bloody fight, then they'll be pointing at us. So it still comes down to a question of whether they're gonna fire the missiles." "That's correct," McCone conceded grimly.

The president reiterated pessimistically that diplomacy alone would not get the missiles out, nor would air strikes or an invasion eliminate the possibility "that they might be fired." The CIA director had no easy answers for the commander-in-chief, agreeing that an invasion was going to be "a much more *serious* undertaking than most people realize." The Russians, he observed, have "very lethal stuff" in Cuba—rocket launchers, self-propelled gun carriers, and half-tracks—and will "give an invading force a *pretty bad* time. It would be no cinch by any manner or means." JFK asked if U.S. air control over Cuba would make it possible to "chew those up," but McCone swept aside that premise: "It's *damn* hard to knock out these field pieces." The CIA chief recalled that in World War II and Korea, "where you had *complete* air [supremacy] and [would] go and pound hell out of these gun sites, . . . *they're still there.*"

JFK asked again, "What course of action does this lead you to?" McCone answered unflinchingly, "Well, this would lead me to moving quickly on an air strike." President Kennedy had apparently heard enough and turned off the tape recorder.

The president, as the October 26 meetings suggest, was again leaning towards military action to eliminate the missiles before they could be fired. After the briefing, JFK and Bundy worked out a public statement emphasizing that "there is no evidence to date indicating that there is any intention to dismantle or discontinue work on these missile sites. On the contrary the Soviets are rapidly continuing their construction of missile support and launch facilities, and serious attempts are underway to camouflage their efforts." Operation Mongoose discussions in the Pentagon that afternoon focused on sending Cuban sabotage squads to attack the sites and on setting up a civil government after an invasion.

The U.N. moratorium plan, JFK finally decided, was not acceptable unless the U.S.S.R. suspended arms shipments, ceased construction on the bases, and immobilized the missiles within forty-eight hours. The U.S. would lift the quarantine only after compliance had been independently verified. The president nonetheless followed through on the Ex-Comm agreement to attempt a back-channel diplomatic contact with Castro. The cable to be delivered to Castro by Brazil's ambassador in Havana admonished the Cuban leader that the missiles represented a danger to the survival of Cuba and stressed that the U.S.S.R. was angling to betray Cuba for concessions from NATO. The message concluded with "the seduction" mentioned by Rusk that morning, an assurance that the U.S. would be unlikely to invade if the missiles were removed.

Shortly after 6:00 p.m., a new message from Khrushchev began arriving at the State Department from the U.S. embassy in Moscow. The letter was lengthy, emotional, and personal, and the copy delivered to the embassy included Khrushchev's handwritten notations. State Department and White House officials assumed that the letter was a direct private appeal by the Soviet leader to the president—likely sent without the approval of the Presidium. However, recently declassified documents confirm that Khrushchev had consulted the Central Committee as well as the Presidium before sending the message. This shift in Soviet strategy "had already been approved."

Khrushchev appeared to be offering an olive branch, but his Marxist belief system remained firmly in place: "Everyone needs peace: both capitalists, if they have not lost their reason, and, still more, communists, people who know how to value not only their own lives, but, more than anything, the lives of the people." The Soviet leader argued passionately that the weapons in Cuba were defensive, but no longer denied their presence. The knot of nuclear war could be untied, he proposed, if the Soviet Union ceased sending armaments to Cuba and the United States pledged not to invade. Khrushchev's language was vague, especially on inspection, but his meaning seemed clear: the missiles would be removed if the U.S. promised not to invade Cuba.

Scali met again with Fomin later that evening and relayed a message from Rusk: "I have reason to believe that the [United States] sees real possibilities and supposes that the representatives of the two governments in New York could work this matter out with U Thant and with each other. My impression is, however, that time is very urgent." Fomin rushed off to communicate with the "highest Soviet sources." JFK and the ExComm continued to act on the assumption that Fomin's offer and Khrushchev's message were connected. In fact, Fomin's initial report did not arrive in Moscow until after Khrushchev's letter had been written and delivered to the U.S. embassy.

General Taylor and the JCS, however, rejected the message as a transparent attempt to stall for time while the missile sites were rushed to completion. General LeMay was typically blunt, ridiculing the argument that the missiles were defensive as "a lot of bullshit" and declaring that Khrushchev must believe "we are a bunch of dumb shits, if we swallow that syrup."

In Cuba, Castro received new intelligence that U.S. air strikes and an invasion were only days away. He arrived at the Havana apartment of Soviet ambassador Aleksandr Alekseev in the early morning hours and dictated, in Spanish, an emotional letter to Khrushchev. "The situation is developing in such a way that it's either we or they. If we want to avoid receiving the first strike, if an attack is inevitable, then wipe them off the face of the earth." The U.S.S.R., he further admonished, "must never allow the circumstances in which the imperialists could launch the first nuclear strike against it." Castro seemed to be writing "a last testament—a farewell." Alekseev translated the message into Russian and urgently cabled Moscow.

Saturday, October 27, 10:00 A.M., Cabinet Room

"I think you're gonna have it very difficult to explain why we are
going to take hostile military action in Cuba, against these sites . . .
when he's saying, 'If you get *yours* out of Turkey, we'll get *ours* out
of Cuba.' I think you've got a very tough one here."

President John F. Kennedy

The president turned on the recorder after McCone revealed that most
MRBM sites were operational and the Soviets were installing antiaircraft guns—increasing the danger to American pilots. Also, despite
Khrushchev's statement to U Thant, there was no firm proof that Soviet
ships had changed course. McNamara reported that the *Grozny* was
only six hundred miles from Cuba and steadily approaching the quarantine line.

The president accepted a proposal by Ball to alert U Thant on the
precise location of the blockade so that Soviet ships could be advised
when to turn around safely. McNamara, with McCone's backing,
claimed that pressure was building to take some action and, even
though the *Grozny* was unlikely to be carrying prohibited materials, "I
think we ought to *stop it*, anyhow, and use force if necessary." He also
recommended two extensive low-level surveillance missions later that
day.

Suddenly, JFK interrupted to read aloud a United Press/Associated
Press statement just handed to him: "Premier Khrushchev told President
Kennedy in a message today he would withdraw offensive weapons
from Cuba if the United States withdrew its rockets from Turkey." The
president and the ExComm were clearly startled and puzzled. "He
didn't really say that, did he?" Sorensen recalled. "No, no," Bundy insisted. But JFK speculated, "He may be putting out another letter," and
called in press secretary Pierre Salinger. "I read it pretty carefully,"
Salinger asserted, "and it didn't read that way to me either." "Well,"
the president concluded, "let's just sit tight on it." Rusk asked an aide
to check the news ticker to see whether the message might actually be
the same one Khrushchev had sent the previous evening and pointed out
that "the Turkish thing" had not been raised at the U.N. and "wasn't in
the letter last night." He finally articulated the emerging realization in
the Cabinet Room: "This appears to be something *quite* new."

McNamara and Bundy urged the president to "keep the heat on" by
approving new reconnaissance missions, especially night missions. But,

they both seem to have sensed JFK's doubts—since he waited some six seconds to reply—and each asked if he preferred to hold off the night missions. "I think we ought to go ahead if they want it," the president instructed at first. But, exposing his lingering misgivings, he opted for a delay after all: "I think we might have one more conversation about it . . . just in case during the day we get something that's important." The defense chief, in an unusually reassuring tone of voice, declared, "Plenty of time. We'll keep it on alert," and, along with Bundy, endorsed postponing a formal announcement. Lyndon Johnson asked if night missions required flares, and McNamara replied, "Yes, it does, Mr. Vice President."

Rusk, only moments before, had asserted that Khrushchev's reported proposal to swap missiles in Turkey and Cuba was something new. In fact, President Kennedy had been probing that option for more than a week, and in light of Khrushchev's new public announcement asked, "where are we with our conversations with the Turks?" Nitze responded firmly, "The Turks say that this is *absolutely* anathema" and view it "as a matter of prestige and politics." Ball pointed out that the Jupiter deployment had been a NATO decision. JFK understood the world of prestige and politics as well as anyone in the room, but nonetheless told Nitze, "Well, I don't think we can" take that position "if this is an *accurate* [report]."

Bundy argued that if Khrushchev had backed away from the "purely Cuban context" in last night's letter, "There's nothing wrong with our posture in sticking to that line." "Well maybe they changed it overnight," JFK persisted. "He's in a difficult position to change it overnight," Bundy reasoned, "having sent *you* a personal communication on the other line." "Well now, let's say he *has* changed it," JFK snapped, "and this is his latest position." "Well, I would answer back," Bundy retorted testily, "saying that 'I would prefer to deal with your interesting proposals of last night.'" Someone egged Bundy on, whispering, "Go for it!"

President Kennedy's reply represents a turning point in the discussions—leaving no doubt about his evolving position: "Well now, that's what we oughta be thinkin' about. We're gonna be in an *insupportable* position on this matter if this becomes his proposal. In the first place, we last year tried to get the missiles out of there because they're not militarily useful, number one. Number two, it's gonna—to any man at the United Nations or any other *rational* man, it will look like a very fair trade." "I don't think so," Nitze countered, as someone muttered

"No, no, no" in the background. "Deal with this Cuban thing. We'll talk about other things later."

Salinger brought in a news ticker report which JFK read aloud, confirming Khrushchev's new public offer to link the missiles in Cuba and Turkey. "Now we've known this might be coming for a week," Kennedy asserted impatiently, "*This* is their proposal." "How much negotiation have we had with the Turks this week?" JFK grumbled again, "Who's done it?" "We haven't talked with the Turks," Rusk tried to explain, "The Turks have talked with us." "Where have they talked with us?" JFK demanded. "In NATO," Rusk replied. "I've talked about it now for a week," the president protested again. "Have we got any conversations *in Turkey* with the Turks?" Rusk reiterated, "We've not actually talked with the Turks."

Ball declared that approaching the Turks on withdrawing the Jupiters "would be an *extremely* unsettling business." "Well," JFK barked, "*this* is unsettling *now* George, because he's got us in a pretty good spot here. Because most people will regard this as not an *unreasonable* proposal. I'll just tell you *that*." "But, what '*most* people,' Mr. President?" Bundy asked skeptically. The president shot back: "I think you're gonna have it very difficult to explain why we are going to take hostile military action in Cuba . . . when he's saying, 'If you get *yours* out of Turkey, we'll get *ours* out of Cuba.' I think you've got a very tough one here." "I don't see why we pick *that track*," Bundy repeated, "when he's offered us the other track in the last twenty-four hours." JFK interrupted irritably, "Well he's *now* offered us a new one! . . . I think we have to assume that this is their *new* and *latest* position, and it's a *public* one."

Ball and Bundy suggested pulling the rug out from under Khrushchev by releasing his private October 26 letter. "Yeah, but I think we have to," the president countered, not quite suppressing an exasperated laugh, "be now thinking about what our position's gonna be on *this* one, because this is the one that's *before* us and *before* the world." Sorensen speculated that "practically everyone here would favor the secret proposal," but JFK pointed out that the Friday offer also had "serious disadvantages . . . which is this guarantee of Cuba [against invasion]." But, he reiterated, "this is *now* his official one. We can release his other one, and it's different, but this is the one that the Soviet government obviously is going on."

Nitze tried to shake the president's determination by suggesting that the Soviets might be pursuing a private track with Cuba and a public track with the U.S. "to confuse the public scene and divide us." JFK readily admitted, "It's possible." The opponents of the trade refused to back down. "They've got hundreds of missiles looking down the throat of every NATO country," Rusk argued; "The Cuba thing is a Western Hemisphere problem." Nitze warned against linking Cuba and Turkey, and Bundy chimed in, "if we *accept* the notion of the trade at this stage, our position will come apart very fast." Ball cautioned that any discussion with the Turks would inevitably leak and undermine American credibility. "If we had talked to the Turks," Bundy lectured, "it would *already* be clear that we were trying to sell our allies for our interests. That would be the view in all of NATO. Now it's *irrational* and it's *crazy*, but it's a *terribly powerful fact*." Ambassador Thompson urged the president to instruct Stevenson at the U.N. to say that "we will not discuss the Turkish bases." "The problem is *Cuba*," Bundy contended; "The Turks are not a threat to the peace."

President Kennedy brushed aside Thompson's proposal and instructed instead that Stevenson should try to get clarification of this new Soviet proposal: "As I say, you're going to find a lot of people thinking this is rather a reasonable position." "That's true," Bundy admitted, and JFK advised, "Let's not kid ourselves." At least until Soviet intentions had been spelled out, the president concluded, "we ought to go with this last night's business" and not get bogged down about Turkey until Khrushchev's new offer has been officially received. "Okay," Bundy replied, and Rusk added, "There's nothing coming in *yet* on our tickers." Thompson wondered if Khrushchev might have mistakenly concluded that Austrian foreign minister Bruno Kreisky's October 25 speech proposing a Cuba-Turkey trade had been "inspired by *us*." Perhaps, McCone suggested suspiciously, "the Russians got Kreisky to do it."

JFK, after talking briefly with Rusk, temporarily left the meeting. Robert Kennedy soon cut in, insisting that the missiles in Cuba had nothing to do with NATO. But, he nonetheless conceded, "*We* would obviously consider negotiating the giving up of bases in Turkey" if NATO's security could be guaranteed. Perhaps, he speculated, an agreement might include inspection in Cuba and "assurances that we are not going to invade . . . Something along those lines."

The informal conversation that continued, with the president still out of the room, exposed the depth of ExComm hostility to a Cuba-Turkey link. Ball reported that Stevenson had called to say that the U.S. delegation at the U.N. wanted "to keep it strictly separate—keep the Turkey business out." "We must insist," Rusk demanded, "that *U Thant* not fall for this." RFK still had doubts as well: "I don't see how we can ask the Turks to give up their defense" unless the Soviets give up their weapons aimed at Turkey—and, McNamara added, "agree not to invade Turkey" and to permit inspections. RFK declared that the United States would "feel that this is a *major* breakthrough and we would be glad to discuss that." But, he contended, the first order of business was the removal of the threat to the U.S. and Latin America from the missiles in Cuba.

The discussion returned to whether to release Khrushchev's October 26 letter: Ball seemed reluctant to make public a secret message between heads of state for the first time and Thompson asserted, with Bundy's backing, "I would *not* release this." "Attack this Turkish thing *hard*," Nitze interjected abruptly. "It's an *entirely* separate situation." Bundy and Taylor, backed by McNamara and Gilpatric, agreed that the U.S. should not be diverted from the real issues: halting construction on the bases and the inoperability and removal of the missiles.

Rusk was handed copies of the new public message from Moscow— just as the president returned to his seat—and read aloud Khrushchev's new public offer: "I propose that we agree to remove from Cuba the means which you consider aggressive. Your representatives will then remove analogous means from Turkey." McNamara reacted incredulously, asking "Dean, how do you interpret the addition of still another condition over and above the letter that came in last night? We had one *deal* in the letter, now we've got a different deal." "And in *public*," Taylor declared. "I suppose," Rusk speculated, "the boys in Moscow decided this [Friday proposal] was too much of a setback for 'em." "How can we negotiate," McNamara repeated angrily, "with somebody who changes his deal before we even get a chance to reply and *announces publicly* the deal before we receive it?" "I think there must have been an overruling in Moscow," Bundy conjectured.

Rusk guessed that the personal Friday night letter had been sent "without clearance," and a consensus quickly developed that "The Politburo intended *this one*." "*This* should be knocked down publicly," Bundy demanded. "*Privately* we say to Khrushchev: '*Look*, your public statement is a very *dangerous* one because it makes *impossible* immediate discussion of your *private* proposals and requires us to proceed urgently with the things that we have in mind. You'd *better* get straightened out!'" McCone, backed by several others, affirmed, "This is exactly right!"

Bundy still resisted releasing Khrushchev's Friday letter, but suggested a subtle threat: "We say, 'we are reluctant to release this letter which displayed the inconsistency in your position, but we don't have very much time.'" RFK, however, questioned the wisdom of publicly exposing Khrushchev's flip-flop: "What is the advantage? . . . *He's* gonna have a ploy publicly that's gonna look rather satisfactory, as the president says. How are we going to *have him* do anything but take the ball away from us publicly if we don't agree?" McNamara responded firmly, "Just turn it down publicly," but the attorney general replied, "Yeah, but I think that's *awful tough*." McCone pointed out that a public rejection would also require revealing Khrushchev's October 26 proposal.

RFK, thinking out loud, proposed combining the removal and inspection of the Cuban missile bases with an American non-invasion pledge and U.N. inspections in the U.S. "to ensure that we're not getting ready to invade." He also suggested linking the withdrawal of the Turkish Jupiters to a Soviet guarantee to stand down its bases for invading Turkey, backed up by inspections in Turkey and the U.S.S.R. "I think it's *too* complicated, Bobby," Bundy protested, but RFK snapped, "Well, *I* don't think it is!"

The president, convinced that Khrushchev's public letter had made discussion of the Turkish missiles unavoidable, spoke up for the first time since rejoining the meeting: "It seems to me, the *first* thing we oughta try to do is not let the Turks issue some statement which is wholly unacceptable"—i.e., rejecting Khrushchev's offer. He reiterated that work on the missile sites had to stop "before we talk about *anything*. At least then we're in a defensible position." But, JFK repeated, "We gotta have a talk with the Turks because I think they've got to understand the *peril* that they're going to move into next week if we take some action in Cuba. I think the chances are that he'll take some action in Turkey. They oughta *understand* that."

Ball, Rusk, and Taylor defended the right of the Turks to say that NATO military arrangements have nothing to do with Cuba. "It seems to me," Bundy insisted, "it's important that they *should*. If anyone pulls them in it will be us, and they *can't* be expected to do *that*." "No, but we want to give 'em some guidance," the president countered stubbornly; "These are *American* missiles, not *Turkish* missiles. They're under *American* control, not *Turkish* control." McNamara and Taylor, however, made clear that the missiles belonged to Turkey and the warheads, although in U.S. custody, were committed to NATO. "In other words,"

JFK observed grudgingly, "we couldn't withdraw the missiles anyway, could we? They belong to the Turks. All we could withdraw is the warheads?" McNamara explained that the president could only remove the warheads in accordance with NATO nuclear policy procedures.

President Kennedy nonetheless remained determined to restrain the Turks "until we've had a chance to think a little more about it." But, he cautioned, "We *cannot* permit ourselves to be *impaled* on a long negotiating hook while the work goes on on these bases." If the UN can arrange "for cessation of the work," he maintained, "*then* we can talk about *all* these matters, which are *very* complicated."

"The current threat to peace is *not* in Turkey," Bundy reiterated firmly, "it is in *Cuba*." "Let's not kid ourselves," JFK reaffirmed, "They've got a *very good* proposal, which is the reason they've made it public." Bundy explained that a consensus had developed during the president's brief absence: the Friday message was written by Khrushchev, but the Saturday public message reflected "his own hard-nosed people overruling him. . . . They didn't like what he said to you last night." "Nor would I," Bundy added colorfully, "if I were a Soviet hardnose." Thompson repeated that the Soviets might have interpreted the Kreisky speech as "*our* underground way of suggesting this."

President Kennedy, nonetheless, underscored again that the public offer could not be ignored: "the fact that work is going on is the one *defensible* public position we've got. They've got a very good prod and this one is gonna be *very tough*, I think, for us. It's gonna be tough in England, I'm sure, as well as other places on the continent." An attack on Cuba would give the U.S.S.R "not a blank check but a pretty good check to take action in Berlin on the grounds that we are *wholly* unreasonable. Most people will think this is a rather even trade and we ought to take *advantage* of it."

But rapid-fire criticism of the president's stance continued. Dillon argued that Khrushchev's reference to U.S. bases surrounding the U.S.S.R. could apply to countries other than Turkey. "That was propaganda," the president countered dismissively. "The *direct* trade is suggested with Turkey." Thompson warned that the phrase "the means which you consider aggressive" could also include planes and technicians; Bundy speculated that Khrushchev might demand a missile-for-missile trade, "which wouldn't be good enough from our point of view" because there are more missiles in Cuba than in Turkey. "But the problem," JFK contended again, "is to get work on their bases stopped. That's, in my opinion, *our* defensible position."

McNamara shot back: "It isn't enough to stop work on a base that's already operable," and Nitze insisted that hesitating over the differences in Khrushchev's messages "looks to the public as though *we're* confused. . . . I think we've got to take a *firmer* line than that." Bundy agreed: "*I myself* would send back word by [Aleksandr] Fomin, for example, that last night's stuff was pretty good. . . . If they want to stop something further in Cuba they have to do better than *this* public statement." JFK abruptly sidetracked the increasingly contentious discussion by asking to have a call placed to Ambassador Stevenson at the U.N.

The president, waiting for the connection to New York, asked how many Soviet missiles "may be facing Turkey." Nitze estimated one hundred—compared to fifteen Jupiters in Turkey. But, McNamara added, "we have a lot of planes with nuclear weapons. Those are the 'analogous weapons' he's speaking of here." Evelyn Lincoln interrupted to say that Stevenson was on the line. The tape picked up only JFK's part of the conversation—while several ExComm members whispered quietly in the background. President Kennedy, on the phone for several minutes, asked for Stevenson's judgment about Khrushchev's last two messages and asserted, "What we gotta do is get them to agree to stop work while we talk about *all* these proposals."

After hanging up, perhaps prompted by something Stevenson said, JFK alluded to Soviet pressure for a U.S. pledge not to invade Cuba and exclaimed with a chuckle, "What about our putting something in about Berlin? . . . just to try to put some sand in *his* gears for a few minutes." "In what way?" Bundy inquired, apparently puzzled. The president responded sharply, "*Well, satisfactory guarantees for Berlin!*" But, he promptly conceded, "which he's not gonna give. I'm just tryin' to think of what the public problem is about this . . . because everybody's gonna think this [offer] is *very* reasonable."

"Who has talked to the Turks?" JFK pressed again. Dillon, perhaps momentarily reconsidering the missile trade, speculated "that the Turkish proposal opens the way to a *major* discussion of relaxed tensions in Europe, including Berlin." Nitze strenuously objected, "Oh, no, no, no, no, no, no! . . . If you mention that, you've lost the Germans." "That's right," McCone declared. "Right then and there," Nitze reaffirmed.

The recording suddenly cut off—probably because the backup recorder ran out of tape. Alexis Johnson, according to the minutes, re-

ported that the Turks, as expected, had publicly denounced the Soviet scheme to remove the Jupiters. RFK, still ambivalent about a missile trade, demanded "that we make doubly clear that Turkish NATO missiles were one problem and that Cuba was an entirely separate problem." Gilpatric argued that the U.S. could not negotiate "while the Soviet missile threat is growing in Cuba."

The president did not retreat: "We are now in a position of risking war in Cuba and in Berlin over missiles in Turkey which are of little military value. . . . We are in a bad position if we appear to be attacking Cuba for the purpose of keeping useless missiles in Turkey." The Turks, he maintained, must understand the dangers they face, "and we have to face up to the possibility of some kind of a trade over missiles." JFK soon left to meet with a delegation of state governors. RFK speculated that talks with the Soviets could drag on for weeks or months while the Cubans refused to allow inspections to verify that the missiles were inoperable—but, he added with obvious interest, "we could then decide to attack the bases by air." Several ExComm members agreed to meet at the State Department without the president at 2:30, before reconvening in the Cabinet Room at 4:00 p.m.

Just before leaving for the State Department meeting, McNamara learned that the morning U-2 flight over Cuba was more than thirty minutes overdue. The small meeting focused again on eliminating the missile bases. RFK recommended allowing Soviet tankers to pass through the quarantine line: "if we attack a Soviet tanker, the balloon would go up." Instead, he again urged preparation for air attacks on the missiles. McNamara revived the idea of issuing a warning before air strikes. As they were about to leave for the 4:00 p.m. meeting with the president, McNamara learned that the U-2 was still missing and that the low-level missions had been fired on over Cuba.

JFK greeted the Civil Defense Committee of the Governor's Conference cordially, but several participants later recalled that he seemed "unusually somber and harried." California's Edmund Brown, a Democrat, asked bluntly, "Mr. President, many people wonder why you changed your mind about the Bay of Pigs and aborted the attack. Will you change your mind again?" "I chose the quarantine," Kennedy retorted harshly, "because I wondered if our people are ready for the bomb."

A report soon arrived that a U-2 from a SAC base in Alaska, presumably on a "routine air-sampling mission" to check on nuclear testing, had accidentally strayed into Soviet air space. MiGs scrambled to *intercept, but no shots were fired and the plane returned to base escorted by U.S. fighters equipped with nuclear air-to-air missiles. McNamara reportedly shouted when informed, "This means war with the Soviet Union!" But the president, with classic gallows humor, joked, "There is always some son-of-a-bitch who doesn't get the word."*

Meanwhile, Castro's cable from Havana, which would not be declassified for decades, reached the Kremlin. "It became clear to us that Fidel totally failed to understand our purpose," Khrushchev later wrote, clearly horrified by Castro's apocalyptic tone. "Is he proposing that we start a nuclear war?" he asked his son Sergei. "This is insane. We deployed missiles there to prevent an attack on the island, to save Cuba and defend socialism. And now not only is he preparing to die himself, he wants to drag us with him." Khrushchev, in his message to Kennedy the previous evening, before receiving Castro's cable, had already been thinking about people in Washington, Moscow, or Havana who might be tempted to deliberately unleash a nuclear war: "Only lunatics or suicides, who themselves want to perish and to destroy the whole world before they die, could do this."

Later Khrushchev replied to his Cuban ally, "You proposed that we be the first to carry out a nuclear strike against the territory of the enemy. You, of course, realize where that would have led. Rather than a simple strike, it would have been the start of a thermonuclear world war. Dear Comrade Fidel Castro, I consider this proposal of yours incorrect, although I understand your motivation. . . . We struggle against imperialism, not in order to die, but to . . . achieve the victory of communism." Castro's appeal for a nuclear first strike "may well have influenced Khrushchev's decision to proceed with a settlement with the United States."

Saturday, October 27, 4:00 P.M., Cabinet Room

"I just tell you, I think we're better off to get those missiles out of Turkey and out of Cuba because I think the way of getting 'em *out* of Turkey and *out* of Cuba is gonna be *very, very* difficult and *very* bloody, one place or another."

President John F. Kennedy

Kennedy switched on the recorder as McNamara and Taylor explained that low-level reconnaissance flights had been forced to turn back by apparent Cuban ground fire. "Mr. President," Rusk insisted, "we're gonna have to make a decision later today as to what we do about *that*." "Well," JFK replied, "we better wait till we hear more about *why* they aborted it." McNamara pushed for initiating night missions and Donald Wilson suggested Voice of America radio broadcasts in Spanish to explain to the Cubans that the flares for night photos were harmless. "I don't know whether tonight's the night to do it," JFK responded, and Taylor advised evaluating "the technique before we let them go." "I think we'd better wait," the president finally decided, "till we find out what happened to these planes before we put this out about tonight."

McNamara disclosed that one mission had been aborted because of mechanical failure and another for unknown reasons, and, sensing JFK's uneasiness, added, "We don't have to *do* it tonight. . . . I don't see we're committed to it." "What he was gonna do," RFK explained, "the night that you *do* it, he [Wilson] was gonna *tell* people in more *detail* about it." "Okay," JFK agreed.

The conversation then returned to drafting the president's response to Khrushchev's last two letters, focusing initially on linking assurances against invading Cuba to a commitment from the Cubans not to support aggression in Latin America. "I mean, all bets are *off* on this, I would think," RFK declared stubbornly, if Cuba supplies arms to Latin American insurgents. The president objected to RFK's tough "the bets [are] off" wording: "I don't think we can use *this* language." He instead proposed softer language: "'As I was preparing this letter, which was prepared in response to your private letter of last night, I learned of your [new message].'" After a cessation of work in Cuba, "'I shall *certainly* be ready to discuss the matters you mentioned in your *public* message.' You see," he pointed out, "that's more forthcoming." But, he added bleakly, "This isn't gonna be successful. We might as well realize *that*."

JFK nonetheless reasoned that if the U.S. rebuffed Khrushchev on Turkey, "then where are we gonna be?" The cessation of work issue, he repeated, is "the only place *we've got him*. . . . Otherwise he's going to announce that we've rejected his proposal." Kennedy paused dramatically for some six seconds before reiterating darkly, "And then where are we? . . . I think our message oughta be that we're glad to discuss this [Turkey] and other matters, but we've gotta get a cessation of work." "And the dismantling of the bases," RFK added pointedly.

Ball revealed that Ambassador Zorin had told U Thant that Khrushchev's private Friday letter had been "designed to reduce tension but so far as *he* was concerned," the public Saturday message, just as the president had argued, "contained the substantive proposal." JFK proposed putting pressure on U Thant that afternoon. "We oughta make it a *formal* request, I think, George," and he dictated specific wording: "'If we're going to discuss *these* [issues with NATO] we must have *some* assurances which can be *verified* that the Soviet Union will cease work on the missiles and that the missiles which are presently there have been made inoperable. Would the secretary general get from the Soviet Union these assurances? In that case, the United States would be prepared to discuss any proposals of the Soviet Union.'" RFK, convinced that the reference to consulting NATO would reassure the Turks, advised, "Jack, it would be well to get that out pretty quickly . . . so that the Turkey thing isn't a big story."

Bundy disclosed that Ambassador Bohlen in Paris reported that rejecting a Turkey-Cuba link was well received in France, and Rusk candidly expressed hope for "a revolt in NATO" against removing the Jupiters from Turkey. Bundy also revealed, despite the president's determined pressure to start talks with the Turks, that he had instructed Ambassador Finletter to tell NATO that the U.S. *opposed* involving Turkey in a Cuban settlement. Finletter had been authorized, however, to listen if NATO felt that this decision exposed the alliance to an "unusual hazard." JFK did not comment.

At that moment, General Taylor received an update confirming reports that at least one of eight low-level reconnaissance planes had been fired on over Cuba. Rusk probed immediately: "fired on by what?" and Taylor replied, "Presumably low-level ack-ack [antiaircraft]—that's the only thing that could fire." Everyone in the room understood the grim implications—the first shots of the Cuban missile crisis had likely been fired. The president, clearly troubled by this development, asked if reconnaissance missions were scheduled for that night. He seemed more reluctant than ever to give the order for night flights: "Just have it ready," he counseled after further discussion. "I just think we might have one more conversation about the details of this firing on. . . . We may wanna do something else."

Rusk then brought up the even more alarming report that a U-2 had crossed into Soviet air space near Alaska. There appears to be more to this episode than first meets the ear: the secretary of state, reading from a prepared text, proposed a step-by-step scenario to explain the incident. His reference to a possible "advantage" in this explanation also hints that he was proposing a cover story: "Now they will probably be making a big blast out of that in the next day or so," Rusk warned. "The question would be would there be any advantage in our saying that [begins reading] 'an Alaska-based U-2 flight engaged in routine air-sampling operations in an area normally one hundred miles from the Soviet Union had an instrument failure and went off course. Efforts by ground stations and our aircraft to recall it to its course did not succeed in time to prevent it from overflying a portion of the Soviet Union.' [stops reading] Now, whether we should leave the..."

President Kennedy interrupted and argued for toughing it out without an official explanation: "I don't feel there's any advantage now. It just gives him a story tomorrow and it makes it look like we're maybe the offenders." Khrushchev, in his letter the next day, took the U-2 incident *very* seriously: "One asks, Mr. President, how should we regard this? ... An intruding American aircraft can easily be taken for a bomber with nuclear weapons, and this could push us toward a fatal step."

McNamara then jolted the meeting again—confirming that the plane fired on over Cuba had been "hit by a 37-millimeter shell. It's coming back. It's all right, but it simply indicates that there's *quite a change* in the character of the orders given to the Cuban defenders." Two days before, he had reported that the Soviets had instructed the Cubans not to fire on U.S. aircraft. In this new situation, he advised against further escalating tensions by disclosing the Alaska U-2 overflight. The president agreed, "Let's let it go."

Rusk returned to the draft of the proposed letter from JFK to Khrushchev about U.N. negotiating proposals. "Now that they've taken a public position," Kennedy reiterated, "I think we ought to put our emphasis, *right now*, on the fact that we want an indication from him in the next twenty-four hours that he's gonna stand still and disarm these weapons. Then we'll say, that under *those* conditions, we'll be *glad* to discuss these matters. But I think that if we *don't* say that, he's gonna say that we *rejected* his offer and therefore he's gonna have public opinion with *him*."

The president then read the draft message to U Thant aloud and asked, "Does anybody object to that?" "Well," Ball protested, "the only question I'd like to raise about that is that that *really* injects Turkey as a quid pro quo for a..." "That's my worry about it," Bundy broke in. "*No! With negotiations!*" JFK countered testily. The problem, he repeated calmly, was to keep all viable options open: "We have to wait and see what the Turks say. We don't want the Soviet Union or the United Nations to be able to say that the United States *rejected it*. So I think," he concluded impatiently, "we're *better off* to stick on the question of the *freeze* and *then* we'll discuss it. I don't think we..."

Bundy cut the president off with a stinging dissent: "I think if we *sound* as if we wanted to make this trade to our NATO people and to all the people who are tied to us by *alliance*, we are in *real trouble.*" The national security adviser admonished the commander-in-chief: "I think that we'll *all* join in doing this if this is the decision. But I think we *should* tell you that that's the *universal* assessment of everyone in the government that's connected with these alliance problems." He repeated that Ambassadors Finletter and Hare felt strongly that if the U.S. appeared to be trading away the defense of Turkey, "we just *have* to face a *radical* decline" in NATO.

President Kennedy, addressing Bundy as "Mac," nonetheless repeated doggedly, "this trade has *appeal.* Now, if we *reject* it out of hand, and then have to take military action against Cuba, then we'll *also* face a decline" in NATO and in support around the world. He conceded that it was worth trying "to word it so that we don't harm NATO. But the thing that I think *everybody* would agree to is that while these matters, which are complicated, *are* discussed, there should be a cessation of work. Then I think we can *hold* general support for that. If they won't agree to *that*, the Soviet Union, then *we* retain some initiative. That's my response." JFK soon left the meeting to take a call from the NATO supreme commander, General Lauris Norstad.

In the president's stead, RFK argued that the public would think Khrushchev's offer is "quite reasonable. . . . Therefore we just can't out of hand *reject* this . . . and [if] after twenty-four hours we go and make a *bombing* attack, we're going to be in tough shape." The attorney general, however, added his own caveat—"But on the other hand, if we offer them something that they're not gonna accept anyway," such as placing U.N. personnel on the missile sites, "then we're in much better shape throughout the world to go ahead and take whatever [military] steps are necessary." But, RFK stressed, the president's purpose was to "take the initiative away" from the U.S.S.R.

Another version of the draft letter to Khrushchev was cobbled together during several more minutes of give and take on U.S. conditions for negotiations. McNamara, Rusk, Bundy, and Dillon expressed concern that the Soviets might also seek to negotiate removing U.S. bases from Italy and England. Sorensen suggested that Khrushchev had not mentioned bases other than in Turkey; but McNamara, backed by Dillon, replied forcefully, "Oh, he *certainly* did. *Yes,* he did." Bundy also repeated, *"Yes, he did."* Rusk finally exclaimed, "I wonder if this would get us one inch farther," and then read aloud from his updated draft of the message to Khrushchev. McNamara defended the president's reluctance "to turn down a proposal which some people in the world would think was a reasonable proposal," but surmised that JFK *really* "wanted to turn it down. He wanted to *defer* consideration of it, but do it with a good excuse, which was that they hadn't *yet* given us this assurance [on cessation of work]."

RFK, torn between his own combative instincts and his fierce loyalty to the president, pointed out, "Tommy brings up the point" about whether Khrushchev's Saturday message "blows the whole" proposal in the Friday letter. Ambassador Thompson, ExComm's acknowledged "authority" on the Soviet Union, took the cue, contending that Khrushchev's Friday letter "made this proposal that the whole problem's raised by our threat to Cuba and we're prepared to remove that threat [with a non-invasion pledge]. This point [about Turkey] undercuts that effort *entirely*." "For one or two reasons," Thompson deduced, "they've changed their minds on this. One was that they may have picked up this Kreisky thing and thought they could *get* more. The other was Khrushchev may have been overruled. In *either* case, we've gotta *change* that, which means we have to take a tough line."

Rusk urged giving U Thant some more time "to work on the original [Friday] track if possible," but Dillon noted pessimistically that since the firing on the reconnaissance plane, "we haven't got but one more day." Bundy observed bluntly, "Turkey and Cuba is *not* workable for us except in the context of our doing a violent thing. And if we've done a violent thing," the usually self-assured national security adviser admitted, "none of us know *where* to go. The one chance of avoiding that is to impress Khrushchev and get him back where he was last night." Alexis Johnson concurred: "We have to operate on Khrushchev's public warning using a carrot and a stick," and Thompson questioned the president's wisdom in "changing our whole policy for a public relations aspect."

Vice President Lyndon Johnson, who had attended several meetings but had rarely spoken up, particularly if JFK was present, essentially backed the president's position and urged telling Khrushchev that the U.S. would be willing to discuss the security of NATO "as soon as the present Soviet-created threat [in Cuba] has ended." "There it is! That's the proposal to 'em," LBJ asserted, "sayin' we *can* and *will* just as soon as you get rid of these bases." "Well, I see no reason," Bundy interrupted, "why a private message to the chairman shouldn't be a touch more forthcoming," and suggested instead telling Khrushchev, "We understand your sensitivity on this matter but right now we can't get *at this* until we get past the Cuba problem." RFK reminded his colleagues that the Soviet offer, to the man in the street, "is *very* reasonable, and we just turned it down." "We didn't turn it down," LBJ responded irritably; "This says we'll *continue* [talking about Turkey]," he rapped the table, "soon as you stop the work."

As the president rejoined the meeting, RFK quipped, "We really cut it up while you've been out of the room," and JFK, as several people chuckled, asked to read the new draft. Thompson, however, undaunted in opposing the Turkish plan, counseled the president: "you're gonna end up with Soviet control of Cuba..." Bundy also put his own tough spin on the reply to Khrushchev: "The justification for *this* message is that we expect it to be turned down, expect to be acting [militarily] tomorrow or the next day. That's what it's for, and it's *not* good unless that's what happens." Several voices can be heard affirming, "That's right."

Rusk, however, was unsure whether the Turkish scheme was "a *real* sticking point up to the point of shooting with them" or merely "an attempt at the last minute to try to get something *more* after they had indicated last night they will settle for something *less*." RFK endorsed asking U Thant to find out if the Soviets would agree that "work will stop on the missile bases and the missiles remain inoperative under United Nations supervision" during discussions of the messages of the last thirty-six hours. Bundy too proposed "holding him [Khrushchev] to last night while we do this." Several voices affirmed, "Yes," as Bundy concluded, "That's the pattern that would make sense to me."

Bundy, concerned about the evolving diplomatic impasse, pressed McNamara: "What's your military plan?" The defense chief replied unflinchingly, "the military plan now is *very* clear. A limited strike is out"—because aircraft have been fired on. "So the military plan now is *basically* invasion." But, McNamara cautioned, the administration should first try to "minimize the Soviet response against NATO" by alerting the U.S.S.R., *before* air attacks in Cuba, that the Jupiter missiles in Turkey had been rendered inoperable. "Now, on *that* basis," he reasoned, "I *don't* believe the Soviets would strike Turkey."

Rusk, however, raised the threat discussed since the first meeting: the Soviets "might then aim their action at Berlin." McNamara conceded, "They might," and admitted, "I'm not prepared *at this moment* to recommend air attacks on Cuba. I'm just saying that I think we must now begin to look at it more realistically than we have before." Thompson seemed skeptical that the U.S. could replace the Jupiters with submarine-launched Polaris missiles in just twenty-four hours, but the defense secretary insisted, "Oh yes, we can." "If you advertise the Polaris *publicly* as a substitute," Ball noted doubtfully, "then from the point of view of the Soviet Union they've achieved nothing by getting rid of the Jupiters." "But they *sure have less* of a basis for striking Turkey," McNamara retorted, and Ball acknowledged, "Yes, you minimize Turkey as a target."

The wording of JFK's message to U Thant was finalized after a bit more tinkering, and Rusk suggested dictating it over the phone and then releasing it. "Right. Very good," the president agreed. Ball advised calling Stevenson right away, and JFK instructed, "We'll put it out at 6:00, tell him."

Despite the stubborn maneuvering against a Cuba-Turkey trade, especially during his brief absence, JFK quickly put the Turkish option on the fast track. He reported that General Norstad had recommended convening the NATO Council [NAC] to consider the trade, "so that they all have a piece of it. Otherwise, no matter what we do—if we don't take it we're gonna be blamed; if we do take it we're gonna be blamed." "I think," JFK observed, "he's very right." NATO must understand the consequences of rejecting this deal, "Otherwise, it's too easy to say, 'well, let's not take it then.'" The president directed that Ambassador Finletter call a NATO Council meeting the next morning.

RFK again voiced his persistent doubts: the NAC meeting, he muttered, "blows the possibility of this other one, of course, doesn't it?" "Of what?" JFK replied impatiently. "Of getting an acceptance of the [Friday] proposal," RFK insisted. "The *advantage* of the meeting," the president reiterated sharply, "*is* that if we *reject* it [the Turkey deal], they've participated in it. And, if we *accept* it, they've participated in it." "The other possibility," RFK added, "is if you wait twenty-four hours" to see if the Soviets accept the positive reply to Khrushchev's October 26 offer. But, the attorney general admitted, "they won't . . . they're not gonna accept it, yeah."

Ball, backed by Bundy, also urged sticking to the Friday offer in case the public message on Turkey and Cuba "was simply a kind of fishing expedition in Moscow" to see if they could get more. Rusk proposed new language for JFK's message to Khrushchev: "As I was preparing this letter," he read, "I learned of your broadcast message today. That

message raises problems affecting many countries and complicated issues not related to Cuba or the Western Hemisphere." After the crisis
in Cuba is resolved, "we can make progress on other and wider issues."

President Kennedy recognized immediately that Rusk's wording did
not reflect his persistent stance on pursuing a Turkey-Cuba trade—his
advisers appeared to be trying a rather transparent end run around his
position. "Well, isn't that really rejecting their proposal of this morning?" JFK countered impatiently. "I don't think so," Bundy replied,
supported by Rusk. "It's rejecting the *immediate* tie-in [on Turkey],"
Dillon affirmed, "But, we've *got* to do that." "We're *not* rejecting the
tie-in," President Kennedy responded forcefully. "If we go reject it, I
think we ought to have all of NATO rejecting it. What *we* want to insist on now is a cessation of work, etc., while we *discuss* it."

If the NAC meets, Ball predicted, "I think you're gonna get a *flat* rejection of this, which then ties our hands." He also reported that the
NATO-member ambassadors to the U.N. had taken "a *very* strong line
against any discussion of this." "I don't think," the president replied
stubbornly, "the *alternative* has been explained to them"—they don't
realize that Soviet reprisals will be against NATO. "I'd like to have
them have *that* before they reject it." Dillon predicted pensively that
NATO would say, "'*Don't trade*,' but they'd also say, '*Don't* do anything in Cuba!'—which may well be right."

McNamara contended again that the Soviets were likely to strike the
Jupiter missiles in Turkey if the U.S. bombed or invaded Cuba. But, he
reasoned, if the Jupiters in Turkey and Italy were replaced by Polaris
missiles, the Soviets would have no reason to attack Turkey or Italy,
and the U.S. would be "in a *much* better position to present this whole
thing to NATO." What if the Soviets announced, Ball asked abruptly,
that "they were going to deploy atomic missile–carrying submarines off
the United States coast?" McNamara, almost casually, confirmed that
three Soviet submarines had *already* been detected off the coast, but,
"as far as we know, they don't carry missiles." (He learned nearly four
decades later that Soviet submarines near Cuba each carried a nuclear-
tipped torpedo capable of destroying an aircraft carrier.)

This disquieting exchange prompted President Kennedy to point out
again that if the U.S. withdrew the Jupiters, "we'd get the trade the
Russians have offered us." Bundy firmly disagreed: "It's one thing to
stand them down as a favor to the Turks while we hit Cuba; it's quite
another thing to trade them out, I think." McNamara repeated that if

the Jupiters were defused the U.S. could tell the Soviet Union that the threat from Turkey was gone, and might get Khrushchev back to his Friday proposal. Bundy and Dillon predicted that the Soviets would also demand withdrawing missiles from Italy and England, and RFK advised delaying the NAC meeting to pressure Khrushchev, so that "We don't look like we're weakening on the whole Turkey complex." NATO will say, the president replied impatiently, "'Well, God! We don't want to trade 'em off!' They don't realize that in two or three days we may have a military strike which would bring perhaps the seizure of Berlin or a strike on Turkey. And then they'll say, 'By God! We should have taken it!'" JFK decided to request the NAC meeting.

The discussion continued to bog down over the same issues and uncertainties. RFK wondered if Khrushchev might discontinue work and make the missiles inoperable but offer to negotiate U.N. supervision: "That could take three weeks." In that event, McNamara advised continuing surveillance and the blockade until U.N. observers arrived—"an *excellent* course of action." But, he concluded grimly, Khrushchev probably won't stop work on the bases, "And we're faced with a decision tomorrow of what to do." In that case, RFK noted, the U.S. would be in better shape vis-à-vis world opinion.

Thompson, however, again advised a stronger response—releasing Khrushchev's correspondence, including Friday's private letter: "Then you've got to fasten the world focus back on Cuba" instead of Turkey. President Kennedy passed over Thompson's suggestion without comment, but Rusk claimed that if NATO "seems solid" on rejecting Turkey-Cuba linkage, "this has a chance of shaking Khrushchev off this point." Taylor questioned whether Finletter should even discuss U.S. military options with NAC. JFK instructed that Finletter should stress that work was going on and military escalation was likely. "What we *don't* want," he warned, "is sort of a *cheap* turn-down by them without realizing that . . . puts *us* in the position of then having to do something . . . because we wouldn't take the missiles out of Turkey. We're gonna either have to *invade* or have a *massive* strike on Cuba which may *lose* Berlin! That's what concerns me!"

Rusk suggested that the missiles in Cuba and Turkey could be turned over to the U.N. for destruction, but Thompson dismissed the idea: "The Soviets don't want to let anybody . . . see what their technology is." The president preferred more practical steps: "I think the *real* problem is what we do with the Turks *first*." McNamara returned to his earlier scheme for neutralizing the threat to Turkey: "I'd say to the

Turks, 'Look here, we're gonna have to invade Cuba. You're in *mortal danger. . . .* We propose that you defuse those missiles tonight. We're putting Polaris submarines along your coast . . . [to] reduce the pressure on the Soviet Union to attack you.'" RFK replied bluntly, what if the Turks say "And what if the Soviet Union attacks us anyway? Will you use the missiles on the nuclear submarines?" The defense chief admitted, "I'm not prepared to answer that question." The president pointed out again, "Aren't the Soviets gonna take their missiles out if we take 'em out of Turkey? If they don't, they're in an *impossible* position." But, he added, "the question is whether we can get the *Turks* to do it."

Taylor, however, reminded the president, "You're *deeply* in trouble with NATO by this bilateral kind of approach." Bundy suggested adding POL to the blockade instead, and Rusk recommended "shaking Khrushchev off this position of this morning" by declaring a state of national emergency and starting mobilization in the U.S. and NATO. Bundy, backed by McNamara, also pointed out that Khrushchev's Friday message "is not *categorical* about taking the missiles out. It says the *specialists* would go out." JFK responded by again pushing Khrushchev's new proposal: "Well this morning's is more precise, isn't it? More precise." "Mr. President," Thompson snapped, "if we go on the basis of a trade, which I gather is somewhat in your mind, we end up, it seems to me, with the Soviets *still* in Cuba with planes and technicians and so on. Even though the missiles are *out*, that would *surely* be unacceptable and put you in a worse position."

President Kennedy replied with practical and determined logic: "But our technicians and planes and guarantees would still exist for Turkey. I'm just thinking about what we're gonna have to do in a day or so, which is five hundred sorties in seven days and possibly an invasion, *all* because we wouldn't take missiles out of Turkey." Perhaps recalling his own wartime experience, JFK continued, "And we all know how quickly everybody's courage goes when the blood starts to flow and that's what's gonna happen in NATO." If the Soviets "grab Berlin, everybody's gonna say, 'Well, that was a pretty good proposition.' Let's not kid ourselves," he repeated for the third time, "that's the difficulty. *Today* it sounds great to reject it, but it's *not* going to after we *do* something!"

No one in the room could have doubts any longer about the president's attitude toward Khrushchev's public offer. Nitze nonetheless persisted, "I think that there are alternatives"—make "the blockade total and *live* with the missiles [already in Cuba]." He also reminded JFK that reconnaissance planes would be shot down over Cuba. But, as in the case of the blockade decision, Kennedy's advisers began to fall into line behind the commander-in-chief. JFK repeated his concern about NATO taking "a hard position" against the Turkish deal, but Nitze reported that he and Rusk had already talked to the British, French, and West Germans about "how *serious* this was . . . [and] about the *alternatives* they face."

The president again cited General Norstad's view: "We've gotta have NATO have a hand on this thing or otherwise we'll find no matter if we take *no* action or if we take *action*, they're all gonna be saying we should have done the reverse." If the Turks are adamant, he continued, then the U.S. ought to get NATO to "put enough pressure on them. I just tell you," he lectured, "I think we're better off to get those missiles out of Turkey and out of Cuba because I think the way of getting 'em *out* of Turkey and *out* of Cuba is gonna be *very, very* difficult and *very* bloody, one place or another."

Bundy finally seemed to be coming to terms with the president's resolve: "If you . . . are yourself *sure* that this is the *best way out*, then I would say that an immediate personal telegram of acceptance [of the trade] was the best thing to do." But JFK objected to forcing the deal on Turkey and NATO. "I'd rather go the total blockade route, which is a *lesser* step than this military action. What I'd *like* to do is have the Turks and NATO *equally* feel that this is the *wiser* move."

Sorensen pressed the president to delay replying to Khrushchev's public offer and instead respond privately to the Friday letter: "There's always *a chance* that he'll accept *that*. . . . We meanwhile won't have broken up NATO over something that never would have come to NATO." Rusk also read Stevenson's draft of a letter from JFK to Khrushchev, stressing that *after* work on the bases had ceased and the missiles were inoperable, the U.S. could guarantee Cuban independence and discuss NATO defense issues. "The point of the matter is," Kennedy snapped again, "Khrushchev's gonna come back and refer to his thing this morning on Turkey. And then we're gonna be screwing around for another forty-eight hours. . . . He'll come back and say, 'Well we're glad to settle the Cuban matter. What is your opinion of our proposal about Turkey?' So then we're on to Monday afternoon, and the work goes on. . . . He can hang us up for *three days* while he goes on with the work." "For three weeks!" Dillon muttered. "Let's start with *our* letter," JFK continued; "We're gonna take the *cease work* and try to get inoperable. . . . It's got to be finessed . . . we have to finesse him." JFK had no illusions about Khrushchev's response to U.S. pressure to go back to Friday's proposal, "which he *isn't* gonna give us. He's *now* moved on to the *Turkish* thing. So we're just gonna get a letter *back* saying, 'Well, he'd be glad to settle Cuba when we settle Turkey.'"

Rusk pushed for sending Stevenson's draft letter to Khrushchev—rejecting a Cuba-Turkey tie-in. "The only thing is," JFK pointed out, "what he's [Stevenson] saying is that they've gotta get the weapons out of Cuba before we'll discuss the general détente [including Turkey]. . . . [Khrushchev's] not gonna agree to that." Rusk proposed revising the letter, but the president declared compellingly, "It seems to me we oughta *be reasonable*. We're *not* gonna get these weapons out of Cuba, probably, anyway, but I mean, by negotiation. We're gonna have to take our weapons out of Turkey."

"I don't agree, Mr. President," Ambassador Thompson interjected. "You think he'll back down?" JFK asked doubtfully. "Well," Thompson reasoned, "he's already got this other [Friday] proposal." "Yeah," the president observed skeptically, "now this other public one, it seems to me, has become their public position." "This is maybe just pressure on us," Thompson speculated. "The important thing for Khrushchev, it seems to me, is to be able to say, 'I saved Cuba. I stopped an invasion.'"

"In other words, Mr. President," Sorensen summarized, "*your* position is that *once* he meets this condition of halting work and the inoperability, you're *then* prepared to go ahead on either the *specific* Cuban track or what we call a *general* détente track?" The president responded cautiously, "It really depends on whether we believe that we can get a deal on just the Cuban [issue] or whether we have to agree to his position of tying it [to Turkey]. Now Tommy doesn't think we do. I think that having made it public, how can he take these missiles out of Cuba if we just do nothing about Turkey?"

Bundy suggested giving Khrushchev "something else," and Ball urged promising "that when all this is over there can be a larger discussion." Thompson also repeated that Khrushchev might still accept the Friday deal since he could still say that he had removed the U.S. threat to Cuba. "He must be a little shaken up," RFK pointed out, "or he wouldn't have sent the [Friday] message to you in the first place." "That's *last night*," JFK snapped impatiently. "But it's *certainly* conceivable," RFK replied, "that you could get him *back* to that. I don't think that we should abandon it."

JFK halfheartedly agreed that there was no harm in trying. "Well, I think Adlai's letter is all right then [on dealing with Cuba first and Turkey later]." "All right," he finally conceded, "Let's send *this*." But he cautioned that two key questions remained: the timing of a NATO Council meeting and "what are we gonna do about the Turks." "Well, the only thing is," RFK complained, "we're proposing in here the abandonment..." "What? What?" the president cut in testily, "What are we proposing?" "The abandonment of Cuba [to the Soviets]," RFK asserted. "No," Ball objected, backed by Sorensen, "we're just promising not to invade."

Alexis Johnson reported that Stevenson had suggested releasing the new letter to Khrushchev "in order to get this back on the Cuba track and the focus away from *his* letter of this morning about Turkey." JFK, in response, emphasized his political concern about disclosing a U.S. non-invasion guarantee: "No, we don't wanna put it out until we *know* whether there's any chance of acceptance. There's gonna be *a hell of a fight* about that part [the commitment not to invade]. I don't mind takin' it on if we're gonna get somewhere. I don't wanna take on the fight if we're not even gonna get it."

Rusk read aloud the draft presidential letter to Khrushchev: "I have read your letter of October 26 with great care and find in it the indication of a willingness on your part to seek a calm solution to the problem." "We don't really find 'a willingness,'" President Kennedy observed coldly, and proposed substituting, "'your statement of your desire.'" "What's the rest of that?" RFK remarked acerbically. "I thought that was almost *too* nice." Rusk resumed reading: "I note and welcome indications in your second [Saturday] letter, which you've made public, that you would like to work toward a more general arrangement as regards *other armaments*." The president objected again: "'I note your *second* letter,' I don't think we ought to '*welcome*' it." JFK also agreed to Rusk's suggestion to delete a direct reference to Turkey: "We have to keep it vague, unfortunately or fortunately, because we haven't cleared it with Turkey or NATO. So I suppose we have to *fudge it* somewhat."

After Rusk reread the reworded message, RFK renewed his push for trying a positive response to Khrushchev's secret Friday proposal: "Send this letter and say you're accepting *his* offer. He's *made* an offer and you're *in fact* accepting it. ... God, don't bring in Turkey now. We want to settle [Cuba first]." "Well, in any case," JFK observed, "the two letters are ... there's no policy difference, is there?" (Bundy, after listening to this tape, told the author that he was at times unsure which letter was being discussed.)

RFK, however, grumbled about the "*rather* defensive" language in the Stevenson version, which seemed to say, "please don't get into the discussions of NATO or Turkey because we wanna talk about Cuba." The president's draft letter to Khrushchev, he contended, was more direct. "*You* made an offer to us [on Friday] and we *accept* it. And you've also made a *second* offer, which has to do with NATO, and we'll be glad to discuss that at a later time." "What is the reason Adlai's unhappy about our first letter?" JFK inquired; he was told that the U.N. ambassador thought the letter "sounds too much like an ultimatum—that it's making demands."

RFK, trying to break the logjam over the wording of the two messages, told his increasingly impatient brother, "Why do we bother you with it, Mr. President? Why don't you let us work it out?" "There's no question of bothering me," JFK replied. "We're gonna have to decide which letter we send." "Why don't we try to work it out for you without you being able to pick these all open," RFK quipped, and a wave of laughter rolled across the room. (The listener is inevitably struck by the special bond between the Kennedy brothers. It is difficult to imagine any other ExComm member making this remark.) "Yeah, but then you have to worry about ol' Adlai," JFK came back quickly, "so you might as well work it out with him." The room rocked with laughter again.

"Actually, I think Bobby's formula is a good one," Sorensen observed; "we say, 'we are accepting your offer of your letter last night and therefore there's *no need* to talk about these other things.'" The president seemed willing to go along with this scheme on the slim chance that Khrushchev would at least agree to a cessation of work, but he clearly remained unconvinced and unenthusiastic: "As I say, he's not gonna [accept] now [after his public offer on Turkey]. Tommy [Thompson] isn't so sure. But anyway, we can *try* this thing, but he's gonna come back on Turkey." Bundy jumped on the bandwagon as well: "That's right, Mr. President. I think that Bobby's notion of a *concrete* acceptance on our part of how we read last night's telegram is *very* important."

General Taylor, however, reported that the JCS had met that afternoon and recommended that "the big [bombing] strike" should begin no later than Monday morning—"unless there is irrefutable evidence in the meantime that offensive weapons are being dismantled and rendered inoperable"—followed by "the invasion plan, seven days later." "Well," RFK teased, "*I'm surprised!*" and laughter again briefly punctured the unrelenting pressure in the Cabinet Room. The president asked, "What are the reasons why?" The general replied, "The JCS just feel that the longer we wait...," and Dillon added impatiently, "Well, also we're getting *shot at* as we go in for our surveillance."

The president abruptly broke off discussion of an invasion and returned to the option he had been emphasizing throughout the meeting—"Now the next question is the Turkish one and NATO." In the wake of the latest JCS recommendation, JFK seemed even more determined to facilitate the removal of the Jupiter missiles from Turkey as quickly as possible. He again made clear that the decision, in his mind, was not *whether* but *how* to implement a deal on Turkey: "Well, now we have the question of a choice between the *bilateral* arrangements with Turkey, in which we more or less *do* it [defuse the Jupiters and substitute Polaris missiles] *or* whether we go through NATO and let NATO put the pressure on and also explain to the Turks what's gonna happen to them."

McNamara suggested a direct letter from the president to the Turkish prime minister explaining the risks to Turkey, and predicted that "we can get Italy to go along with us, I think ... and this will put some additional pressure on Turkey." "It's going to look like we're caving in," JFK admitted. But, "To get it *done*, probably you have to do it bilaterally, to take all the political effects of the cave-in of NATO. Or do we want to have a meeting in the morning of NATO and say, 'If we *don't* do it, here's the *problem.*'" Bundy countered that "the disadvantage of having a NATO meeting and going to the Turks ... is that you don't give this [Friday] track a fair run, that you just tried out on [Khrushchev]." The president did not respond—he clearly had no confidence in the effectiveness of that supposedly brilliant diplomatic sleight of hand.

McNamara, however, reminded his colleagues that despite discussions "on the deal of last night, we have *intense* ground fire" against the reconnaissance flights. Taylor, strikingly, downplayed the Cuban ground fire: "I wouldn't say 'intense' here. ... Flak came up in front of the flight and they veered away." "What about the *hit?*" Bundy exclaimed, but Taylor replied, "That has not been confirmed." McNamara, nonetheless, insisted that a decision would have to be made whether to discontinue the flights or "send them in with *proper* cover. If we send them in with proper cover and they're attacked, we must attack back."

The defense chief also disclosed that the *Grozny* was entering the quarantine zone. "We have *two* choices, stop it and board it or don't. ... When you put the *two* of these together, *stopping* surveillance and *not* stopping the ship, it seems to me we're *too weak.*" "We *must* continue *surveillance*," Taylor demanded. "That's *far* more important than the ships." "I *don't* think at this particular point," McNamara replied, "we should show a *weakness* to Khrushchev. And I think we would show a weakness if we failed on *both* of these actions." "And we mustn't fail on surveillance," Taylor repeated.

McNamara agreed but advised resuming surveillance "as late as possible in the day to give a little more time." But, he added, "if we go in with surveillance, we *have* to put a cover on, and if we start shooting back we've *escalated substantially*." "I would think we ought to just take a chance on reconnaissance tomorrow without the cover," the president replied doubtfully, "because I don't think the cover's really gonna do you much good. You can't protect . . . [against] ground fire." However, if there was no answer from U Thant, he admitted, air attacks might be necessary by Monday; but "I'm *not* convinced yet of the invasion." "I *agree* with that," Taylor counseled. "My *personal* view is that we be made more ready to go on Monday [with bombing] but then also *ready* to invade, but make no advance decisions."

"I *don't* think we should stop the surveillance tomorrow," McNamara contended, but if "they *fire* on us..." "Now that's a signal then," JFK interjected grimly, "Then we know..." In that event, McNamara proposed, "we're either going to *return* that fire . . . against the things that fired against us or . . . go in the next day" with full air strikes. "One or the other!" "That's right," the president affirmed, "I'm more inclined to take the more general response. . . . I *announce* that we've been fired on, *announce* that work is going ahead, *announce* that we haven't gotten an answer from the Soviets."

President Kennedy, at that moment, was clearly leaning toward ordering comprehensive air strikes if the diplomatic situation remained frozen. But Dillon, a persistent doubter on the Turkey initiative, surprisingly redirected the discussion to JFK's ace in the hole: "Yes, but what about moving ahead with this Turkish...?" "Well that's what I want to come to now," Kennedy quickly affirmed. "Now let's get on to the Turkish thing."

Thompson, finally recognizing the president's determination, endorsed alerting Turkey and Italy that the U.S. might use force in Cuba, which could result in Soviet attacks on the Jupiters; "We are *therefore* considering whether or not it would be in *your* interest for us to *remove* these." "We oughta send that to the Turks," JFK agreed firmly, "cause it's *their* neck. . . . Now they're not gonna want to *do* it, but we may just decide we *have* to do it in *our* interest." It would be far better, he admitted, to have NATO endorse withdrawing the Jupiters. "I don't think we would *get* that, Mr. President," Bundy predicted. "Once you start explaining it to 'em," JFK replied skeptically, "what's gonna happen?" "Even with an offer of a Polaris?" Ball added. Rusk recalled that the Turks had rejected replacing the Jupiters with Polaris in 1961: "the Turkish reaction was, 'Well, the missiles are *here*, and as long as they're here, you're here.'"

"Here's one way to put it," McNamara proposed: the British have accepted the need to replace the obsolescent Thor missiles, and the Turks and Italians have to understand that the Jupiters are even more obsolete. JFK was less sanguine: "they'll say that this is because" the United States wants "to make a trade, if we did it. I don't see how we can put it to 'em without the trade. What we *want*, obviously, is the *Turks* to suggest it, but they're pretty *tough*, and they probably figure that their security is better with them in than it is with them out." But, he added, "They don't know what's coming up. It's not gonna be so *happy*." "If the Turks say no to us," JFK reasoned, it would be much better if all of NATO said no as well, since "what *always* happens, a few days later when the trouble comes," is that they then say "that we should have asked them and they would have told us to get 'em out." "It seems to me," he concluded, we should "begin a negotiation with the Turks now." "What is the *rush* about this?" RFK asked impatiently—except for deciding on the timing of an air strike?

The protracted, repetitive, and vigorous debate over the Turkish Jupiters abruptly became almost irrelevant, and the earlier alarm bells about a U-2 straying into Soviet air space or ground fire on a reconnaissance flight suddenly seemed comparatively unimportant. About two hours into the meeting the crisis lurched to a new level of extreme danger as McNamara was handed a message and made a stunning announcement: "The U-2 was shot down." "The U-2 shot down?" JFK asked in disbelief. "Yes," McNamara confirmed, "it was found shot down." "Was the pilot killed?" RFK pressed. "The pilot's body is in the plane," Taylor explained. (Air Force major Rudolph Anderson was the only known fatality of the Cuban missile crisis.) "This *is*," the president observed unemotionally, "much of an escalation by *them*, isn't it?" "Yes, exactly!" McNamara acknowledged.

The defense chief, nonetheless, recommended caution. Air attacks, he explained, could still be deferred for four to five days if the blockade continued, backed up by armed surveillance, and there would still be "time to go to NATO" about Turkey. The president groped for an explanation for the "change in orders" that resulted in the use of flak and the firing of a SAM missile: "How do we interpret this?" "I don't know how to interpret it," McNamara admitted.

The initial shock in the room gave way to a rising sense of anger. Taylor demanded retaliation against the SAM site that downed the U-2 and the president acknowledged, "How can we send a U-2 fellow over there tomorrow unless we take out *all* the SAM sites?" "This is *exactly* correct," McNamara declared. "I don't think we can." "Can they see the pilot?" JFK probed. "The wreckage is on the ground," Taylor explained, "and the pilot's dead."

McCone demanded "a more stark, *violent* protest" directly to Khrushchev, and Nitze pointed out stridently, "*They've* fired the first shot." "We should retaliate *against* the SAM site," Taylor insisted, "and announce that if any of 'em have any other planes fired on we will come back and attack it." He also reminded the president that an immediate military response to shooting down a U-2 had been decided on days ago. McNamara agreed emphatically: "And if we're gonna carry out surveillance *each day*, we must be prepared to *fire each day*." "We can't very well send a U-2 over there," JFK reiterated, "and have a guy killed again *tomorrow*?" "I think you've just *gotta* take out that SAM site," Nitze asserted, "or you can't maintain surveillance."

President Kennedy and the ExComm seemed more unsettled and uncertain than at any time since the discovery of the missiles. JFK noted that even if the SAM site that shot down the U-2 were destroyed, subsequent flights would still be vulnerable to attacks from other sites. In that case, McNamara declared, the other SAMs and the MiGs could be taken out. "Do we want to announce we're gonna take counteraction," JFK inquired, "or just take it tomorrow morning?" "Just take it," Gilpatric advised, and Ball urged announcing the reprisals *after* they had been carried out. The president was quick to perceive a political advantage in making a statement: "Well, I think we ought to announce it because it throws off Khrushchev's protestations about this."

Several participants seemed troubled about announcing that a U-2 had been shot down and the pilot killed based solely on a claim from Havana. "We haven't confirmed that, have we?" the president asked, almost stifling a caustic laugh about "so goddamn many" rumors. He also worried that announcing the reprisals would make the sorties more dangerous for the pilots. JFK instead directed Gilpatric to prepare a general statement that "action will be taken to protect our aircraft." But, he added a striking coda: "Then we'll go back to what we're gonna do about the Turks and NATO."

McNamara again urged disclosing that a U-2 had been shot down in order to justify protecting surveillance planes with fighter aircraft—a step discouraged by the president just moments before, but JFK remained hesitant about making an announcement without confirmation: "Did they say it should be shot down—the Cubans?" Kennedy finally instructed Gilpatric and Taylor to prepare an announcement to cover all contingencies, since "We don't know if it was shot down." "We don't *know* it," McCone conceded. "If the plane's on the ground there," Dillon observed sarcastically, "it *was* shot down. It didn't just come down and land." But, McNamara countered, "it might have had a mechanical failure." "The only thing that troubles us," JFK pointed out, "is the *other* plane was shot at [with ack-ack]." "That's right, exactly," McNamara noted.

"That's why I'd like to find out," JFK continued, "whether Havana says they *did* shoot it down." Gilpatric, however, put his finger on a critical issue: "We *assume* these SAM sites are manned by Soviets. That's the significant part of it *if* the SAM fired." "This is a *change* of pattern," McNamara conceded. "Now *why* it's a change of pattern, I don't know." "You could have an undisciplined Cuban antiaircraft outfit fire," Gilpatric contended, "But to have a *SAM* site, with a *Russian* crew, fire is not any accident."

(The president left the Cabinet Room for about ten minutes before the meeting resumed.)

Kennedy reported that Castro had just announced that any plane violating Cuban air space would be fired on. He nonetheless puckishly invited Ball, "George, come up and sit here now, you're another civilian," and chuckled as Taylor quipped, "Come on into General Taylor's lap." But JFK promptly returned to the serious business at hand: "Let's talk a little more about . . . NATO and the Turks, that's the *one* matter we haven't settled today." Dillon advised that Castro's statement and the attack on the U-2 would make it difficult to wait four to five days before bombing the missiles. JFK, nervously tapping the table, urged convening the NAC meeting and instructing Ambassador Hare to begin conversations with the Turks. "We need to explain to them what's happening over here. Otherwise, we're gonna be carrying *a hell of a bag.*" Dillon warned that domestic political pressure for reprisals would intensify in the wake of the U-2 loss. The president, however, was determined to push for removal of the Turkish Jupiters rather than speed up the bombing of Cuba: "Therefore, we gotta move. That's why I think we gotta have a NATO meeting *tomorrow.*"

"Of course, it would be relatively easy if we wanted to get NATO to *reject* this," JFK observed, "But I think that isn't necessarily what we *want* right now, is it?" McNamara speculated, "I think we can *force* 'em, and I think we can *do* it in such a way that the aftereffects will not be too severe.... We simply say that we believe this is, as *I do* believe, in the interests of the alliance, and that we will replace those missiles with other fire." "But they're gonna say," JFK predicted, "that we're definitely seeking a trade with the Russians, aren't they? But that's alright isn't it?" "'To free our hands in Cuba,'" Bundy proposed, acknowledging the president's determination, "'we *must* get these missiles out of Turkey,' is what we say." "Yeah," McNamara agreed, "without endangering *you*, the alliance.... We're *not* trading *Turkish* missiles for *Cuban* missiles." "No, no," Bundy affirmed. "*Not a bit,*" McNamara exclaimed, "We're *relieving* the alliance of a *threat* that is presently upon them."

The president again predicted that NATO would say, "Well now, do you have a deal with the Russians if we take 'em out of Turkey?" "It will be *seen* as a trade by a great many people, Mr. President," Bundy stressed. "There's *no doubt* about that. We've looked that one in the eye. If we don't buy that, then it seems to me, Bob [McNamara] has the best way of dealing with it." JFK replied that the best result would be to have the Turks themselves offer the withdrawal, but McNamara cautioned that the Turks "are a *terribly* stubborn people to talk to on this kind of point."

RFK and Sorensen, who had been out of the room completing JFK's letter to Khrushchev, returned with the final draft—essentially accepting his private October 26 offer. JFK tersely approved the letter, in which he clearly had *very* limited confidence, and then resumed the discussion of the Turkish withdrawal. He again dismissed any illusions about concealing American motives: Turkey and NATO would conclude "that this is on the cheap for them, they'll say the United States is pulling out in order to try to make a deal on Cuba. I mean, no matter whether we say it's to protect Turkey or not, that's the way they're gonna think about it."

McNamara, however, continued to resist a direct trade: "We can say ... 'if we attack Cuba, there's a great likelihood that the Soviets will attack the missiles in Turkey.'" "Throw in Italy," the president interjected. The U.S., McNamara continued, is willing to defuse the Jupiter missiles and substitute Polaris submarines, *"before we attack Cuba,* thereby increasing your safety if you wish us to do so. ... If they don't take it, that's *their* decision." "And if they don't take it," the president asserted, Turkey must "accept that danger." JFK urged getting the proposal ready for a Sunday NAC meeting, but Bundy dissented: "No, I would *not* do it tomorrow, Mr. President, myself." President Kennedy simply ignored Bundy's objection: "I think we oughta get moving on it. The fact is, time's running out." Dillon protested, "But the only time we'd say that we've rendered them inoperable is when we've determined that we're gonna attack in Cuba." "*This* is the point," McNamara exclaimed, "if we attack in Cuba." President Kennedy, on the contrary, was thinking of the missile trade not in terms of McNamara's cunning diplomatic scheme to make an attack on Cuba seem less risky for NATO, but rather as a bold political stroke to resolve the crisis without using military force at all.

JFK left the Cabinet Room and the discussion again became less structured and more spontaneous. Vice President Lyndon Johnson, normally assertive and domineering, had been all but silent in Kennedy's presence. Now, with the president gone again, Johnson began to speak out—colorfully and articulately.

LBJ exposed the divide between McNamara and JFK on a Turkish deal: "What you're sayin' is you're willing to give 'em up, as McNamara proposes. Why not trade?" "And then save a few hundred thousand lives," Ball demanded. McNamara, however, tried vigorously to defend his position with four points: 1) "We're gonna send surveillance aircraft in tomorrow. ... We're gonna lose airplanes. ... You just *can't* maintain this position very long. So we must be prepared to *attack* Cuba ("That's right," Dillon interjected)—*quickly*." 2) "*When* we attack Cuba, we are going to *have* to attack with an *all-out* attack ... and I *personally* believe that this is *almost certain* to lead to an invasion." "Unless you get a ceasefire around the world," Dillon muttered. "Or a general war," Bundy added grimly. 3) "*If* we do this ... the Soviet Union *may,* and I think probably *will,* attack the Turkish missiles." 4) "We *cannot* allow a Soviet attack on the Jupiter missiles in Turkey without a military response by NATO. ... The *minimum* military response ... [would be] with conventional weapons by NATO forces in Turkey ... *against* Soviet warships and/or naval bases in the Black Sea area. Now that to me is the *absolute* minimum. ... This is *extremely* dangerous. Now I'm not sure we can avoid anything like that *if* we attack Cuba. But I think we should make *every effort,*" he rapped the table for emphasis, "to avoid it. And one way to avoid it is to *defuse* the Turkish missiles *before* we attack Cuba."

McNamara was clearly taken aback by an eruption of critical responses. McCone backed LBJ's stance: "I don't see why don't you make the trade then!" Ball argued irritably that defusing the Turkish missiles was pointless since the Soviets might strike "in Berlin or somewhere else. Then you're in a position where you've gotten rid of your missiles *for nothing.*" "Well, wait a minute now," McNamara replied defensively, "I didn't say it saves you from a reprisal. I simply said it reduces the chances of military action against Turkey." "Well, what good does that do you," Ball countered testily, if it leads to an attack in Berlin or elsewhere. "I'm not *at all* certain," the defense secretary responded, that the Soviets would attack in Berlin or elsewhere if there were no active Jupiters in Turkey. "Oh, I am," Taylor grumbled.

"Bob," LBJ asked sharply, "if you're willin' to give up your missiles in Turkey . . . *say that* to him [Khrushchev] and say we're tradin'." "Make the trade!" Ball cut in shouting, "Make the trade then!" before LBJ concluded, "Save all the invasion, lives, everything else." McCone asserted impatiently that the U.S. should "be *delighted* to trade those missiles in Turkey for the thing in Cuba." "I'm not opposed to it *now,*" McNamara tried to explain above the din. "All I'm suggesting is *don't* push us into a position where . . . we *are* forced to attack Cuba and the missiles *remain* in Turkey." Last week, Ball countered, "We thought that if we could trade it out for Turkey this would be an *easy* trade and a *very* advantageous deal. Now . . . we don't want it. And we're talking about . . . military action with *enormous* casualties and a *great,* grave risk of escalation."

Ball had shifted ground on the Turkish deal since the U-2 was shot down: "If we're gonna get the *damn* missiles out of Turkey *anyway,* say . . . [to Khrushchev] 'if *this* is a matter of *real* concern to you to have these on your borders, *all right,* we'll get rid of 'em. You get rid of 'em in Cuba.'" The Jupiters were obsolete anyway, he stressed, and Polaris missiles in the Mediterranean would provide a better deterrent for NATO. "And what's left of NATO?" Bundy griped. "If NATO isn't any better than that," Ball retorted brusquely, "it isn't that *good* to us."

McNamara recommended writing two messages to cover the military options *he* had supported: 1) declaring that a missile trade was unacceptable and an attack on Cuba was imminent; 2) offering to defuse the Jupiters in Turkey before striking Cuba. He did *not* propose a message accepting a direct trade in order to avert an attack on Cuba. "I'd like to see *both* of these messages written," Bundy agreed.

The meeting had already been going on for several grueling hours. "Do people want dinner downstairs," Bundy asked, "or they want trays or they want to wait?" "Well, let's wait. You don't have to worry," McNamara muttered despondently and almost inaudibly, "eating is the *least* of my worries." His dismal tone momentarily exposed the depths of exhaustion, insecurity, and anxiety these men had endured virtually around the clock since October 16.

But, the defense secretary quickly returned to the inescapable issues on the table and announced that Taylor and the JCS were working out a low-level surveillance plan for tomorrow: "But we're just gonna get shot up, *sure as hell.* ... We're gonna lose planes." "You know," McCone exclaimed, "I think that we ought to take this occasion to send directly to Khrushchev, by *fast wire*, the most *violent* protest, and demand that he stop this business and stop it *right* away, or we're gonna take those SAM sites out *immediately.* ... And I'd trade these Turkish things out *right now.* ... And I'd make that *part* of the message."

"Lemme go back a second," the usually businesslike defense chief burst out. "When I read that message of last night this morning, I thought, *my God!* I'd never base a transaction on *that* contract. Hell, that's *no* offer! There's not a *damn* thing in it that's an offer! You read that message carefully ... there isn't a *single* word in it that proposes to take the missiles out." McCone, echoing an earlier JFK remark, pointed out, "his message this morning wasn't that way—his public message." "The last night message was twelve pages of ... fluff," McNamara exploded again. "That's *no* contract. You couldn't *sign* that and say we know what we signed. And *before* we got the *damned thing* read," he slapped his hands for emphasis, "the whole deal changed, *completely* changed!"

McCone insisted again, "I'd send him a *threatening* letter. I'd say, 'You've made public an offer; we'll accept that offer. But, you shot down a plane today before we even had a chance to send you a letter.'" If these unarmed reconnaissance planes were fired on again, McCone demanded, Khrushchev had to be told that the U.S. would immediately take out the SAM sites. "But what I'd do," McNamara countered, "is disassociate that from the Turkish missiles, John." McCone sharply disagreed: "No, I wouldn't, because then the pressure gets back at you. You get another proposal. You'll have Berlin thrown in it tomorrow." "That's why," McNamara concluded, "I think we have to be prepared for an attack."

For more than half an hour, only tantalizing fragments of these con-

versations are partially audible in the background. Vice President Johnson, for example, speculated about the position of the Turkish prime
minister on substituting Polaris missiles for the Jupiters: "Why wouldn't
he buy that?" "I'm not sure," Nitze replied, "but the whole proposition
hasn't been made to him, as far as I know." Johnson answered his own
question: "I think the reason he wouldn't buy it would be a fear that
that meant that we were through and we wouldn't come [to Turkey's
defense]."

LBJ continued to ruminate, eventually suggesting that the administration had been backing away "from the president's speech" and that
the American people were becoming insecure. He also claimed that Soviet "ships are comin' through" the blockade. Robert Kennedy reacted
angrily, "No! The ships aren't coming through. They all turned back . . .
90 percent of them." But Johnson stuck to his guns, "I don't think . . . at
this moment, that it looks like we're as strong as we were on the day of
the president's announcement." This exchange, hinting at the bitter
enmity between RFK and LBJ, petered out and the attorney general
soon left the Cabinet Room.

Johnson laughed at times with several colleagues before contending
again that the public was becoming disenchanted: "I don't say it's *wise*.
I just say that's the temperature—it's 101 degrees." Several minutes
later, after discussing the shooting down of the U-2 and the need to continue surveillance, LBJ chuckled softly and declared, in response to
Dillon's question about whether night surveillance was about to begin,
"I hope it hasn't. . . . I've been afraid of those damned flares [for night
missions] ever since they mentioned them. . . . Imagine some crazy Russian captain . . . the damn thing [the flare] goes *blooey* and lights up the
skies. He might just pull a trigger. Looks like we're playin' Fourth of
July over there or somethin'. I'm scared of that, and I don't see what
you get with that photograph. . . . If you're gonna try and psychologi-
cally scare them with a flare, you're liable to get your bottom shot at."

Rusk soon asked Johnson whether he thought the U.S. would shortly
be forced to act. "I think you're at that point," the vice president replied. "There's a *great* feeling of insecurity" in the country. The secretary of state also questioned Johnson about the public reaction to accepting a Cuba-Turkey deal: "I don't know," LBJ admitted candidly.

Johnson, still thinking out loud, hypothesized about telling the
Turkish prime minister directly, "'Now you've got these Jupiters and
they're . . . not worth a damn. And we'll take that old T-Model out,
we'll give you Polaris.'" He pondered again whether the Jupiter missiles

provided the Turks with physical assurance of American support. Rusk pointed out incredulously, "We've got 17,000 *men* there!" and Johnson countered, "We've got 20,000 men there."

LBJ proposed having Ambassador Hare tell the Turks, "'You're more *likely* to get hit *this* way [with the Jupiters] than you are the other way [with Polaris].' Isn't that true, Tommy?" "The trouble with all this," Thompson replied, "is that unless we're *absolutely* decided we're going to hit Cuba ... this would leave us in a *very* weak position." The Soviets will "leave their technicians in Cuba, their bombing planes in Cuba, and we're in a *hell* of a mess." Johnson pointed out that if the U.S. gave up Turkey after the Soviets shot down one plane, Moscow might expect the surrender of Berlin if they shot down another plane: "You know, a *mad* dog, he tastes a little blood."

"I think they've been put off [the October 26 offer] by the Lippmann piece," Thompson conjectured, and Khrushchev has "gotten onto the idea that he can get a lot more." (Journalist Walter Lippmann's proposal for a Cuba-Turkey deal had appeared in the *Washington Post* on October 25.) Dillon predicted that the Soviets would now expect an overall quid pro quo—trading missiles, planes, and technicians in both Turkey and Cuba. "That's why I think," Thompson declared, "any suggestion that we're going to accept this ... is *very* dangerous. ... I *can't* believe it's necessary, when you know the night before he was willing to take this other line."

But Khrushchev might have been overruled, Thompson admitted, or perhaps he had been "deceived by the Lippmann piece" or believed that the U.S. was behind the similar scheme floated by Austrian foreign minister Kreisky. The former ambassador suggested that Khrushchev might be thinking, "'These boys are beginning to give way. Let's push harder.' I think they'll change their minds," he added, "when we take any forceful action, stopping their ship, or taking out a SAM site that ends up killing the Russians." Dillon wondered, if reconnaissance planes were attacked again, whether the U.S. should take out all the SAM sites or just the site which fired the missile. "I'm inclined," Thompson replied, "to take one out," and LBJ quipped, "You war hawks oughta get together," laughing alone and self-consciously at his own joke.

McCone finally read aloud the draft of his proposed "threatening" letter from JFK to Khrushchev. He asserted that firing on unarmed reconnaissance planes and shooting down a U-2 was a "*shocking* further provocation on your part." He nonetheless left the door open to negotiations on *all* of Khrushchev's recent messages, but demanded an immediate cessation of work on the bases, steps to make the missiles inoperable, and progress toward their verified removal. Dillon noticed that the letter did not mention the Jupiters in Turkey, but McCone explained that a deal on Turkey was implicit in the offer to talk about *all* of Khrushchev's proposals.

"The Cubans are beginning to realize that something serious is up," Rusk observed, predicting that gunfire would begin over Cuba very soon. LBJ stressed that Khrushchev was "behind the eight ball a little bit and he's got to get a little blood—and he's *got* it. . . . I guess we'll be doin' somethin' tomorrow. . . . I imagine they'll shoot, we'll shoot..." "That's your main concern," Thompson conceded grimly, but he remained opposed to any deal involving Turkey: "You can see that we have two conflicting things here: one is to prepare for an attack on Cuba, and the other is to get a peaceful solution along the lines which he proposed [on Friday]. . . . If you want to get him to accept this thing that he put in his letter last night, then you shouldn't give *any* indication that we're ready to talk about the Turkish thing." "To mention this," the ambassador concluded, "as McCone does [in his draft letter] . . . [is] a further sign of weakness." Johnson observed sarcastically: the President is "*really* sayin' . . . 'I'm gonna *dismantle* the foreign policy of the United States for the last fifteen years in order to get these missiles out of Cuba.'" LBJ paused dramatically for some ten seconds before rebuking JFK's stance: "Then we say, we're glad, and we appreciate it, and we want to discuss it with you."

Thompson also reasoned that if JFK's latest letter to Khrushchev were released, "that offsets a lot of things . . . that worried the president. . . . The public will *realize* that he's suddenly stepped up the ante." LBJ contended that the downing of a U-2 "is not gonna make the folks too anxious to trade anyway." Dillon, however, seemed uneasy about disclosing Khrushchev's Friday letter since such a move could shut down a private channel of communication with the Soviets.

The rump discussion briefly returned to resuming reconnaissance over Cuba and taking out the SAM site that had brought down the U-2. "You just ask yourself," LBJ asserted vividly, "what made the greatest impression on you today, whether it was his [Khrushchev's] letter last night, or whether it was his letter this morning, or whether it's about that U-2 boy's downing." "U-2 boy," Dillon echoed. "That's *exactly* what did it," the vice president affirmed, "That's when everybody's color changed a little bit, and sure as hell that's what's gonna make the impression on *him* [Khrushchev]—not all these ... [letters] that each one of us write. He's expert at that palaver."

President Kennedy returned to the Cabinet Room at about 7:30 after an absence of some forty-five minutes. During the time away from the meeting he had approved the final version of the letter to Khrushchev. He did not reveal to the full ExComm that he had also arranged to have RFK meet with Ambassador Dobrynin in the Attorney General's office at 8:00 p.m. to explain the president's latest letter to Khrushchev.

JFK apologized for the excessive length of the meeting and immediately turned to the pending messages to Turkey and NATO. "We have *really* to agree on the *track*, you see, Mr. President," Bundy pointed out boldly, "and I think that there's a *very* substantial difference between us." "Let's see what the difference is," JFK replied patiently, "then we can think about that. What is the difference?"

Thompson eagerly recapitulated the arguments he had made during the president's absence: "The Turkish proposal is, I should *think*, *clearly* unacceptable. It's missile for missile, plane for plane, technician for technician, and it ... would leave the Russians installed in Cuba." The ambassador shrewdly appealed to the president's political instincts, predicting that if Khrushchev's October 26 message were released "the public will be pretty solid on that, and that we ought to keep the heat on him and get him back on a line which he obviously was on the night before." The Friday message, he deduced, seemed "almost incoherent and showed that they were *quite* worried," and the Lippmann article and the Kreisky speech "has made him think they can get more and they backed away from it."

The president moved again to conciliate the opponents of a Turkish deal by agreeing that "*first* we oughta *try* to go the first route which you suggest and get him back [to the Friday offer]. That's what our letter's doing." But, at the same time, he again underscored his lack of confidence in that strategy and made clear that he was determined to keep the Turkish option alive: "Then it seems to me we *oughta* have a discussion with NATO about these Turkish missiles."

Lyndon Johnson, speaking at length for the first time with JFK in the room, summarized the options discussed during Kennedy's absence: McNamara's plan to substitute Polaris missiles for the Jupiters before attacking Cuba; McCone's ultimatum—"You shot down our man there and we're not gonna *take* any more of this"—sweetened by a willingness to trade the Jupiters; Ball's offer of a direct trade. Rusk preferred "putting the bee on Cuba on that one" and counseled, "Mr. President, Ball's track would just get us *completely* out of Turkey *in every respect or* leave the Soviets *very much* in Cuba. It's the track of last night we want to get him back to. I think if we step up our actions tomorrow against Cuba..." Instead of "a lot of talk," Dillon cut in sharply. Take out a SAM site immediately: "Don't say anything—Just *do* that!" "But we don't know whether that plane was shot down yet, do we?" JFK replied. Informed that Havana radio had announced that the plane had been destroyed by antiaircraft fire, Kennedy admitted, "Oh, I'm sorry. I didn't know that." Thompson seized the chance to apply even more pressure: "I also think that . . . if that Soviet ship [*Grozny*] comes within this [quarantine] line, we ought to stop it."

After a brief run-through on the *Grozny's* likely cargo, JFK again shifted the discussion back to Turkey. "Didn't he say if we took out the missiles in Turkey, he'd take out the missiles in Cuba?" Thompson repeated that the offer was a trap: "That's why I think it's *very* dangerous to indicate any tentative play on this thing. He's *really* got us there. . . . We either get out of Turkey completely, or we leave the Soviets [technicians and bombers] in Cuba and have only missiles out."

Ball countered that the U.S. could make a counterproposal and Bundy suggested offering to take everything out of *both* Turkey and Cuba. Dillon dissented emphatically, "You can't do that!" President Kennedy again cut through the opposition to make his position unmistakably clear: "We can't very well invade Cuba, with all its toil and blood there's gonna be, when we could have gotten 'em out by making a deal on the same missiles in Turkey. If that's part of the record then you don't have a very good war." He paused for some six seconds before concluding, "But other than that, it's really a question now of what to say to NATO."

Vice President Johnson, in the sharpest challenge to the president's judgment since the harsh attacks by General LeMay and Senators Russell and Fulbright the previous week, flatly disagreed: "It doesn't mean just missiles. He takes his missiles out of Cuba, takes his men out of Cuba, and takes his planes out of Cuba—why then your whole foreign policy is gone. You take everything out of Turkey—twenty thousand men, all *your* technicians, and all *your* planes, and all *your* missiles—and crumble."

"How else are we gonna get those missiles out of there then?" JFK replied impassively, again refusing to make a direct response to tough criticism. "That's the problem." "Well, *last* night he was prepared," Rusk reiterated, "to trade them for a promise not to invade." "That's right, now he's got something completely new," the president pointed out yet again. "*Somebody* told him to try to get a little more," LBJ cut in. McCone suggested sending Khrushchev "a pretty tough message" and JFK countered, "Well, I've already sent him one." "Well, this is a thoughtful one," McCone teased, referring to his own "threatening" draft—producing a brief spurt of laughter.

The stressful and draining meeting had finally run out of steam after almost four hours. The strain, after nearly two weeks, was clearly taking a toll "on people's stamina and composure." But, Rusk later recalled, nervousness and fatigue never led to panic or despair because JFK's "great control . . . gave leadership to ExComm in a way that stabilized the attitudes and the emotions of ExComm members." The president suggested reconvening at 9:00 P.M.—"everybody get a bite to eat, then let's come back" to decide whether to send McCone's letter and "to see about what we do about this trade . . . [and] about our two messages to the U.N. and, I mean, this Turkish thing."

"I remember the sunset," McNamara recalled years later. "We left at about the time the sun was setting in October, and I, at least, was so uncertain as to whether the Soviets would accept replying to the first instead of the second [Khrushchev message] . . . that I wondered if I'd ever see another sunset like that." The meeting actually ended at about 7:45, after the late-October sunset, but the anecdote surely reflects McNamara's state of mind at the time.

After the ExComm had dispersed, Ball, Bundy, Gilpatric, RFK, McNamara, Rusk, Sorensen, and Thompson met with President Kennedy, at his invitation, in the Oval Office. (Unfortunately, this brief but critical discussion was not taped.) "The best available evidence indicates that the president was the dominant person at that small session. He called the meeting, selected the participants, and excluded about another eight men." JFK revealed that his brother was about to hand-deliver the new letter for Khrushchev to Dobrynin and requested advice on what to tell the ambassador. The group quickly agreed that RFK should warn Dobrynin that military action against Cuba was imminent and make clear, consistent with Khrushchev's Friday letter, that the U.S. was prepared to pledge not to invade Cuba if the missiles were withdrawn.

But the president continued to press for a deal on the Turkish mis-

siles. Rusk, attentive to JFK's determination, suggested that RFK advise the ambassador that a public quid pro quo for the missiles in Turkey was unacceptable, but the president was prepared to remove them once the Cuban crisis was resolved. "The proposal was quickly supported by the rest of us," Bundy wrote decades later, "and approved by the president. It was also agreed that knowledge of this assurance would be held among those present . . . that no one not in the room was to be informed of this additional message. Robert Kennedy was instructed to make plain to Dobrynin . . . that any Soviet reference to our assurance would simply make it null and void." "The fact of a private deal undoubtedly met the objections of some of the serious opponents of a public deal. But the central fact was," Barton Bernstein has concluded, "that the president made clear that he cared deeply about this issue, he chose the policy, and nobody would resist him. They were the president's men, and he was the president."

Sometime later that evening, without the knowledge of virtually the entire ExComm, the president participated in another attempt to head off military action in Cuba. JFK had no confidence in the ExComm strategy of accepting Khrushchev's Friday offer and ignoring his public Saturday message. (This scheme, celebrated in much of the missile crisis literature as the "Trollope Ploy," is a reference to a plot device by nineteenth-century British novelist Anthony Trollope in which a woman decides to interpret a man's casual romantic interest as an offer of marriage.) The president instead worked secretly with Dean Rusk, apparently at the secretary's suggestion, to cobble together a fall-back plan. Rusk arranged to have former deputy U.N. secretary general Andrew Cordier put in place an emergency back-channel strategy by which U Thant would announce, after receiving private word from Rusk that negotiations had failed, a U.N. plan through which the U.S. and the U.S.S.R. would mutually agree to remove their missiles from Turkey and Cuba. JFK was prepared to gamble that if the U.S. publicly accepted this supposedly neutral plan, it would be very difficult for the Soviets to reject it. Khrushchev's unexpected decision the following morning made the Cordier gambit moot, and Rusk did not reveal this closely held secret for over twenty-five years.

Meanwhile, John Scali, informed about Khrushchev's Friday letter, met again with Aleksandr Fomin and demanded an explanation of Khrushchev's conflicting offers. Fomin tried to blame the change on inadequate communications, but Scali exploded, calling the new message "a stinking double cross" and warned that an invasion of Cuba was imminent. Fomin pleaded with Scali to persuade U.S. officials that the Soviet Union was serious about reaching a settlement. Scali agreed to convey the message.

The president was also informed that Soviet ships were continuing toward Cuba, and Stevenson reported that Ambassador Zorin had refused to accept information on the precise location of the quarantine line. Fidel Castro rejected U Thant's appeal to suspend work on the missile sites unless the U.S. lifted the quarantine. But Castro did invite the acting secretary general to Cuba for talks.

Declassified Soviet sources have confirmed that the fatal launch of the SAM missile was ordered by local air defense officers without permission from General Pliyev in Cuba or from Khrushchev. "Castro's joy was indescribable," but the Kremlin boss was furious and ordered that no firings take place without his direct order: "No independent initiatives. Everything is hanging by a thread as it is."

When General LeMay received word that the U-2 had been lost, he ordered air-to-surface rocket-carrying fighters readied for an attack on the SAMs. "The White House, realizing that there was a standing order for the immediate destruction of a firing SAM site," ordered LeMay "not to launch the aircraft until he received direct orders from the president." "He chickened out again," LeMay growled. "How in hell do you get men to risk their lives when the SAMs are not attacked?" The Strategic Air Command, nonetheless, had already been placed on full nuclear alert. Nearly 1,600 Air Force bombers and just over 275 missiles (177 ICBMs and 100 Polaris) were armed and ready if the president should decide to order a nuclear attack on the U.S.S.R.

RFK returned to the White House at about 8:45 p.m. after telling Dobrynin that time was running out. The attorney general had reiterated the president's willingness to renounce invading Cuba and suggested that removing the Jupiters from Turkey was possible—but not as a written quid pro quo. RFK was nonetheless convinced that the chances for a peaceful settlement were slim at best. Determined to avoid creating a paper trail of the secret offer to Dobrynin, Robert Kennedy later falsified his memo to Rusk about the meeting by actually crossing out a reference to this secret understanding. Only about half of the ExComm knew about RFK's secret mission, and the remaining half were never formally told. JFK's letter and Dobrynin's personal account of his meeting with RFK were in Khrushchev's hands by early morning on Sunday, October 28.

Saturday, October 27, 9:00 P.M., Cabinet Room

"Then we need to have two things ready, a government for Cuba, because we're gonna need one after we go in with five hundred aircraft. And secondly, some plans for how to respond to the Soviet Union in Europe, cause *sure as hell* they're gonna do *something* there."

Secretary of Defense Robert McNamara

The president switched on the recorder during Rusk's update on the diplomatic situation. Khrushchev has "got to worry a *great deal* about how far he wants to push this thing," the secretary of state observed; "He's *on* a bad footing on his relations with the United States, his relations with *you*, the *actual* strategic situation." Rusk urged the president "to build up the pressure" by continuing surveillance, shooting "at anybody who gets in our way," intercepting the *Grozny*, and adding POL to the blockade. He also advised keeping "the monkey on *Cuba's* back." "If we *do* have to enforce our right to overfly," he declared, reminiscent of Senator Fulbright on October 22, "the accidental fact that some Russian technicians may be around at the time we have to shoot, since they've already fired the first shot" is regrettable. "We're enforcing this with respect to *Cuba,* not the Soviet Union." Dillon asked again about attacking the SAM that brought down the U-2 and JFK replied evasively, "We don't know if it did yet, Doug."

Taylor reported that low-level flights were "becoming difficult" because of ack-ack fire. "We're approaching the point, I think, Mr. President, where low-level reconnaissance will be entirely impossible." Sending in medium- or high-level missions, he advised, would require knocking out ten SAM sites if not "the whole works." McNamara added that the U-2 mission planned for Sunday was "just *too* dangerous," but "*if* our low-level planes are fired on tomorrow," he counseled, "we ought to fire back." President Kennedy endorsed waiting until Sunday for a possible breakthrough if U Thant went to Cuba. But, he declared, if the planes were attacked again and the Soviets failed to respond, the administration should make a public statement and "then go in and take out *all* the SAM sites." Despite these tough words, JFK had, in effect, stepped back from his October 23 commitment to order *immediate* air strikes against any SAM site that fired on a U-2. (The delay, as it turned out, made it much less awkward for Khrushchev to announce on Sunday that he would withdraw Soviet missiles from Cuba.)

McNamara also urged keeping "*some* kind of pressure on tonight and tomorrow night that indicates we're firm. Now if we call up these air squadrons tonight, I think that settles that." The president agreed. The defense chief revealed that he had prepared a statement calling up "twenty-four air reserve squadrons, roughly three hundred troop carrier transports, which are required for an invasion. And this would both be a preparatory move and also a *strong* indication of what lies ahead." Several voices can be heard in the background affirming, "That's right." JFK asked whether fighter planes would also be called up. "Just the troop carriers," McNamara explained; "We *could* call up some fighters. But they're just cats and dogs, Mr. President. It isn't worth it." Rusk questioned whether calling up fighter planes would have some "effect on Khrushchev," but Taylor pointed to the danger from the SAM sites and McNamara concluded, "Dean, it isn't worthwhile."

Attention shifted to the imminent arrival of the *Grozny* at the quarantine line. Robert Kennedy, likely shaken by his just-completed secret meeting with Dobrynin, suggested letting the *Grozny* through the blockade since by Monday, "we're gonna perhaps fire on all of Cuba. Whether this ship gets in or not is not really gonna count in the big picture." "Hell, we oughta wait and see tomorrow," JFK cut in; if this ship, contrary to Khrushchev's assurances, actually challenged the quarantine, then "no ships come through beginning the next morning." Sorensen, backed by Bundy, pointed out that those assurances had been given to U Thant rather than JFK. The president therefore proposed having Stevenson ask U Thant to alert Zorin on the approach of the *Grozny*. RFK, however, again questioned whether it was advisable to intercept a ship at this moment, and JFK declared, "We don't need to say what we're gonna do about it, but we ought to say this [ship] is approaching and we'd like to have him know about it."

There was no reason to be defensive about a delay, Rusk insisted, since the administration had already taken major steps that day, "to see whether we're building up the pressures on Khrushchev to get back to a pact [the Friday offer] that we can live with." These steps included: the White House statement on Khrushchev's public message; clarifying the quarantine intercept zone; announcing enforced surveillance; responding to Khrushchev's October 26 message and U Thant's initiative; calling up air reserve squadrons; and warning U Thant and Zorin on the approach of the *Grozny*. JFK suggested that if Khrushchev broke his promise to avoid the quarantine zone, pressure could be increased by adding POL and by stopping all ships. McNamara also observed that the call up of 14,000 air reservists constituted only a small portion of the congressional authorization to mobilize 150,000 reserves.

President Kennedy, turning again to the planned Sunday morning meeting of the North Atlantic Council, read aloud a private letter he had received from General Norstad. The supreme NATO commander advised that Ambassador Finletter should be "brief, factual, ... cool, and skeptical" at the NAC meeting; "In any event, it should help to avoid a situation in which you *can* be wrong *whatever* you do and your allies can be *right* and *wise* regardless of developments"—the same point JFK had referred to that afternoon. Norstad nonetheless concluded that a NATO Council meeting "will not, I fear, substantially relieve you of the burden of making a difficult decision." The general rejected equating the missiles in Cuba with the missiles in Turkey and predicted that a trade would undermine NATO confidence in American resolve. He urged the president to instruct Ambassador Finletter "to indicate this as the general direction of U.S. thinking."

After drafts of the instructions to Finletter were distributed, Rusk cautioned, "If we were asked for an *especial* preference, *of course* the preference is that we go ahead with this Cuban business without regard to bargaining with NATO—but that *NATO* must understand the nature of the risks that are involved for NATO." "It seems to me though, Mr. Secretary," JFK responded, "even if we *want* them to end up that way, we don't want it to look like that's where we *urged* them and therefore they have accepted, some reluctantly, some eagerly, the United States' opinion. Then this goes bad, which it may well, and they say, 'Well, we followed you and you bitched it up.'" President Kennedy, in short, wanted to be sure that the ambassadors at the NAC meeting fully understood that "'This is it! This situation's getting *worse*, and we're gonna have to take some action.'" Rusk expressed a hope that some members of the NATO Council "may come up with an idea that would unlock this *damn* thing, something that we haven't thought of." He added, with little conviction, "It's *just* possible." But the president reiterated, "if they want to get off, then *now* is the time to speak up."

Recognizing the continuing division over the Turkish missiles, McNamara asked bluntly, "Mr. President, do we believe that we will be able to settle Cuba more easily with or without the Jupiters in Turkey? I think we ought to decide this point, before we open a door to NATO—to make up our own minds." RFK cut in irritably before JFK could answer: "Can't we wait?" If the Soviets conclude "we're willing to make some deal, if I were they, I'd *push* on that, and then I'd *push* on Italy." RFK also urged trying to get Khrushchev back to his October 26 offer by remaining "*hard* and tough on this." But even the hawkish attorney general, mindful of the secret understanding on the Turkish missiles reached in the Oval Office earlier that evening, as well as his own discussion with Dobrynin shortly thereafter, acknowledged that if U Thant is "not successful and the whole thing looks like it's collapsing and we're gonna have to go in there," then we go to the NATO allies with the Turkish proposal despite our preference to keep the issue "completely in the Western Hemisphere."

RFK recommended that Finletter should remain non-committal at the NAC meeting and should stress that "the president is *very* reasonable." But, if the Russians rejected the U.S. acceptance of their Friday message and still insisted on their latest offer involving Turkey, NATO must be given an opportunity to make a decision affecting their own security. The attorney general, despite the secret offer to Dobrynin, still seemed to be anticipating—or perhaps even hoping—that Khrushchev might say "nyet" and NATO would decide, "We want to hold fast, and then on Tuesday we go into" Cuba.

JFK asked Bundy and Sorensen to draw up instructions for Finletter "based on what Bobby said," directing the ambassador to "take the temperature" in NATO without overtly pressuring the allies to adopt any position. But the president was far less ambivalent than RFK on a missile trade. The European allies must be prepared, he repeated again, "for a *disaster* to NATO later in the week in Berlin or someplace; you ought to be *saying* to them that the reason we're consulting with them is that the situation's deteriorating, and *if we take action* we think there *will* be reprisals..." RFK suggested sending someone from ExComm to the NAC meeting to "explain all of this," but Bundy pointed out that the session was only seven hours away. "Is it?" the surprised president replied. Sorensen asked if the NATO Council should discuss military options, but McNamara strenuously objected, "they may split up, and you may have chaos."

McCone tried to redirect attention to his proposed tough note to Khrushchev on shooting down the U-2. But a consensus quickly developed for continuing the flights without additional announcements. "We've got enough messages right now, John," the president gently told the CIA director; "I think that he [Khrushchev] knows about the plane. We've announced it." Sorensen was more blunt: "I think in some ways it's a sign of weakness if we just keep responding in messages." President Kennedy agreed, concluding that the urgent question was whether the Soviets would turn the *Grozny* around before it reached the quarantine line. He also recommended sending letters to key European leaders "because it involves Berlin," particularly de Gaulle, because "his view is *key* in this."

"What about the Turks now?" JFK asked again, "What do we gotta say to [Ambassador] Hare?" However, since only eight other people in the room knew about the confidential consensus reached after the last meeting and only Rusk knew about the secret Cordier initiative, JFK became cagey and ambiguous: "Let's give him [Hare] an explanation of what we're tryin to do. We're tryin to get it *back* on the original proposition of last night because we don't wanna get into this trade. If we're *unsuccessful*, then it's *possible* that we may have to get *back* onto the Jupiter thing. If we *do*, then we would of course want it to come from the Turks themselves and NATO, rather than just the United States. We're *hopeful*, however," JFK observed disingenuously, having already acted secretly to accept Khrushchev's proposal on Turkey, "that that won't come. . . . We'll be in touch with him in twenty-four hours when we find out if we are successful in putting the Russians back on the original track."

People began gathering their papers and getting up from the table as the discussion started to break up. McNamara, however, insisted that a decision on tomorrow's low-level reconnaissance missions had to be made soon. "We'll do that by tomorrow morning," JFK replied, "*or* when they *say* they've shot down our U-2." But McNamara exhorted the president, "This time we would make it *perfectly* clear if they attack our aircraft, we're going in after some of their MiGs." "Yeah, but we *won't* do the ground thing," against the SAMs and the antiaircraft batteries, JFK cautioned; "I think we oughta save that for a *real* [bombing] operation, which under this schedule you wouldn't do until Tuesday morning, because we'll have to go back to NATO again Monday in which we say the situation is getting worse . . . and give them their *last* chance" to avoid an attack by removing the Jupiters.

The defense secretary also raised another difficult subject—preparing an interim government for Cuba—and mentioned that a task force was working on that problem. RFK, referring to the president's September 30 decision to send federal troops to Oxford, Mississippi, to put down a riot sparked by the enrollment of James Meredith, a black Air Force veteran, at the University of Mississippi, quipped that the Army might actually be going directly from Mississippi to Cuba. After some mixed laughter and conversation, the president joked, "Well, I just wanted to go to Boston," and soon left the Cabinet Room.

A few ExComm members remained during the following exchange: "How you doing, Bob?" RFK teased. "Well," McNamara joked, "how about yourself?" "All right," RFK replied. "Got any doubts?" McNamara asked. "No," RFK responded, "I think we're doin' the only thing we can do." "I think the one thing, Bobby," McNamara added, "before we attack them, you've gotta be *damned sure they* [the U.S.S.R.] *understand it's coming.* In other words, you need to *really* escalate this." "Yeah," RFK murmured. "Then we need to have two things ready," McNamara continued. "A government for Cuba, because we're gonna need one after we go in with five hundred aircraft. And secondly, some plans for how to respond to the Soviet Union in Europe, cause *sure as hell* they're gonna do *something* there."

Dillon suggested that even "the smallest thing" the Soviets might try in Europe could aggravate tensions. But McNamara advised restraint: "*I* would suggest *a half* an eye for an eye." "That's right," Dillon replied. "If it isn't too serious an attack," McNamara added as a qualification. "I'd like to take Cuba back," RFK interposed wistfully. "That would be nice." Someone wisecracked, amidst laughter, "Yeah, how are they gonna partition that [Cuba]?" Someone else teased, "Well, suppose they make Bobby mayor of Havana?" provoking even more laughter.

The tape recorder suddenly cut off—ending the toughest day of the crisis and one of the most riveting documents in American history. Several members of ExComm spent restless or sleepless nights in their offices.

Just after 6:00 a.m., the CIA provided new evidence that Soviet technicians had rushed all twenty-four MRBM sites to operational status. The Soviets also knew that the Strategic Air Command had already targeted nearly six dozen Russian cities for nuclear attack. "The situation was fraught with dangers of slipping out of control."

By early on Sunday morning, October 28, Khrushchev, "in complete control of the Soviet leadership," had made up his mind: the danger was simply too great. "Anyone with an ounce of sense," Khrushchev later wrote, "can see I'm telling the truth. It would have been preposterous for us to unleash a war against the United States from Cuba. Cuba was 11,000 kilometers from the Soviet Union. Our sea and air communica-

tions with Cuba were so precarious that an attack against the U.S. was unthinkable." "Remove them," the Soviet leader ordered, "as soon as possible. Before something terrible happens." He promptly sent an order to General Pliyev: "Allow no one near the missiles. Obey no orders to launch and under no circumstances install the warheads." The earlier authorization to use tactical nuclear weapons without a direct order from Moscow was also revoked. Khrushchev told Gromyko, "'We don't have the right to take risks. . . . We have to let Kennedy know that we want to help him.' Father hesitated at the word 'help,'" Sergei Khrushchev later recalled, "but after a moment's silence repeated firmly, 'Yes, help. We now have a common cause, to save the world from those pushing us toward war.'" He instructed Gromyko to direct Dobrynin to contact Robert Kennedy at once and tell him that a positive reply to the president's message would arrive shortly.

The Kremlin had received a report from the Soviet embassy in Washington that President Kennedy had scheduled a television address on Sunday afternoon—presumably to announce an invasion of Cuba. In fact, the broadcast was a repeat of JFK's October 22 speech, but Soviet leaders had little understanding of a free media and assumed that the telecast of a presidential speech had originated at the highest government levels. Khrushchev therefore decided to broadcast his message immediately over Moscow radio. "This was an unusual, perhaps unprecedented, step in international practice, but an effective one. The answer would be on the president's desk in just a few minutes."

In Washington, President Kennedy was preparing to attend 10:00 Mass at St. Stephen's Church when intelligence sources reported that the Grozny had come to a stop before reaching the quarantine. McCone had gone to Mass an hour earlier after hearing on his car radio that the Kremlin would shortly make a significant announcement; he later joked that it seemed like the most interminable Mass he ever sat through. JFK reacted to Khrushchev's message with surprise, relief, and some skepticism. The Soviets had deceived the administration about placing missiles in Cuba and Gromyko had personally lied to the president on October 18. It seemed entirely possible that the announcement might be a trick.

The Joint Chiefs remained extremely suspicious and urged JFK to order sweeping air strikes in Cuba in twenty-four hours, followed by an invasion, unless indisputable evidence proved that the missile sites were being dismantled. Admiral Anderson moaned, "We have been had." General LeMay denounced the agreement as "the greatest defeat in our

history" and banged the table demanding, "We should invade today!"
McNamara later recalled that JFK was so stunned by LeMay's outburst
that he could only stutter in response. The president later remarked,
"The first advice I'm going to give my successor is to watch the generals
and to avoid feeling that because they were military men their opinions
on military matters were worth a damn." JFK "never felt closer to
Khrushchev than when he imagined him having to cope with a Curtis
LeMay of his own."

By the time JFK returned from Mass a groundswell of elation had
overwhelmed the White House. Nuclear war had apparently been
averted. One participant described the mood as "a miasma of self-
congratulation." McCone, however, reminded his colleagues that many
issues remained unresolved—such as inspection and verification, the
presence of MiG fighters and IL-28 nuclear bombers, and the precise
terms of the U.S. non-invasion pledge.

Sunday, October 28, about 11:00 A.M., Cabinet Room

"Now in this situation . . . there's some gratification for everyone's
line of action, except 'do nothing.'"

Secretary of State Dean Rusk

The president and the ExComm read through the full text of Khrushchev's message offering to withdraw the missiles from Cuba under
U.N. supervision. JFK turned on the tape recorder as Rusk commended
the president and the ExComm for a job well done. He recalled Kennedy's sardonic remark at an earlier meeting "that whichever line of action you adopt, those who were in favor of it were gonna regret it" because there were really no satisfactory choices. "Now in this situation,"
he continued, "there's some gratification for everyone's line of action,
except 'do nothing.'" The secretary of state concluded that those who
favored invading Cuba had backed the course that "turned out to be the
major quid pro quo for getting these weapons out of Cuba." But, just as
he mentioned those who supported air strikes, the tape inexplicably cut
off.

"Bundy interrupted to say that everyone knew who were hawks and
who were doves, but that today was the doves' day." Rusk and
McNamara recommended, and the president agreed, "that no air re-
connaissance missions be flown today."

JFK, concerned about possible Soviet treachery, insisted that "every

*effort be made to get the U.N. to fly reconnaissance missions Monday,"
and he authorized the release to the U.N. of photographs and refugee
reports, "to facilitate the inspection task which we expected the U.N. to
promptly undertake." He also "suggested that we tell the U.N. they
must carry out reconnaissance or else we will."*

*Kennedy also approved a public statement "welcoming the Soviet
decision to withdraw offensive weapons from Cuba" but cautioned his
advisers "to be reserved in all comment" in order to strengthen Khrushchev's position against sniping by Soviet or Cuban hawks. Rusk reported that Vasily Kuznetsov, first deputy minister of foreign affairs,
was coming to New York for the U.N. negotiations.*

*Finally, President Kennedy urged a private approach to Khrushchev
on removing the IL-28 bombers but admonished that the U.S. "should
not get hung up on this issue." Taylor recommended that "our objective
should be the status quo ante." JFK agreed, but added that "he did not
want to get into a position where we would appear to be going back on
our part of the deal." The president's reply to Khrushchev was released
to the press that afternoon.*

*Around noon, JFK phoned former presidents Eisenhower, Truman,
and Herbert Hoover—and deliberately misinformed them. He accurately reported that Khrushchev, on Friday, had privately suggested
withdrawing the missiles in exchange for an American promise not to
invade Cuba; but, on Saturday, the Kremlin leader had sent a public
message offering to remove the missiles if the U.S. pulled its Jupiters out
of Turkey. President Kennedy informed Eisenhower, "we couldn't get
into that deal"; told Hoover that Khrushchev had gone back "to their
more reasonable [Friday] position"; and assured Truman, "they . . . accepted the earlier proposal." Eisenhower, who had dealt personally
with Khrushchev, asked skeptically if the Soviets had tried to attach any
other conditions. "No," Kennedy replied disingenuously, "except that
we're not gonna invade Cuba." The former president, aware of only
half the truth, concluded, "this is a very, I think, conciliatory move he's
made." Such deceptions shaped the administration's cover story and
helped generate the notion of the "Trollope Ploy"—which, as suggested
above, is essentially a myth.*

*Castro heard the news of Khrushchev's decision over the radio. He
spoke at the University of Havana several days later and ridiculed
Khrushchev for lacking the "cojones" (balls) for a final showdown with
American imperialism. He also demanded an end to the U.S. economic
embargo against Cuba, the cessation of aerial reconnaissance, a halt to*

exile attacks, and the withdrawal of American forces from Guantanamo.

Soviet personnel in Cuba received instructions within hours to start dismantling the missile bases, and the work began by late on Sunday. Later that evening, Scali met again with Fomin, who reported, "I am under instructions to thank you. The information you provided Chairman Khrushchev was most helpful to him in making up his mind quickly. And that includes your explosion of Saturday."

JFK, after scheduling an ExComm meeting for Monday morning, left the White House to join his family at their private retreat in the Virginia countryside. NBC News White House correspondent Sander Vanocur later noticed that Kennedy had scrawled five words on his desk pad before leaving: "Berlin, Berlin, Berlin, Berlin, Berlin."

Kuznetsov met on Monday morning with U Thant in New York to finalize details on dismantling the bases and removing the missiles from Cuba. The Soviet envoy agreed to report directly to the Security Council, "which would then authorize a U.N. team to visit Cuba for 'on-site' inspection." Meanwhile, a task force met at the Defense Department to begin planning the withdrawal of the Jupiters from Turkey. In Moscow, the Presidium voted to send Anastas Mikoyan, Khrushchev's first deputy, to Havana to negotiate with Castro about implementing the October 28 agreement.

Monday, October 29, about 10:00 A.M., Cabinet Room

"This photography will tell us much more than *his* [U Thant's] words. He doesn't know *what the hell to look for*, any more than *I would.*"

President John F. Kennedy

Barely twenty-four hours after Khrushchev's surprise announcement, no one could be sure that the crisis was really moving toward a peaceful resolution. President Kennedy read his announcement establishing a coordinating committee "to give full time and attention to the matters involved in the conclusion of the Cuban crisis." Rusk recommended continuing the quarantine and counseled, "I *do* think we need surveillance today," but urged waiting to find out "what Kuznetsov is up to" at the U.N.

President Kennedy, reflecting the uncertainty, apprehension, and suspicion in Washington, recommended that the coordinating committee meet right away to determine, "How are we gonna maintain a satisfactory degree of knowledge about Cuba? We can't rely on the U.N. to do it." McNamara agreed that this was "a *very* difficult problem." Joseph Charyk, under secretary of the Air Force, who had discussed inspection with U Thant and his military adviser, Indian general Indar Rikhye, reported that the U.N. had been unable to finalize arrangements for flights later that day. But U Thant would be in Cuba in twenty-four hours and U.N. observers would be flown "to the sites to observe the actual status of the dismantling operation." Rikhye had also suggested suspending the blockade during U Thant's visit and keeping Kuznetsov informed on all decisions relating to reconnaissance and the quarantine.

McNamara advised Kennedy to approve surveillance missions that afternoon, and Rusk again urged keeping the quarantine in place, "Because if we give up *that* point we may be subject to a *massive* trick here." JFK agreed that U.S. ships should continue to challenge vessels as required and also objected to excluding American observers from any U.N. surveillance missions. "We ought to be *very hard*," he contended, "that there's gonna be an American on that plane"—with a copy of the film going to the U.S. The president also observed that aerial reconnaissance was "the least obtrusive ... to the sovereignty of Cuba, because one way or another it's gonna be inspected."

JFK further demanded having an American in the group traveling to Cuba with U Thant: "We said we'll let a Russian go, but let's have an American in there. If we *can't* get an American, then we shouldn't have a Russian." He also sided with Taylor and McNamara about relying on low-level flights, despite the political/military risks, because U-2 photos could be obscured by cloud cover. Paul Nitze urged a tough stance on surveillance until the U.N. took over: "I think we ought to *attack* the general *principle* of the *propriety* of surveillance." Rusk and Nitze also explained that Khrushchev had not specifically demanded a halt to low-level reconnaissance in his October 28 message. Rusk warned, quite presciently, that "U Thant has two big hurdles to get over to bring this thing [inspection] home. ... And he's gonna have, I think, more trouble with Castro perhaps than Kuznetsov." Taylor also expressed doubts about the technical competence of U.N. ground observers.

Nitze suggested informing the Soviets and the Cubans privately about the flights to "save their face," and JFK interjected, "I agree with you about that." Kennedy also recommended informing Kuznetsov in advance. "We don't wanna *bitch* this thing up, just to do a flight." Ambassador Thompson defended the flights as the only way to confirm that the Soviets were keeping their word on dismantling the sites. "We want to *see* that," Taylor murmured in the background.

JFK, mindful of Taylor's concern about competent U.N. observers, declared bluntly, "This photography will tell us much more than *his* [U Thant's] words. He doesn't know *what the hell to look for* any more than *I would*. Unless we know that there are technical people on this mission in whom we have confidence," we really need those photos very soon. McNamara noted skeptically that the U.N. force flying to Cuba with U Thant totaled only ten to fifteen people. JFK seemed genuinely worried that Khrushchev's offer to withdraw the missiles might still unravel. "We're not sure *ourselves* that we can get the photography *today*. So they're going ahead with the work. Well then, that means the whole deal *blows*." McNamara asserted firmly, "I *don't* believe there'll be U.N. reconnaissance flights. I think it's almost *impossible* the way they're working and talking . . . [and] we need to show our people that we're properly protecting their interests." Rusk was somewhat more upbeat: "I'm not discouraged *yet* . . . this may be for real." "I think they're gonna *dismantle* these things now," JFK also contended; "There's no *logic* to their going *ahead* now with the construction."

"Mr. President," McNamara reiterated, "*I* don't think we're gonna have U.N. reconnaissance capabilities develop without *tremendous* pressure from us. . . . they're not *at all* interested, and they're *particularly* not interested in doing it in any *practical* way." JFK, as a result, finally decided to tell the U.N., "We're gonna do this reconnaissance today, . . . and if they *don't* do it, then we're gonna have to continue the surveillance." McNamara added, "I don't think we'll *ever* get them to do it." The president recommended telling U Thant and Kuznetsov that we are "doing this in order to give *our own* people . . . and others, including the OAS," verifiable assurances. "Either we're gonna do it or the UN's gonna do it. If the U.N. does the procedure, we'll withdraw." As they were about to leave the Cabinet Room, the president ordered that U Thant be told that a low-level mission would be flown later that day.

The president returned to the Oval Office for a briefing on military options in Cuba.

Monday, October 29, about 12:30 P.M., Oval Office

"If they continue this conventional buildup into Cuba, then we just
have to draw conclusions from *that*. So I think we just stay *on* it."
President John F. Kennedy

JFK turned on the tape recorder during an exchange about the possible
use of any Soviet tactical nuclear weapons in Cuba to counter a U.S. invasion. General David Shoup admitted, "we *really* don't know how
much they've got [in Cuba]. ... What they would do with the nuclear
weapons if they had 'em? I don't know. I think they'd *shoot* 'em. Then
the question is, are we at nuclear war?"

The president, referring to historic anti-American sentiment in Cuba,
something he had overlooked before the Bay of Pigs, expressed concern
that American invasion forces might get bogged down: "probably the
younger Cubans *are* loyal to Castro and have enough nationalist spirit,
even ones that don't like Castro, so that we would certainly run into a
hard-core situation with a lot of guerrilla [resistance]. ... Your judgment is that it's *not* a major military effort, or is it?" "It would be a
major military effort, *yes sir*," Shoup replied firmly, but he was confident that the U.S. could inflict significant damage on Castro's forces
anywhere in Cuba. JFK asked if Cuban armored vehicles could be taken
out by air with conventional weapons and was assured by Admiral
George Anderson that with "250-pound low-flying bombs ... we'd
really make a shambles of it." Shoup also suggested that ports and
beaches might be mined. "Well, we just have to watch," Kennedy concluded, "and if they continue this conventional buildup into Cuba, then
we just have to draw conclusions from *that*. So I think we just stay *on*
it."

Kennedy recalled scornfully that the Russians had shipped missiles to
Cuba despite assurances from Dobrynin, who "is regarded *very well* in
Russia. ... So now he's liquidated as a source, cause nobody believes
him anymore, and the chances are he probably *didn't know*! He looked
so *shocked* that day, when Rusk showed him. He still wouldn't believe
it." JFK concluded that the Russians could not be trusted: "When
you're dealing under those conditions, where there's *no* basis [for trust]
... We just have to assume that we're gonna be back with Cuba in two
or three months if they start to build up their conventional forces."

As the briefing started to break up, President Kennedy and Admiral
Anderson chatted about college football and JFK remarked, "I see

you're on the cover of *Time*, Admiral." "Sir," Anderson replied, "I haven't read the article yet." "I'm sure they'll be kinder to you," Kennedy observed sarcastically, "than they are yet to me." The president also speculated about the practical limitations on the use of nuclear weapons, but Shoup observed: "the sixty-four-dollar question" is whether the Soviets might still use tactical nuclear weapons in Cuba "because they would deal bloody hell with Guantanamo." JFK seemed skeptical: "Everybody sort of figures that, *in extremis*, that everybody would use nuclear weapons. The decision to use any kind of a nuclear weapon, even the tactical ones, presents *such a risk* of it getting out of control." "If that joker [Castro] ever had the control," Shoup remarked, but the Soviets are "tellin' him that they have the keys, like we've got the keys." "I'm sure they do," JFK agreed. "The Russians say [to the U.S.]," Shoup continued, "'We have the keys; you have the keys. You trust us; we trust you.'" "No," JFK responded forcefully, "we don't *trust* each other. But we figure that they're never gonna give 'em [tactical nuclear weapons] to the Cubans anymore than we'd give them to, you know, *the Turks*. . . . I don't think anybody wants that weapon to escape from their control."

The president also mused about using the Cuban crisis as an opportunity for progress on Berlin: "Berlin really is a *paralyzing*" problem. "Because everything you want to do, you say, 'Oh, well, it will screw us in Berlin.' And I think if we can ever get any kind of a decent deal in Berlin..." "I *certainly* agree," Anderson replied. "It *really* gives them the *initiative* all the time." "It always makes us look like it divides the Allies," JFK continued, citing Rusk's recollection that General George Marshall, during World War II, had predicted that Berlin would "become an *impossible* situation over the years. . . . So that's what I think what we oughta do now while we've got some initiative here."

After the two JCS officers left the Oval Office, Sorensen came by and the conversation turned to possible press speculation about the negotiations at the U.N. Despite having sent McCloy to New York to look over Stevenson's shoulder in the talks with Kuznetsov, JFK insisted, "Adlai's in charge of the U.N. delegation." The president did not want the Republicans to "have a piece of this" potential political issue "just ten days before [the mid-term] election." There won't be a political problem, he repeated emphatically, "providing we don't make it *look* like it's a problem. . . . We want *U Thant* to know that Adlai is our voice. So I think that that's the general line." "Yeah, I'll see to that," Sorensen promised.

Rusk (and possibly Walt Rostow) came in soon after Sorensen left and the president can be heard suggesting, "I'm gonna decorate that widow some time"—a reference to the wife of Major Rudolph Anderson, the U-2 pilot killed over Cuba. The president, however, after bringing up the secret agreement on withdrawing the Jupiters from Turkey, abruptly became angry: "Now listen. ... I gotta tell you this in private." When the Soviets made the Turkish proposal on Saturday, he recalled, "there was *nothing* done, really. ... Now it seemed to me that it was *obvious* that was coming along, and as I say in my notes" from last Saturday, "I *asked* them to review this, particularly asked *Nitze*, because it's a NATO commitment."

JFK cited his written notes at least two more times to back up his charge—likely hinting at his rationale for making these secret recordings. Kennedy respected his advisers and the fact that they had strong views of their own, but he was distressed because single-minded resistance to the Turkish trade at the ExComm meetings had, he suspected, been accompanied by bureaucratic foot dragging and possible obstruction by high-ranking officials. "We had it [the Soviet offer on Turkey] for twenty-four hours," the president continued irritably, "and *now* we're trying to figure out whether we turn it down, and nobody had any idea *really* what the Turks would go for and all the rest." Rusk, rather diffidently, referred to some State Department policy papers, but JFK snapped, "Well *I'd like* to *get* them," and cut him off sharply, "I never get your stuff! *You* talk to Mac [Bundy] *now*," he ordered, "and have somebody over in the White House that's responsible for liaison with you, so I can see some of these things." He calmed down quickly, however, explaining in a much more composed tone of voice, "Can you get 'em to me more?" Rusk, likely taken aback by the president's sudden and uncharacteristic outburst, left the Oval Office.

A few minutes later, JFK pushed a button on the phone console and told an aide, "I want to get a president's commemorative for the Executive Committee of the National Security Council who've been involved in this matter. What I thought of is something that would have the month of October on it and ... have a line drawn around the calendar days. ... In other words just like a page out of a calendar. ... How could you get that so it wouldn't be too expensive? It's about twelve [days]." (The subsequent association of the missile crisis with "thirteen days" did not really become indelible until the publication of RFK's book in 1969.) Kennedy then switched off the tape recorder.

Each silver calendar, with highlighted engraving of the thirteen days from October 16 to 28, was inscribed with the initials of the president and those of the individual recipient and designed by Tiffany's for the members of ExComm and for several aides—as well as for Evelyn Lincoln and Jacqueline Kennedy. JFK had sometimes walked around the White House grounds alone after late ExComm meetings, "trying to clear his mind," then had dinner with his wife and told "her everything that was happening." He later made "a special point" of giving Jackie a calendar of her own.

Epilogue: The November Post-Crisis

JFK's decision to create commemorative calendars, engraved through October 28, suggests that he was hopeful that the nuclear standoff over missiles in Cuba had been resolved. However, the secret understanding between the Kremlin and the White House began to fray almost immediately—largely because of resistance from Castro. The missile crisis was not *really* over after all.

Ambassador Dobrynin delivered a letter from Khrushchev to Robert Kennedy on October 29. The message identified the terms of the agreement reached on that fateful weekend: Soviet withdrawal of "those weapons you describe as offensive;" on-site verification by U.N. inspectors; a U.S. pledge not to invade Cuba; plus an American commitment to remove the Jupiters from Turkey. After consulting with the president, RFK returned the letter and, in line with the strategy adopted in the Oval Office on October 27, refused to formalize the secret agreement about the Jupiters in writing. RFK admitted, according to Dobrynin, that he could not "risk getting involved in the transmission of this sort of letter, since who knows where and when such letters can surface or be somehow published—not now, but in the future—and any changes in the course of events are possible. The appearance of such a document could cause irreparable harm to my political career in the future. This is why we request that you take this letter back." Dobrynin chose not to press the issue.

U Thant arrived in Cuba on October 30 and found Castro in an "impossible and intractable mood." The Cuban leader railed about Soviet betrayal and "declared categorically that there would be no inspection of any kind by any outside agency on Cuban soil." JFK ordered the resumption of reconnaissance flights despite threats that Cuban forces would fire on U.S. aircraft.

Negotiations at the U.N. between Ambassador Stevenson (assisted by John McCloy) and Ambassador Zorin (assisted by Vasily Kuznetsov) quickly bogged down over whether the IL-28 bombers should be considered "offensive" weapons. JFK, in several ExComm meetings, had argued that the U.S. should learn to live with Soviet bombers in Cuba. But, in the wake of Khrushchev's unanticipated retreat, and with the mid-term elections barely a week away, he gradually hardened his position.

Khrushchev's principal deputy, Anastas Mikoyan, arrived in Havana in early November to persuade Castro to accept outside inspection and removal of the IL-28s. Castro "grudgingly" met Mikoyan's plane, but refused to confer with him for days and finally presented a list of demands, including suspension of the economic embargo, an end to U.S. sabotage and overflights, and the return of the Guantanamo naval base. Castro told Khrushchev's emissary, "we oppose this inspection," insisting that Cuba had "the right to defend our dignity." The refusal of the Kennedy administration to make direct contact with Castro "placed the entire burden of coping with Cuba on the Soviet government, which, in effect, was being asked to serve as a U.S. ally in the handling of relations with Cuba."

Tensions between the Soviets and their Cuban allies bubbled over at a Soviet embassy dinner marking the forty-fifth anniversary of the Bolshevik Revolution. The Soviets neglected to offer a toast to Castro, and a Cuban official shocked his hosts by proposing "a joint toast to Fidel and Stalin." Khrushchev, furious after learning of this incident, became alarmed that Castro's intransigence might derail the entire October 28 agreement.

By the end of the first week of the post-crisis, the president had concluded that the presence of the IL-28 bombers and the failure to implement ground inspection had thrown into question any U.S. non-invasion pledge. JFK pressed McNamara to be prepared for "an unforeseen turn of events in Cuba that offered a worthwhile opportunity ... [to launch] an airborne assault in the vicinity of Havana by two airborne divisions, followed as quickly as possible by an amphibious assault ... over beaches to the east of Havana." "With this election now over," JFK candidly admitted, "we ought to just play it...," "Cool for a while," Bundy interjected." "Well, *no*," the president replied revealingly, "*very straight*, say what is pleasing and what is not. We're not being . . . this constant thing of somebody gouging us. I think we'll have a little *time* now. . . . We wanna get the IL-28s out of there and . . . then we probably wouldn't invade," unless there was a major appeal from the Cuban people or the Soviets reintroduced offensive weapons. "Then we would invade. Otherwise our commitment ought to stay. We don't plan to invade Cuba. *But*, we're ready to give that in a more formal way when they meet *their* commitments."

JFK also speculated about pressuring other nations to put "the squeeze" on Castro to remove the bombers. If the U.S. strictly enforced the quarantine, the president argued, it would cause many countries "a lot of grief." He added, somewhat hopefully, "I think that under those conditions they should be willing to *join us*." "I think," Rusk quipped, as Bundy chuckled, "they would go to great lengths to avoid that situation."

The Defense Department announced on November 8 that all known Soviet missile bases in Cuba had been dismantled, but, on the same day, a sabotage team carried out an attack on a Cuban factory—despite the suspension of Operation Mongoose at the end of October. The president also continued to lean toward linking the IL-28 removal and the U.S. non-invasion guarantee: "I don't think we'd look very good to say, 'Well, we withdraw our commitment that we won't invade.' . . . [But] I think that it's gonna be *damned* important" to make clear to the international community that the withdrawal of the IL-28s would determine the viability of the non-invasion pledge. In an effort to break this impasse, RFK invited Bolshakov to his home and later explained that the United States could not resolve the crisis without "the rapid removal of the IL-28s." The administration was also concerned about rumors that the Soviets had concealed some missiles in Cuba. Nitze estimated a 10 percent chance of deception, but McNamara contended that the likelihood "was far less than that, a tenth of 1 percent chance," but joked that 30 percent of the public and 80 percent of the Congress would probably believe these reports.

Stevenson informed the president on November 12 that negotiations with Zorin and Kuznetsov on the IL-28s had deadlocked. Nevertheless, JFK worried that enforcing the full quarantine would be very risky politically, since, with the missiles out of Cuba, the U.S. would no longer command unified support in Latin America or Europe. Instead, he proposed putting the screws on Khrushchev through "our refusal to give the assurances on invasion and the continued surveillance [of Cuba]. . . .

I think we're probably in maybe better shape to do *that* than we are to put back the kind of a quarantine which we never *really* enforced, which was to stop everybody and search 'em." That evening, RFK informed Dobrynin that the U.S. expected the IL-28s to be withdrawn in thirty days, but suggested that a Soviet promise "to remove the bombers according to a definite schedule" could be sufficient to allow lifting the quarantine.

In Havana, Mikoyan again pressed Castro to remove the IL-28s—which he described as militarily insignificant—and promised that this concession would be the last from the Soviet side. He also argued that the Americans would not lift the blockade unless the bombers were withdrawn. Khrushchev, on November 14, privately assured JFK, "those planes will be removed from Cuba with all the equipment and flying personnel. It can be done in two to three months."

Castro, however, vowed again that he would not permit U.S. planes to violate Cuban sovereignty, admonishing Mikoyan that "we will open fire on all American military planes" regardless of Soviet objections. Mikoyan complained to Khrushchev that the Cubans were too emotional and "bitter feelings often overcome reason." The angry and frustrated Soviet leader declared, "Either they cooperate or we will recall our personnel." Khrushchev felt that the American non-invasion pledge constituted a major step to assure the survival of the Cuban revolution, which had been the Kremlin's principal goal, and demanded that Castro "must show more flexibility."

JFK repeated his concern a few days later that "cranking on the quarantine to get the IL-28s out is not particularly satisfactory," and Bundy provoked general laughter by drolly interjecting, "There are two people to whom it's *wholly* unsatisfactory, Mr. President, you and the chairman [Khrushchev]." The president was determined not to let Khrushchev off the hook and declared that the non-invasion pledge was on hold "*until* he gets the IL-28s *out*." The overflights would also continue and if "they shoot at us and we shoot back ... he [Khrushchev] gets the kind of escalation which he can't *like very much*.... And in addition ... any other negotiation which he may want more to go on in Berlin or anything else are held up because of our public charge that he did not *fulfill* his agreement." Amphibious landing exercises also continued in North Carolina, and the JCS reported that 100,000 Army troops, 40,000 Marines, and nearly 15,000 paratroopers, as well as 550 combat aircraft and 180 ships, were poised to invade Cuba.

"We're *not* going to invade Cuba," JFK nonetheless continued to insist. "What we want from the Russians is the withdrawal of their military presence ... or certainly a great lessening of it. It isn't just taking out the IL-28s." The ultimate goal is to guarantee "that Cuba is not an armed camp [and then] we would not *invade* Cuba." But Kennedy had also decided to keep *all* military options open, especially if Castro continued to support political subversion in Latin America. "Now let's just see," JFK hypothesized, "the conditions under which we'd invade. ... We'd invade Cuba only if a military threat came to us, or if they were carrying out their threat against their neighbor. Now, that's *quite* obvious. Then we'd invade Cuba probably only if there was a real outbreak of civil war where our presence might be a *decisive* factor. I don't think *otherwise* we're gonna find the condition in the next two or three years where we're gonna be able to justifiably, *in our interests*, taken around the world, of *invading* Cuba." JFK also conceded, "We'd like to get him [Castro] out. But I don't think we're probably gonna be able to get Castro *out of there* by an invasion by the United States forces. So we don't wanna tie our hands too much 'cause these other conditions might arise."

On November 18, Stevenson told the president that Soviet negotiators at the U.N. remained obdurate on the IL-28s. John McCloy tried to break the logjam by telling Kuznetsov that the president would overlook the on-site inspection issue, despite persistent rumors about missiles hidden in Cuba, and would "guarantee the non-invasion of Cuba from other Latin American countries" if the bombers were withdrawn. JFK, however, grimly notified the leaders of England, France, and West Germany that Khrushchev was unlikely to back down again.

Castro, the next day, finally gave in to intense pressure from the Kremlin and advised U Thant that he would not stand in the way of withdrawing the IL-28s. A formal letter from Khrushchev, agreeing to pull the nuclear bombers out of Cuba, was delivered to JFK by Bolshakov on November 20. "Well," Khrushchev wrote to his adversary in Washington, "I think, this answer of mine gives you not bad material for your statement at your press conference."

Hours before the president's statement to the nation, RFK, McCone, and several other NSC members urged JFK not to make a public non-invasion commitment. With the quarantine removed, they reasoned, the non-invasion promise was the only remaining lever for putting pressure on Khrushchev. President Kennedy seemed uneasy: "Now how do we prevent this from looking too much like we're welching on it as well?" The attorney general, despite his personal negotiations with Dobrynin, continued to take a hard line: "I don't think that we owe anything as far as Khrushchev is concerned; nor does he expect it at the moment." RFK did concede, "maybe we wanna throw this in as a piece of cake." JFK also pondered whether the non-invasion pledge might make it politically easier for Khrushchev to withdraw Soviet conventional forces from Cuba.

In the end, Kennedy toughened his stance. Despite announcing at his press conference that the Soviets would withdraw the IL-28s within thirty days, and that the quarantine would be lifted, he added that since on-site inspection and verification had not been implemented, the preconditions for the U.S. non-invasion pledge had not been met. He did affirm, however, that if offensive weapons were kept out of Cuba, and Castro ended "the export of aggressive Communist purposes, there will be peace in the Caribbean." Khrushchev seemed satisfied, telling Mikoyan, "Evidently, Kennedy himself is not an extremist."

Over the next few months, Khrushchev worked to repair damaged relations with Cuba and invited Castro to visit the U.S.S.R. in the spring of 1963. Castro's travel plans were kept secret because Khrushchev believed "there was a real possibility of an 'accidental' attack on the plane carrying Fidel over the ocean. It was well known that one of the aims of the 'Mongoose' operation was his physical elimination." Castro's trip was not announced publicly until after his plane had landed safely in the U.S.S.R.

Historians of the missile crisis and its aftermath continue to wrestle with a murky question: in the wake of the allegedly sobering lessons of those thirteen days, did President Kennedy adopt "a dual-track policy toward Castro of ideological antagonism and accommodation"— including rethinking plans to get rid of the Cuban leader? Operation Mongoose, for example, was terminated in late October. In the spring, after anti-Castro exiles attacked Soviet vessels in Cuba, JFK suspended operations against Soviet interests. José Miró Cardona, the zealous head of the Cuban Revolutionary Council, resigned in protest. In May, journalist Lisa Howard interviewed Castro in Havana and later reported to the CIA on "possible interest in rapprochement with the United States." JFK agreed in September to explore contacts with the Cuban government through intermediary William Attwood, former ambassador to Guinea. The president also met privately with French journalist Jean Daniel, just before the reporter's November trip to Cuba. Kennedy acknowledged America's share of culpability for the suffering caused by Batista and expressed sympathy for a revolutionary Cuba free from ex-

ternal Soviet control. Castro, after later talking to Daniel, seemed receptive to pursuing a secret dialogue with the U.S. The Daniel contact appears to have been initiated by Cuban intelligence, which "considered
the signals Kennedy gave in response to these overtures highly positive.
Castro was very enthusiastic, and became convinced that a settlement
was possible." But, "this hopeful period" ended on November 22, 1963.

On balance, however, these tentative and ad hoc steps do not out-
weigh the remaining evidence. On December 29, 1962, before some
40,000 Cuban exiles in Miami's Orange Bowl, JFK paid tribute to the
just-released Bay of Pigs prisoners and pledged that their brigade flag
would fly over a "free Havana." The Cubans chanted, "Guerra!
Guerra!" Only a month later, Kennedy reconstituted covert operations
under a new Interdepartmental Cuban Coordinating Committee. He
also continued to press forward with "contingency invasion plans," personally approved sabotage against Cuban shipping and infrastructure,
and supported economic warfare "to tighten the noose around the Cuban economy." Contrary to private assurances to Khrushchev, JFK even
authorized "inciting Cubans" to assault Soviet military forces in Cuba
"provided every precaution is taken to prevent attribution." Thirteen
major CIA covert operations against Cuba were approved for just the
last few months of 1963, "including the sabotage of an electric power
plant, a sugar mill, and an oil refinery." Attempts to kill Castro continued as well. U.S.-Soviet relations did moderate in the year after the missile crisis, but there was no comparable thaw in U.S.-Cuban relations.

Conclusion

The objective of this book has been to provide a new avenue of access to the often neglected core event of the Cuban missile crisis: the secret ExComm meetings. Historians regularly quote from notes or transcripts of these discussions, but verbatim transcripts alone simply cannot capture the full human dimension of these meetings. A narrative account derived directly from the tapes, however, fine tunes the inner history of the missile crisis by underscoring the personal, political, and intellectual dynamic between JFK and his advisors.

Most importantly, the narrative approach provides special insight into the off-the-record depth and color of President Kennedy's handling of these secret meetings. JFK's leadership style rarely comes across in paper records (or even in his speeches—notwithstanding the flashes of wit and intelligence). So much that cannot be captured, even in the most accurate transcripts, is there on the tapes for the listener with a discerning ear: the nuances of his voice and temperament, his impatience, his Cold War assumptions and convictions, his doubts, his blind spots, his political instincts, his quick mind, his dispassionate self-control, his persistence, his caution, his skepticism about military solutions to political problems, and his ironic sense of humor.

Kennedy's management of the ExComm discussions was subtle and understated, but remarkably effective. He virtually never lost his temper, at least, Dean Rusk might add, not during the high point of the crisis, and remained all but imperturbable in the face of sometimes severe criticism from the Joint Chiefs, the ExComm, or the leaders of Congress. JFK was never arrogant or egotistical, never put anyone down harshly, and barely raised his voice even when obviously irritated or angry—except in the Rusk incident on October 29. Even when Kennedy chastised Rusk, however, he specifically pointed out that his criticism was being leveled in private. JFK was always willing to let people have their say—confident that in the end the constitutional authority to decide remained entirely in his hands.

The views of ExComm members, of course, shifted, evolved, and even reversed direction in response to the changing diplomatic, political, and military situation, their own beliefs and values, and the arguments of their colleagues. Some participants were nearly always diffident and reflective; others were tough and assertive; some were eager to lead, despite the enormous stakes involved; others were content to follow and say very little.

The author has made a determined effort to capture as much of the nuance of the meetings as a written narrative can possibly convey; but, only the tapes themselves can fully portray the human reality of these discussions. Imagine, for example, if it suddenly became possible to *hear* a recording of the actual Gettysburg Address. Our understanding of Lincoln's words, meaning, and intent would certainly be changed by exposure to the unique power of the spoken word—especially when heard in its original historical context. It is hard to imagine that anyone would *first* choose to read the speech if the option to actually hear the original presentation existed as well.

The ExComm conversations, of course, were not consciously crafted public oratory. Nonetheless, a narrative based on a careful hearing of the tapes inevitably generates insights beyond those of tone and mood. Was Secretary Rusk, for example, merely reviewing the facts or proposing a cover story about the U-2 that "strayed" into Soviet air space on an air-sampling mission near Alaska?

The so-called "Trollope Ploy," however, provides the most striking case in point. Historians and missile crisis participants, largely as a result of Robert Kennedy's *Thirteen Days*, have often overestimated the importance of this celebrated decision to respond to Khrushchev's secret Friday offer while "ignoring" his public Saturday proposal. Indeed, this ExComm tactic, initially attributed to RFK alone, has become a fixture in the legend and lore of the crisis. At least in part, RFK overstated the significance of this clever diplomatic maneuver simply because the U.S.-Soviet understanding on the Turkish missiles was still secret when his book was written and remained secret for decades afterwards.

In fact, listening to the October 27 meeting tapes suggests that scholars and ExComm members have read far too much cunning and coherence into the discussion of that thorny issue. President Kennedy, as the tapes document, stubbornly and persistently contended that Khrushchev's Saturday offer could not be ignored precisely because it had been made public. In fact, JFK's eventual message to Khrushchev did *not* "ignore" the Saturday proposal on Turkey, but left the door open to settling broader international issues once the immediate danger in Cuba had been neutralized. JFK ultimately offered the Kremlin a calculated blend of Khrushchev's October 26 and 27 proposals: the removal of the Soviet missiles from Cuba, an American non-invasion pledge (contingent on U.N. inspection), a willingness to talk later about NATO-related issues, *and* a secret commitment to withdraw the Jupiters from Turkey. The "Trollope Ploy," in that sense, is basically a myth.

Robert Kennedy did tirelessly press his brother not to give up on Khrushchev's Friday proposal. JFK, although skeptical and reluctant, finally agreed to try this scheme despite repeatedly predicting that the Soviet leader would inevitably "come back" to his public offer on the Turkish missiles. The President had no illusions about forcing Khrushchev to settle for the terms in his earlier message and assented to this strategy largely to placate unyielding ExComm opposition. In fact, as revealed by RFK's meeting with Dobrynin and other secret steps taken later that day and kept from much of the ExComm, JFK was determined not to allow this chance to avert nuclear catastrophe to slip away. As he reminded the gung-ho Joint Chiefs on October 19, an attack on Cuba could prompt the firing of nuclear missiles against American cities and result in 80–100 million casualties—"you're talkin' about the destruction of a country!"

In addition, the continuing importance of the ExComm discussions in helping the President to make up his mind, even in the final hours of the crisis, can only be fully grasped by either listening to the tapes or reading a narrative that captures the nuances in voices, tone, and words—*when heard together.* There can be no question, after listening painstakingly to these recordings, that the often rough give-and-take with the ExComm played a decisive role in continuing to shape JFK's perspective and decisions. The President, for example, surely understood the alarming implications of Taylor's almost casual assertion that using nuclear weapons in Cuba would not necessarily provoke a nuclear response from the Soviet Union; or McNamara's confident assurances about using practice depth charges to "harmlessly" force Soviet submarines to surface; or Bundy's self-important claim that everyone in the government involved in alliance problems would be hostile to a Cuba-Turkey missile trade; or Nitze's inflexibility over amending JCS procedures to prevent the firing of the Turkish Jupiter missiles and advocacy of shooting down Soviet planes in the Berlin air corridor.

In several of these cases, not to mention the taut exchanges with General LeMay and Senators Russell and Fulbright, JFK barely managed to conceal his disdain in the face of inflexibility, doctrinaire thinking, and lack of imagination. Even in the final days and hours of the crisis, the ExComm had an enormous emotional and psychological impact on President Kennedy's commitment to averting nuclear war. Every major option was discussed, frequently in exhaustive and exhausting detail—providing both the context and sounding board for the President in making his final decisions.

In fact, President Kennedy's inclination to pursue the Turkish option actually seems to have hardened in response to the dogged intractability of his advisers. The tapes indicate that the ExComm continued to have a major impact, especially during the final meetings, simply by repeatedly and all but unanimously *opposing* JFK's preferred course of action. It is a serious mistake to underestimate the importance of these discussions in prodding the President to implement this potential settlement—while there was still time.

Studying history, of course, is not like assembling a neatly-cut jigsaw puzzle. Pieces of historical evidence do not have to fit together tidily or logically within fixed and predetermined borders. Indeed, despite the best efforts of historians, they do not have to fit together at all. History defines its own parameters, and real historical figures often defy our assumptions and expectations. Contradictions and inconsistencies are the rule rather than the exception in human affairs.

As a historian trained in the turbulent 1960s and influenced by New Left historiography, I took for granted that John Kennedy had been a tough and relentless Cold Warrior. And, as discussed earlier, JFK and his administration bear significant responsibility for precipitating the missile crisis. The ExComm tapes, nonetheless, prove conclusively that President Kennedy consistently dug in his heels in the face of determined pressure to bomb or invade Cuba. He also repeatedly acted to prevent, postpone, or at least question the wisdom of potentially provocative measures such as:

mining international waters around Cuba
declaring war in conjunction with announcing the quarantine

extending the quarantine to Soviet aircraft flying to Cuba
resisting Russian efforts to inspect U.S. truck convoys entering Berlin
using belligerent language in an official proclamation
using the word "miscalculate" in a presidential letter because Khru-
    shchev had misinterpreted this concept when translated into Rus-
    sian at the Vienna summit
seizing a Soviet ship that had reversed course
risking gunfire if the crew of a disabled ship resisted boarding
allowing the Navy to photograph a bloody clash at sea
enforcing the quarantine by attacking a Soviet submarine
arming U.S. reconnaissance planes and returning Cuban ground fire
initiating night surveillance using flares
immediately destroying a SAM site if a U-2 was shot down.

JFK repeatedly tried to rise above the simplistic Cold War rhetoric he had exploited in his October 22 speech announcing the discovery of Soviet missiles in Cuba. And, to a remarkable degree, he succeeded— although not without some "help" from Khrushchev and some genuine luck.

The evidence from the missile crisis tapes is anomalous and even surprising, but no less true: Kennedy often stood virtually alone against warlike counsel from the ExComm, the JCS, and the leaders of Congress during those historic 13 days. Nonetheless, he never abandoned his commitment, even *after* the missile crisis, to undermine the Cuban revolution and get rid of Fidel Castro. It was one thing, however, to support efforts to overthrow or even eliminate the Cuban leader, and quite another to recklessly risk unleashing "the final failure."

JFK confided to Ambassador John Kenneth Galbraith after the crisis, "You will never know how much bad advice I had." Now, thanks to the tapes President Kennedy never imagined would be made public, we *all* know.

Notes

The numbers at the left are page numbers.

2 *transcripts . . . can be dense and impenetrable*: for the author's discussion of errors in the published transcripts, see *Averting 'The Final Failure': John F. Kennedy and the Secret Cuban Missile Crisis Meetings*, xx–xxi, 427–40.

7 *might have . . . listened to some of the tapes in 1963*: see Timothy Naftali, "The Origins of 'Thirteen Days,'" *Miller Center Report* 15 (Summer 1999): 23–24.

7 *"There pose the Kennedy brothers . . ."*: William Safire, New *York Times*, October 12, 1997.

12 *"For Stalin there were always two worlds"*: Vladislav Zubok and Constantine Pleshakov, *Inside the Kremlin's Cold War: From Stalin to Khrushchev* (Cambridge, Mass.: Harvard University Press, 1996), 12.

14 *"most acute and dangerous confrontation"*: Laurence Chang, "The View from Washington and the View from Nowhere: Cuban Missile Crisis Historiography and the Epistemology of Decision Making," in James A. Nathan, ed., *The Cuban Missile Crisis Revisited* (New York: St. Martin's, 1992), 132.

15 *"Don't worry about this"*: Chester Bowles Oral History Interview, John F. Kennedy Library [JFKL], 61–62.

16 *"How could I have been so far off base?"*: Theodore C. Sorensen, *Kennedy* (New York: Harper and Row, 1965), 309.

16 *Guevara . . . peace feeler*: Richard Goodwin, "Conversation with Commandante Ernesto Guevara of Cuba," August 22, 1961, JFKL.

17   *"All one can say is"*: Lawrence Freedman, *Kennedy's Wars: Berlin, Cuba, Laos and Vietnam* (New York: Oxford University Press, 2000), 150–52.

17   *expel . . . from the Organization of American States*: The OAS administered the Rio Treaty, a mutual defense pact of the nations of the Americas signed in 1947—two years before the creation of NATO.

17   *"From the Cuban perspective"*: Philip Brenner, "Thirteen Months: Cuba's Perspective on the Missile Crisis," in Nathan, ed., *The Cuban Missile Crisis Revisited*, 201, 206.

18   *"It is hard to imagine"*: Fred Kaplan, "JFK's First-Strike Plan," *Atlantic Monthly 288* (2001): 81–86.

18   *"imprisoned by Berlin"*: Hugh Sidey, *John F. Kennedy, President* (New York: Athenaeum, 1963), 218.

18   *"one thought kept hammering"*: Strobe Talbott, ed. and trans., *Khrushchev Remembers* (Boston: Little, Brown, 1970), 493.

19   *"a little of their own medicine"*: Ibid., 492–94.

19   *"With forty missiles staring at Florida"*: Aleksandr Fursenko and Timothy Naftali, *"One Hell of a Gamble": Khrushchev, Castro and Kennedy, 1958–1964* (New York: W. W. Norton, 1997), 189.

19   *Khrushchev . . . acting to . . . implement the Marxist view of history*: Strobe Talbott, ed. and trans., *Khrushchev Remembers: The Last Testament* (Boston: Little, Brown, 1974), 511–14.

20   *these huge missiles could be "disguised . . ."*: Sergei Khrushchev, *Nikita Khrushchev and the Creation of a Superpower* (University Park: Pennsylvania State University Press, 2000), 502, 559–62. Sergei Khrushchev, now an American citizen and a senior fellow at the Brown University Watson Institute for International Studies, was shocked that his father fell for "such primitive reasoning."

21   *Soviet medium-range ballistic missiles were delivered*: Fursenko and Naftali, *"One Hell of a Gamble,"* 217.

21   *"If we cooperate"*: James Schefter, *The Race* (New York: Doubleday, 1999), 145.

21   *plans . . . for a nuclear first strike*: Fred Kaplan, "JFK's First-Strike Plan," 81–86.

22   *"He can't do that to me"*: McGeorge Bundy, *Danger and Survival: Choices About the Bomb in the First Fifty Years* (New York: Random House, 1998), 684–85.

22   *RFK upon seeing the photos*: Dino Brugioni, *Eyeball to Eyeball: The In-*

side Story of the Cuban Missile Crisis, ed. Robert F. McCort (New York: Random House, 1991), 223.

23 *JFK's "strategy of annihilation"*: Thomas G. Paterson, "John F. Kennedy's Quest for Victory and Global Crisis," in Thomas G. Paterson, ed., *Kennedy's Quest for Victory: American Foreign Policy, 1961–1963* (New York: Oxford University Press, 1989), 5, 7, 20; Thomas G. Paterson, "When Fear Ruled: Rethinking the Cuban Missile Crisis," *New England Journal of History* 52 (Fall 1995): 26.

23 *"not immune to mistakes"*: Sergei Khrushchev, *Nikita Khrushchev*, 460–61.

23 *"In the future"*: Ibid., 466.

24 *JFK preventing nuclear war*: Fred Kaplan, "Kennedy Legacy Shines," *Boston Globe*, January 13, 2001; Robert Kuttner, "Watching '13 Days,'" *Boston Globe*, January 28, 2001; John L. Gaddis, *We Now Know: Rethinking Cold War History* (New York: Oxford University Press, 1997), 272.

24 *"I am dissatisfied"*: Hugh Sidey, Introduction, *Prelude to Leadership: The European Diary of John F. Kennedy—Summer 1945* (Washington, D.C.: Regnery, 1995), xix–xxi.

24 *"He had read the books"*: Ibid., xxiv–xxv, xxix.

24 *"deep core of realism"*: Ibid., xvi, xx, xxviii.

25 *"a return to barbarism"*: John F. Kennedy, *Harvard Crimson*, October 9, 1939.

25 *"a hell of an attack"*: John F. Kennedy to K. Lemoyne Billings, May 6, 1943, Billings Papers, JFKL.

25 *"I would like to write you"*: John F. Kennedy to Inga Arvad, no date, spring 1943, Nigel Hamilton Research Materials, Massachusetts Historical Society [NHRM, MHS].

26 *"Dearest Inga Binga"*: John F. Kennedy to Inga Arvad, no date, NHRM, MHS.

26 *"Just had an inspection"*: John F. Kennedy to Inga Arvad, no date, NHRM, MHS.

27 *"Don't let anyone"*: John F. Kennedy to Rose and Joseph Kennedy, May 14, 1943, JFKL.

27 *"When I read"*: John F. Kennedy to Rose and Joseph Kennedy, September 12, 1943, JFKL; John F. Kennedy to Inga Arvad, no date, spring 1943, NHRM, MHS.

27 *"That whole story was fucked up"*: Herbert S. Parmet, *Jack: The Struggles of John F. Kennedy* (New York: Doubleday, 1980), 111–12.

27 *"The war goes slowly here"*: John F. Kennedy to Inga Arvad, September 26, 1943, NHRM, MHS.

28 *"The greatest danger"*: John F. Kennedy, "Aid for Greece and Turkey," *Record of the House of Representatives*, April 1, 1947.

28 *"We should bear in mind"*: John F. Kennedy, Review of B. H. Liddell Hart, *Deterrent or Defense*, *Saturday Review*, September 3, 1960.

28– *he loathed the brutality and carnage of war*: Charles Bohlen Oral History
29 Interview, JFKL; Richard Goodwin, *Remembering America: A Voice from the Sixties* (Boston: Little Brown, 1988), 218; Geoffrey Perret, *Jack: A Life Like No Other* (New York: Random House, 2001), 326.

29 *"How did it all happen?"*: Sorensen, *Kennedy*, 513.

29 *"There's no doubt that any man"*: JFK and J. William Fulbright, Tape 26B.5, August 23, 1963, JFKL.

37 *first ExComm meeting*: the term "Executive Committee of the National Security Council" (ExComm) was created by Executive Order on October 22.

38 *"confidence and coolness"*: U. Alexis Johnson Oral History Interview, JFKL.

45 *daily meetings with the Special Group (Augmented)*: The other members of the Special Group (Augmented) were Roswell Gilpatric (Defense), McGeorge Bundy (White House), Alexis Johnson (State), John McCone (CIA), and Maxwell Taylor (Joint Chiefs).

51 *JFK slapping his knee*: Kennedy's nervous habit is vividly captured in Robert Drew's 1963 cinema verité documentary, *Crisis: Behind a Presidential Commitment*.

54 *JCS plans for bombing*: *Foreign Relations of the United States [FRUS]: Cuban Missile Crisis and Aftermath*, XI, Documents #22 and #23.

64 *Acheson's hard-line response*: Walter Isaacson and Evan Thomas, *The Wise Men* (New York: Simon and Schuster, 1986), 622.

65 *"that lying bastard"*: Brugioni, *Eyeball to Eyeball*, 287.

66 *SIOP briefing*: Thomas J. Schoenbaum, *Waging Peace and War: Dean Rusk in the Truman, Kennedy and Johnson Years* (New York: Simon and Schuster, 1988), 330.

66 *JFK and LeMay*: Carl S. Anthony, *As We Remember Her* (New York: HarperCollins, 1997), 179; Arthur M. Schlesinger, Jr., *A Thousand*

Days: John F. Kennedy in the White House (Boston: Houghton Mifflin, 1965), 912; Brugioni, *Eyeball to Eyeball*, 265.

68   *"He was just choleric"*: Roswell Gilpatric Oral History Interview, JFKL, 116.

71   *"These brass hats"*: Kenneth O'Donnell and David Powers, with Joe McCarthy, *Johnny We Hardly Knew Ye: Memories of John Fitzgerald Kennedy* (Boston: Little, Brown, 1970), 318.

71   *Bundy's reversal on bombing the missiles*: Kai Bird, *The Color of Truth: McGeorge Bundy and William Bundy: Brothers in Arms* (New York: Simon and Schuster, 1998), 234.

72   *"The minute you get back"*: Pierre Salinger, *With Kennedy* (Garden City, NY: Doubleday, 1966), 252; Pierre Salinger, *John F. Kennedy: Commander in Chief* (New York: Penguin, 1997), 116.

72   *"You should all hope"*: Brugioni, *Eyeball to Eyeball*, 314.

72   *"there is something to destroy in Cuba"*: Minutes of the 505th Meeting of the National Security Council, October 20, 1962, JFKL.

74   *"We are very, very close to war"*: Theodore Sorensen Oral History Interview, JFKL, 64; Sorensen, *Kennedy*, 2–3.

75   *"the clandestine manner"*: Minutes of the 506th Meeting of the National Security Council, October 21, 1962, JFKL.

79   *"a feeling of impending doom"*: Fursenko and Naftali, *"One Hell of a Gamble,"* 240–41.

80   *"a reasonable consensus"*: Minutes of the 507th Meeting of the National Security Council, October 22, 1962, JFKL, 2–3.

81   "this would be the first time": Matthias Uhl and Vladimir Ivkin, "'Operation Atom': The Soviet Union's Stationing of Nuclear Missiles in the German Democratic Republic, 1959," *Cold War International History Project Bulletin* [CWIHPB] 12/13 (Fall/Winter 2001): 299–307.

84   *lack of emergency planning*: Orville Freeman to Dino Brugioni, January 4, 1978, cited in Brugioni, *Eyeball to Eyeball*, 353–54; Alice L. George, *Awaiting Armageddon: How Americans Faced the Cuban Missile Crisis* (Chapel Hill: University of North Carolina Press, 2003), 2.

85   *range of Soviet missiles*: A nautical mile is 6,080 feet but a statute mile is only 5,280 feet—1,020 nautical miles are equivalent to 1,175 statute miles.

91   *"I slept on a couch"*: Fursenko and Naftali, *"One Hell of a Gamble,"* 241, 248; Talbott, ed., *Khrushchev Remembers*, 497.

91– *signs of panic*: Discussion with Edwin G. Quattlebaum III, Phillips Acad-
92   emy history faculty; George, *Awaiting Armageddon*, 68.

92   *"I'll see you in the morning"*: Harlan Cleveland Oral History Interview,
      JFKL, 34.

98   *"'Well, I'm still here'"*: Dean Rusk Oral History Interview, JFKL, 134.

99   *"show prudence"*: Nikita Khrushchev to John F. Kennedy, October 23,
      1962, *FRUS, 1961–1963, VI, Kennedy–Khrushchev Exchanges*, Docu-
      ment #61.

99   *Bolshakov and journalists*: Fursenko and Naftali, *"One Hell of a Gam-
      ble,"* 248–52.

105   *"haphazard and . . . almost comical"*: George, *Awaiting Armageddon*,
      42, 61, 70.

105   *"I am going to keep this one"*: *New York Times*, October 24, 1962; Bru-
      gioni, *Eyeball to Eyeball*, 383.

106   *no-nonsense discussion*: The Kennedy brothers were clearly not thinking
      about the fact that their conversation was being taped.

107   *"I am concerned"*: John F. Kennedy to Nikita Khrushchev, October 23,
      1962, *FRUS, 1961–1963, VI, Kennedy–Khrushchev Exchanges*, Docu-
      ment #62.

107   *"The President felt himself deceived"*: Anatoly Dobrynin, October 24,
      1962, Cable to Moscow, *CWIHPB* 5 (Spring 1995): 71–75; Robert F.
      Kennedy, *Thirteen Days: A Memoir of the Cuban Missile Crisis* (New
      York: W. W. Norton, 1999), 50–51.

110   *"we stared at each other across the table"*: Ibid., 53–54.

112   *"everyone looked like a different person"*: Ibid., 55.

119– *McNamara-Anderson confrontation*: James G. Blight and David A.
 20   Welch, *On the Brink: Americans and Soviets Examine the Cuban Missile
      Crisis* (New York: Noonday Press, 1989), 63–64; Gilpatric Oral History,
      61.

120   *"This was political chess"*: Maxwell Taylor Oral History Interview,
      JFKL, 57–58.

120   *National Press Club incident*: Fursenko and Naftali, *"One Hell of a
      Gamble,"* 257–61.

120   *"I cannot agree to this"*: Nikita Khrushchev to John F. Kennedy, Octo-
      ber 24, 1962, in Laurence Chang and Peter Kornbluh, eds., *The Cuban
      Missile Crisis, 1962: A National Security Archive Document Reader*
      (New York: The New Press, 1998), 173–74.

121 *"I regret very much"*: John F. Kennedy to Nikita Khrushchev, October 25, 1962, in Chang and Kornbluh, *Cuban Missile Crisis*, 183.

121 *"Comrades, let's go to the Bolshoi"*: Fursenko and Naftali, *"One Hell of a Gamble,"* 259–60; Talbott, ed., *Khrushchev Remembers*, 497.

133 *response to Stevenson's U.N. presentation*: A misleading article by journalists with close Kennedy ties later undermined Stevenson by claiming that he had backed "a Munich" at the ExComm meetings.

135– *photo leaflets*: The leaflets were never dropped over Cuba because of
36   Khrushchev's surprise October 28 decision to withdraw the missiles.

138 *"Let's send this off"*: Khrushchev agreed to remove the missiles before the message could be delivered to Castro.

146 *Mongoose discussions*: David L. Larson, *The Cuban Crisis of 1962: Selected Documents, Chronology and Bibliography* (Lanham, Md.: University Press of America, 1986), 171–72.

146 *"the seduction"*: U. Alexis Johnson to McGeorge Bundy, October 26, 1962, JFKL; Chang and Kornbluh, *Cuban Missile Crisis*, 386.

146 *shift in Soviet strategy*: Fursenko and Naftali, *"One Hell of a Gamble,"* 263.

147 *"Everyone needs peace"*: Nikita Khrushchev to John F. Kennedy, October 26, 1962, in Larson, *The Cuban Crisis*, 175–80.

147 *"a lot of bullshit"*: Brugioni, *Eyeball to Eyeball*, 448.

147 *"wipe them off the face of the earth"*: Fursenko and Naftali, *"One Hell of a Gamble,"* 272–73, 292; Sergei Khrushchev, *Nikita Khrushchev*, 628, 642.

155– *quotes from minutes*: Bromley Smith, Summary of NSC Executive Com-
56   mittee Meeting No. 7, October 27, 1962, JFKL, 4–5.

156 *JFK's meeting with governors*: Governor Elmer Anderson to Dino A. Brugioni, March 23, 1978, cited in Brugioni, *Eyeball to Eyeball*, 453–57.

156– *Alaska U-2 incident*: Roger Hilsman, *To Move a Nation: The Politics of
57   Foreign Policy in the Administration of John F. Kennedy* (New York: Doubleday, 1967), 221; Sergei Khrushchev, *Nikita Khrushchev*, 605.

157 *Khrushchev's reaction to Castro's "first strike" cable*: Jerrold L. Schechter, ed. and trans., Nikita Khrushchev, *Khrushchev Remembers: The Glasnost Tapes* (Boston: Little, Brown, 1990), 177; Sergei Khrushchev, *Nikita Khrushchev*, 625.

157 *Khrushchev's reply to Castro*: Nikita Khrushchev to Fidel Castro, October 30, 1962, in James G. Blight, Bruce J. Allyn, and David A. Welch,

Cuba on the Brink: Castro, the Missile Crisis and the Soviet Collapse (New York: Pantheon, 1993), 485–88; Jorge E. Domínguez, "The @#$%& Missile Crisis: (Or, What Was Cuban about U.S. Decisions During the Cuban Missile Crisis)," *Diplomatic History* 24 (Spring 2000): 313.

160 *Khrushchev response to "stray" U-2*: Nikita Khrushchev to John F. Kennedy, October 28, 1962, in Chang and Kornbluh, *Cuban Missile Crisis*, 238.

165 *Soviet submarines and nuclear torpedoes*: Fursenko and Naftali, "*One Hell of a Gamble,*" 242.

178 *JFK–LBJ relationship*: see George Reedy, *Lyndon B. Johnson: A Memoir* (Kansas City, Mo.: Andrews McMeel, 1982).

186 *ExComm stress and fatigue*: Gilpatric Oral History, 58–59; Rusk Oral History, 128.

186 *"I remember the sunset"*: Cited in Bernstein, "Reconsidering the Missile Crisis," 94.

186– *Oval Office discussion*: Barton J. Bernstein, "Understanding Decision
87   making: U.S. Foreign Policy and the Cuban Missile Crisis," *International Security* 25 (Summer 2000): 160.

187 *"The proposal was quickly supported"*: Bundy, *Danger and Survival*, 432–33; Robert Kennedy to Dean Rusk, October 30, 1962, JFKL; Bernstein, "Understanding Decisionmaking," 161.

187 *Cordier gambit*: Dean Rusk, as told to Richard Rusk, *As I Saw It* (New York: W. W. Norton, 1990), 240–41; Bernstein, "Reconsidering the Missile Crisis," 100–101, 127.

187– *Scali's explosion*: Chang and Kornbluh, *Cuban Missile Crisis*, 389–
88   90.

188 *"No independent initiatives"*: Sergei Khrushchev, *Nikita Khrushchev*, 609.

188 *"He chickened out again"*: Brugioni, *Eyeball to Eyeball*, 463–64.

188 *readiness to attack Cuba*: Fursenko and Naftali, "*One Hell of a Gamble,*" 258; Raymond L. Garthoff, *Reflections on the Cuban Missile Crisis*, rev. ed. (Washington, D.C.: Brookings, 1989), 98–99.

188 *RFK–Dobrynin October 27 meeting*: Kennedy, *Thirteen Days*, 80–84; James G. Hershberg, "Anatomy of a Controversy: Anatoly F. Dobrynin's Meeting With Robert F. Kennedy, Saturday, 27 October 1962," *CWIHPB* 5 (Spring 1995): 75, 77–80; Hershberg, "More on Bobby and the Cuban Missile Crisis," *CWIHPB* 8–9 (Winter 1996–97): 274, 344–47.

194   *"The situation was fraught with dangers"*: Chang and Kornbluh, *Cuban Missile Crisis*, 391; Garthoff, *Reflections*, 96.

194–   *Khrushchev's retreat*: Fursenko and Naftali, *"One Hell of a Gamble,"*
95   273, 276–77; Talbott, ed., *Khrushchev: The Last Testament*, 511; Sergei Khrushchev, *Nikita Khrushchev*, 626–30.

195   *"This was an unusual, perhaps unprecedented, step"*: Sergei Khrushchev to Sheldon M. Stern, October 2, 2001; Zubok and Pleshakov, *Inside the Kremlin's Cold War*, 267; Sergei Khrushchev, *Nikita Khrushchev*, xiv.

195–   *JCS response to Khrushchev announcement*: Taylor Oral History, 57;
96   Michael Beschloss, *The Crisis Years: Kennedy and Khrushchev, 1960–1963* (New York: Harper Collins, 1991), 544; Benjamin Bradlee, *Conversations With Kennedy* (New York: W. W. Norton, 1975), 122; Freedman, *Kennedy's Wars*, 208.

196   *"miasma of self-congratulation"*: Brugioni, *Eyeball to Eyeball*, 489.

196–   *minutes of meeting*: Bromley Smith, Summary Record of NSC Executive
97   Committee Meeting No. 10, October 28, 1962, 11:10 AM, JFKL, 1; McGeorge Bundy, NSC Executive Committee Record of Action, October 28, 1962, 11:00 AM, Meeting No. 10, JFKL, 1.

197   *JFK calls to Hoover, Truman, and Eisenhower*: Cassette L, Side 1, Dictabelts 41.2, 41.3, and 41.4, JFKL.

197–   *Castro's reaction to Khrushchev announcement*: Blight et al., *Cuba on the
98   Brink*, 23; Fursenko and Naftali, *"One Hell of a Gamble,"* 288–89; Chang and Kornbluh, *Cuban Missile Crisis*, 392.

198   *"I am under instructions to thank you"*: Ibid., 392–93.

198   *JFK's Berlin preoccupation*: Conversation with Sander Vanocur, September 12, 2003; Brugioni, *Eyeball to Eyeball*, 491.

198   *Kuznetsov/Mikoyan missions*: Chang and Kornbluh, *Cuban Missile Crisis*, 393; Garthoff, *Reflections*, 99; Fursenko and Naftali, *"One Hell of a Gamble,"* 290–315.

198   *coordinating committee members*: John McCloy (chair), George Ball, Roswell Gilpatric, Robert McNamara, and Adlai Stevenson.

204   *Jackie Kennedy's calendar*: Hugh Sidey, cited in Anthony, *As We Remember Her*, 181.

205   *RFK returns Khrushchev letter to Dobrynin*: Hershberg, "More on Bobby and the Cuban Missile Crisis," 274, 344–47.

205–   *Castro's intransigence*: Chang and Kornbluh, *Cuban Missile Crisis*, 394;
6   Adlai Stevenson to Dean Rusk, November 1, 1962, in Chang and Kornbluh, *Cuban Missile Crisis*, 259.

206 *U.S. refusal to negotiate with Castro*: Brenner, "Thirteen Months," 202; Domínguez, "The @#$%& Missile Crisis," 307.

206 *Cuban-Soviet tensions*: Fursenko and Naftali, *"One Hell of a Gamble,"* 295, 296–97.

206– *JFK on possible invasion of Cuba*: John F. Kennedy to Robert McNa-
7   mara, *FRUS: Cuban Missile Crisis and Aftermath, 1961–1963*, XI, Document #150; Meeting recording, JFKL, November 7, 1962.

207 *squeezing Castro*: Meeting recording, JFKL, November 8, 1962.

207 *IL-28 standoff and possible concealed Soviet missiles*: Brenner, "Thirteen Months," 203; Meeting recording, JFKL, November 9, 1962; Fursenko and Naftali, *"One Hell of a Gamble,"* 299–300.

207– *IL-28 negotiations*: Meeting recording, JFKL, November 12, 1962; Fur-
8   senko and Naftali, *"One Hell of a Gamble,"* 303.

208 *Khrushchev promises to remove IL-28s*: Ibid., 302; Nikita Khrushchev to John F. Kennedy, November 14, 1962, *FRUS: The Cuban Missile Crisis and its Aftermath*, XI, Document #176.

208 *Castro refuses to give up IL-28s*: Fursenko and Naftali, *"One Hell of a Gamble,"* 304–7.

208– *increased U.S. pressure on Khrushchev*: Meeting recording, JFKL, Novem-
9   ber 16, 1962; Chang and Kornbluh, *Cuban Missile Crisis*, 401.

209 *JFK on conditions for invading Cuba*: Meeting recording, JFKL, November 16, 1962.

209 *JFK's pessimism on settlement*: Fursenko and Naftali, *"One Hell of a Gamble,"* 307–8; Chang and Kornbluh, *Cuban Missile Crisis*, 402.

209 *Khrushchev November 20 letter*: Fursenko and Naftali, *"One Hell of a Gamble,"* 309.

209– *RFK and McCone oppose public non-invasion pledge*: Meeting record-
10   ing, JFKL, November 20, 1962.

210 *JFK toughens public stance*: *Public Papers of the Presidents: John F. Kennedy, 1962*, II (Washington, D.C.: U.S. Government Printing Office, 1963), 830–38.

210 *"Evidently, Kennedy himself is not an extremist"*: Fursenko and Naftali, *"One Hell of a Gamble,"* 310.

210 *Castro's secret 1963 trip to USSR*: Sergei Khrushchev, *Nikita Khrushchev*, 658; Fursenko and Naftali, *"One Hell of a Gamble,"* 327–30.

210– *JFK post–missile crisis Cuban policy*: Stephen G. Rabe, "After the Mis-
11   siles of October: John F. Kennedy and Cuba, November 1962 to November 1963," *Presidential Studies Quarterly* 30 (December 2000): 716, 724.

210– *post–missile crisis secret U.S.–Cuban contacts*: FRUS: *Cuba, 1961–*
11 *1962*, X, 738–46; Schlesinger, *A Thousand Days*, 998–1000; Arthur
Schlesinger, Jr., *Robert Kennedy and His Times* (Boston: Houghton Mifflin, 1978), 552–53; Peter Kornbluh, ed., "Kennedy and Castro: The Secret Quest for Accommodation," National Security Archive Electronic Briefing Book No. 17, August 16, 1999; Rabe, "After the Missiles of October," 723–24; Domingo Amuchastegui, "Cuban Intelligence and the October Crisis," in Blight and Welch, eds., *Intelligence and the Cuban Missile Crisis*, 107.

211 *U.S. anti-Castro policies continue*: O'Donnell and Powers, *Johnny, We Hardly Knew Ye*, 276–77; FRUS: *Cuban Missile Crisis and Aftermath*, XI, Document #376, November 12, 1963; Rabe, "After the Missiles of October," 717–21, 725; Brenner, "Thirteen Months," 205–7; Raymond L. Garthoff, "Documenting the Cuban Missile Crisis," *Diplomatic History* 24 (Spring 2000): 302–3.

Selective Bibliography

For a comprehensive bibliography, see Sheldon M. Stern, *Averting 'The Final Failure': John F. Kennedy and the Secret Cuban Missile Crisis Meetings*, 441–49 (Stanford, Calif.: Stanford University Press, 2003).

Archives

John F. Kennedy Library, Boston, Massachusetts [JFKL]
John F. Kennedy Personal Papers
John F. Kennedy Presidential Papers, 1961–63
    National Security Files
    Oral History Collection
    President's Office Files
    Presidential Recordings Collection
Nigel Hamilton Research Materials, Massachusetts Historical Society, Boston, Massachusetts [NHRM, MHS]

Secondary Sources

Amuchastegui, Domingo. "Cuban Intelligence and the October Crisis." In James G. Blight and David A. Welch, eds., *Intelligence and the Cuban Missile Crisis*, 88–119. London: Frank Cass, 1998.

Bernstein, Barton J. "Commentary: Reconsidering Khrushchev's Gambit—Defending the Soviet Union and Cuba." *Diplomatic History* 14 (Spring 1990): 231–39.

———. "Reconsidering the Missile Crisis: Dealing with the Problems of the American Jupiters in Turkey." In James A. Nathan, ed., *The Cuban Missile Crisis Revisited*, 55–130. New York: St. Martin's, 1992.

———. "Understanding Decisionmaking: U.S. Foreign Policy and the Cuban Missile Crisis." *International Security* 25 (Summer 2000): 134–64.

Blight, James G., Bruce J. Allyn, and David A. Welch. *Cuba on the Brink: Castro, the Missile Crisis and the Soviet Collapse.* New York: Pantheon, 1993.

Blight, James G., and David A. Welch. "The Cuban Missile Crisis and Intelligence Performance." In James G. Blight and David A. Welch, eds., *Intelligence and the Cuban Missile Crisis,* 173–217. London: Frank Cass, 1998.

———. *On the Brink: Americans and Soviets Examine the Cuban Missile Crisis.* New York: Noonday Press, 1989.

———. "What Can Intelligence Tell Us About the Cuban Missile Crisis, and What Can the Cuban Missile Crisis Tell Us About Intelligence?" In James G. Blight and David A. Welch, eds., *Intelligence and the Cuban Missile Crisis,* 1–17. London: Frank Cass, 1998.

Brenner, Philip. "Thirteen Months: Cuba's Perspective on the Missile Crisis." In James A. Nathan, ed., *The Cuban Missile Crisis Revisited,* 187–219. New York, St. Martin's, 1992.

Brugioni, Dino. *Eyeball to Eyeball: The Inside Story of the Cuban Missile Crisis,* edited by Robert F. McCort. New York: Random House, 1991.

Bundy, McGeorge. *Danger and Survival: Choices About the Bomb in the First Fifty Years.* New York: Random House, 1998.

Chang, Laurence. "The View from Washington and the View from Nowhere: Cuban Missile Crisis Historiography and the Epistemology of Decision Making." In James A. Nathan, ed., *The Cuban Missile Crisis Revisited,* 131–60. New York: St. Martin's, 1992.

Chang, Laurence, and Peter Kornbluh, eds. *The Cuban Missile Crisis, 1962: A National Security Archive Document Reader.* New York: The New Press, 1998.

Domínguez, Jorge E. "The @#$%& Missile Crisis: (Or, What Was Cuban about U.S. Decisions During the Cuban Missile Crisis?)." *Diplomatic History* 24 (Spring 2000): 305–15.

Foreign Relations of the United States [FRUS], vols. V–XVI. Washington, D.C.: United States Government Printing Office, 1994–98. Also on the World Wide Web: state.gov/r/pa/ho/frus/kennedyjf/.

Freedman, Lawrence. *Kennedy's Wars: Berlin, Cuba, Laos and Vietnam.* New York: Oxford University Press, 2000.

Fursenko, Aleksandr, and Timothy Naftali. "Soviet Intelligence and the Cuban Missile Crisis." In James G. Blight and David A. Welch, eds., *Intelligence and the Cuban Missile Crisis,* 64–87. London: Frank Cass, 1998.

———. *"One Hell of a Gamble": Khrushchev, Castro and Kennedy, 1958–1964.* New York: W. W. Norton, 1997.

Garthoff, Raymond L. "Documenting the Cuban Missile Crisis." *Diplomatic History* 24 (Spring 2000): 297–303.

———. *Reflections on the Cuban Missile Crisis.* Rev. ed. Washington, D.C.: Brookings, 1989.

———. "US Intelligence in the Cuban Missile Crisis." In James G. Blight and David A. Welch, eds., *Intelligence and the Cuban Missile Crisis*, 18–63. London: Frank Cass, 1998.

George, Alice L. *Awaiting Armageddon: How Americans Faced the Cuban Missile Crisis.* Chapel Hill: University of North Carolina Press, 2003.

Gribkov, Anatoli I., and William Y. Smith. *Operation ANAYDR: U.S. and Soviet Generals Recount the Cuban Missile Crisis.* Chicago: Edition Q, 1994.

Hershberg, James G. "Anatomy of a Controversy: Anatoly F. Dobrynin's Meeting with Robert F. Kennedy, Saturday, 27 October 1962." *Cold War International History Project Bulletin* 5 (Spring 1995): 75, 77–80.

———. "Before 'The Missiles of October': Did Kennedy Plan a Military Strike Against Cuba?" *Diplomatic History* 14 (Spring 1990): 163–98; also in different form in Blight, James G., and David A. Welch, eds., *Intelligence and the Cuban Missile Crisis*, 237–80. London: Frank Cass, 1998.

———. "More on Bobby and the Cuban Missile Crisis." *Cold War International History Project Bulletin* 8–9 (Winter 1996–97): 274–77.

Kennedy, Robert F. *Thirteen Days: A Memoir of the Cuban Missile Crisis* New York: W. W. Norton, 1999.

Khrushchev, Nikita. *Khrushchev Remembers: The Glasnost Tapes.* Ed. and trans. Jerrold L. Schechter. Boston: Little, Brown, 1990.

Khrushchev, Sergei. *Nikita Khrushchev and the Creation of a Superpower.* University Park: Pennsylvania State University Press, 2000.

Larson, David L. *The Cuban Crisis of 1962: Selected Documents, Chronology and Bibliography.* Lanham, Md.: University Press of America, 1986.

Mastny, Vojtech. *The Cold War and Soviet Insecurity.* New York: Oxford University Press, 1997.

McCauliffe, Mary S., ed. *CIA Documents on the Cuban Missile Crisis, 1962.* Washington, D.C.: Central Intelligence Agency, 1992.

Naftali, Timothy. "The Origins of 'Thirteen Days.'" *Miller Center Report* 15 (Summer 1999): 23–24.

Nash, Philip. *The Other Missiles of October: Eisenhower, Kennedy and the Jupiters, 1957–1963.* Chapel Hill: University of North Carolina Press, 1997.

Paterson, Thomas G. "When Fear Ruled: Rethinking the Cuban Missile Crisis." *New England Journal of History* 52 (Fall 1995): 12–37.

Paterson, Thomas G., ed. *Kennedy's Quest for Victory: American Foreign Policy, 1961–1963.* New York: Oxford University Press, 1989.

Rabe, Stephen G. "After the Missiles of October: John F. Kennedy and Cuba, November 1962 to November 1963." *Presidential Studies Quarterly* 30 (December 2000): 714–26.

Rusk, Dean, as told to Richard Rusk. *As I Saw It*. New York: W. W. Norton, 1990.

Sidey, Hugh. Introduction to *Prelude to Leadership: The European Diary of John F. Kennedy—Summer 1945*. Washington, D.C.: Regnery, 1995.

Stern, Sheldon M. *Averting 'The Final Failure': John F. Kennedy and the Secret Cuban Missile Crisis Meetings*. Stanford, Calif.: Stanford University Press, 2003.

Talbott, Strobe, ed. and trans. *Khrushchev Remembers*. Boston: Little, Brown, 1970.

———. *Khrushchev Remembers: The Last Testament*. Boston: Little, Brown, 1974.

Zubok, Vladislav, and Constantine Pleshakov. *Inside the Kremlin's Cold War: From Stalin to Khrushchev*. Cambridge, Mass.: Harvard University Press, 1996.

Index

In this index an "f" after a number indicates a separate reference on the next page, and an "ff" indicates separate references on the next two pages. A continuous discussion over two or more pages is indicated by a span of page numbers, e.g., "57–59." *Passim* is used for a cluster of references in close but not consecutive sequence.

Stanford Nuclear Age Series

General Editor, Martin Sherwin

Robert Oppenheimer: Letters and Recollections. Edited by Alice Kimball Smith and Charles Weiner. New foreword by Martin J. Sherwin. 1980. Reissued 1995.

The Advisors: Oppenheimer, Teller, and the Superbomb. By Herbert F. York. With a new Preface and Epilogue. Historical essay by Hans A. Bethe. 1976. Reissued 1989.

The Voice of the Dolphins and Other Stories. Leo Szilard. 1961. Reissued 1991.

Atomic Energy for Military Purposes. Henry D. Smith. Preface by Philip Morrison. 1945. New foreword 1989.

Acknowledgments

The original, full-length version of this book, *Averting 'The Final Failure': John F. Kennedy and the Secret Cuban Missile Crisis Meetings*, began, at least in my mind, over twenty years ago when, as JFK Library historian, I first listened to the still-classified ExComm tapes. I was especially intrigued by the October 26 morning meeting in which U.N. ambassador Adlai Stevenson, my hero in the 1950s, attempted unsuccessfully to overcome the hostility of his ExComm critics. I later told my wife that a narrative account of these meetings would make a fascinating book. But the project had to wait until all the tapes from these historic thirteen days were finally declassified in the late 1990s.

This revised and condensed version of *Averting 'The Final Failure'* aims to make this unique historical event completely comprehensible—especially for students and general readers. And, of course, genuinely interested readers can always move on to the full-length version.

I am particularly indebted to Muriel Bell, director of acquisitions at Stanford University Press, and Professor Martin Sherwin, general editor of the Stanford Nuclear Age Series, in which the original version of this book first appeared.

Finally, I can never adequately sum up the support from my wife Helen, my daughter Jennifer, and especially my son Jeremy, a historian in his own right, throughout this project.

Sheldon M. Stern

Newton, Mass.